Praise for
Ivy Briefs

"Entertaining and funny."

—*Publishers Weekly*

"An antic case study illuminating how a lawyer is made in frisky prose infused with attitude."

—*Kirkus Reviews*

"*Ivy Briefs* follows Kimes's journey from LSAT to new associate—a journey that's sometimes snarky, always emotional and ultimately enjoyable."

—*ABA Journal*

"Ha[s] former colleagues buzzing."

—*New York Law Journal*

"Set your coffee pot going now, because you're not going to want to put this book down until you finish."

—lawvibe.com

"It is precisely Kimes's breezy, fast-paced, tongue-in-cheek tone that makes *Ivy Briefs* a thoroughly enjoyable memoir, and a worthwhile read, even for those of us who think we've already had enough of law school."

—*Georgetown Law Weekly*

This title is also available as an eBook.

"Take a little bit of *The Paper Chase* but without those awful sideburns. Take a little bit of *Legally Blonde* but with a bit less irony and fewer gadgets. Take a bit of Scott Turow's memoir, *One L,* but change the gender of the main character. Mix. They say the sum is greater than all of its parts. Martha Kimes's new memoir . . . is definitely proof of that adage."

—blogcritics.org

"With self-deprecating humor, ditzy dithering, and gossipy bluntness, author Martha Kimes tells what it's like to be out of your (ivy) league. . . . If you're a Perry Mason fan, a real-life Judd for the Defense, or if you just want something different to read, here's a book to court. *Ivy Briefs* is one you'll want to adjourn with, and that's no joke."

—(Yankton) *Press & Dakotan*

"Sharp and insightful wit."

—nylawblog.typepad.com

"*Ivy Briefs* is compulsively readable and should appeal to a wide variety of people—lawyers and non-legal types alike."

—curledup.com

"[Kimes's] lacerating wit and knack for human portraiture enable the reader to appreciate each and every one of her spirited characters."

—Saira Rao, author of *Chambermaid*

"A must-read for anyone contemplating law school; and for those who have already graduated, a sidesplitting review of the law school experience—torts and all."

—Karen Quinn, author of *The Ivy Chronicles*
and *Wife in the Fast Lane*

"Martha Kimes's candid tale of attending Columbia Law School is *Legally Blonde* meets *One L,* told with sweet self-awareness and pervasive wit. I couldn't help but cheer Kimes on as she faced every daunting law school challenge, transforming herself from fearful Midwesterner to cool and confident Ivy League grad. *Ivy Briefs* makes me want to hug Kimes . . . and then hire her as my attorney."

—Jen Lancaster, author of *Bitter Is the New Black* and *Bright Lights, Big Ass*

"It's a fun and compelling journey through a lofty world most of us will never experience, guided by the girl next door."

—Robert Rummel-Hudson, author of *Schuyler's Monster*

"With pitch-perfect dialogue and witty observations, Martha Kimes delivers a funny and charming look at the trials and tribulations of law school. I give *Ivy Briefs* an A."

—Alison Pace, author of *Pug Hill* and *Through Thick and Thin*

IVY BRIEFS

True Tales of a Neurotic Law Student

MARTHA KIMES

ATRIA BOOKS

New York   London   Toronto   Sydney

 BOOKS

A Division of Simon & Schuster, Inc.
1230 Avenue of the Americas
New York, NY 10020

Copyright © 2007 by Martha Kimes

First Atria Books trade paperback edition December 2008

ATRIA BOOKS and colophon are trademarks of Simon & Schuster, Inc.

For information about special discounts for bulk purchases,
please contact Simon & Schuster Special Sales at
1-800-456-6798 or business@simonandschuster.com.

Manufactured in the United States of America

10   9   8   7   6   5   4   3   2   1

The Library of Congress has cataloged the hardcover edition as follows:

Kimes, Martha.
    Ivy briefs : true tales of a neurotic law student / Martha Kimes.
        p. cm.
        1. Women lawyers—United States—Biography.   2. Columbia
    University. School of Law—Alumni and alumnae—Biography.   I. Title.
    KF373.K473A3 2007
    340.071'17471—dc22
    [B]   2007060651

ISBN-13: 978-0-7432-8838-5
ISBN-10:   0-7432-8838-6
ISBN-13: 978-0-7432-8839-2 (pbk)
ISBN-10:   0-7432-8839-4 (pbk)

For Joe, who has been with me through it all
And for Donovan and Simon,
who are my proudest accomplishments

Contents

Author's Note

This memoir is based on real events, and the essence of this book is true. To protect those who deserve to be protected (and also those who probably don't) I have changed many names, places, and identifying characteristics. I've combined some characters and altered the chronology of events in order to organize the narrative. Certain details were fictionalized, and some specific dialogue was exaggerated. (Oh, hell, some of the dialogue was invented altogether. The people I knew in law school weren't always as amusing as I would have liked.)

Memories fade over the years, but I believe this book presents an accurate picture of my experience at Columbia Law School (the exception being the fact that I intentionally omitted all references to the Rule Against Perpetuities—a small kindness that will undoubtedly be appreciated by anyone who has ever studied the law). I hope you enjoy it.

Prologue

THE THICK AND THE THIN

"When the gods wish to punish us, they answer our prayers."
—OSCAR WILDE

The letter that arrived in the mail on that early December day was thin. More than thin. It was sickly, it was malnourished, it was positively *anorexic*. I knew at first glance what that meant. Good news from law school admissions offices does not come in anorexic envelopes. Good news comes in thick, heavy packages of impressive heft, packages that look like they've just feasted on filet mignon and chocolate soufflé, packages that scream out "We want you!" The thin envelopes? Those quietly whisper in your ear "You suck." You might as well just toss them into the trash, as there's no sense in torturing yourself with letters that are certain to begin with the overly polite "After a careful review of your application, we are sorry to inform you that . . ." and always finish with a nice version of "We've decided you're not worthy. But thanks for trying, and we do appreciate having received your $60 application fee." They only need one page to tell you that.

But I am a sucker for punishment, so I opened the anorexic letter. To my sheer and utter shock, the words on the crisp ivory page read "Congratulations. We are happy to welcome you into the Columbia Law School Class of 1997." *Accepted. Not rejected. Accepted? To an Ivy League school? OH. MY. GOD.* But what kind of law school sends acceptance letters in skinny envelopes? Are these people living in some sort of alternate reality where they don't understand the universal significance of the thin envelope? Or is this all some sort of cruel joke?

With shaking hands, I called my husband, Joe.

"I got in," I croaked.

"What?" he replied.

"Accepted not rejected got in Columbia early admission law school accepted they said yes Ivy League oh *shit!!!!!!*"

"What?" he asked. "Honey, slow down—I can't understand you."

I believe it was then that I started hyperventilating. "Columbia. *Wheeze.* Law school. *Wheeze.* Columbia Law School? Accepted? *Wheeze.* Early decision program? New York City? CAN'T BREATHE."

"Take a cleansing breath, Martha. Slowly. Breathe in and out."

"Why? Is that how they do it in the Ivy League? *Wheeze.* Are you trying to tell me that I don't even know how to breathe like the other fancy students there? You don't think I'm good enough? *Wheeze wheeze.* I mean, I know that I don't exactly come from a long line of Harvard-educated lawyers, but, my God, what kind of person are you? We're still newlyweds—the ink is barely dry on the marriage license. You're not allowed to be cruel yet. You're supposed to be supportive! *Wheeze.* Congratulatory! And instead you criticize? How dare you? *Wheeeeeeze!*"

Yeah, that was a harbinger of things to come.

There's no doubt that I'm a smart enough person, but I hardly border on the brilliant. If you skip class and are looking to borrow a day's worth of notes, I'm a good person to ask. But if you're desperate for an A and hoping to copy from someone's test, you might have better luck looking elsewhere. Unless, of course, it's a standardized test, in which case I'm your woman. (Not that there's a chance in hell that I'm letting you copy.) You know how people always argue that standardized tests are unfair because "they don't test people's intelligence or knowledge, they just test people's ability to take standardized tests?" Well, I'm a proud supporter of that system because, intelligence and knowledge be damned, I happen to have a *spectacular* ability to take standardized tests.

The Law School Admission Test changed the course of my life. Before I took that exam, I was just an average Midwestern girl with average grades and a degree from an average college. Sure, my parents had stressed the importance of education, but always within certain limits. I was expected to do well in my studies and I consistently did, without ever trying all that hard. I was the product of public schools, and that was just a given in my house—when your parents drive a used Ford Escort, there's not a lot of extra money to throw around for private school tuition. (Not that there was a private school anywhere near the small town where we lived.) When it came time to go off to college, it was not a matter of researching universities near and far in order to choose the very best school to fit my needs and allow me to grow personally, socially, culturally, and intellectually. My mailbox was not filled with glossy brochures from small liberal arts colleges across the country picturing gorgeous quads and ivied buildings. That just wasn't our style. In my house, it was more a matter of "Okay, which state school do you want to go to? And don't go giving some crazy answer like UCLA or Colorado State. We mean which state school *in this state that we now live in called Wisconsin where resident tuition is inexpensive.*"

To my parents' credit, their philosophy pretty well matched that of most other families in my town. Except for a privileged few, we kids were destined to be Wisconsinites for at least four more years. My high school fantasies about breaking away mostly involved sitting around on the burnished orange velvet couch in the living room of my family's modest ranch home with my best friend Leah, snacking on Doritos and off-brand diet cola, and dreaming about the virtual Eden that was Madison, where the main campus of the University of Wisconsin was housed—all of ninety-nine miles away. Sure, I would have rather ventured off far away, but you can make a lot out of ninety-nine miles' worth of distance if you try. Especially if your parents are on the verge of a divorce and you're trying the best you can to separate yourself from all of their issues.

During high school, I waited tables at the local Pizza Hut three or four nights a week, serving carbo-loaded food to overweight people, and squirreling away tip money into my college savings account. Each extra basket of breadsticks that I could talk a table into ordering would transfer into an extra twenty cents or so tip-wise, so I always tried to do the hard sell. I came home each night exhausted, stinking of sweat, dough, and pepperoni, but bounded into my bedroom, dumped the tips out of my waitress apron onto my bed, and excitedly counted up the pile of one-dollar bills and heaps of change that I had earned.

Leah and I both applied to and were accepted by the University of Wisconsin in Madison, and we excitedly headed off to be college roommates. A few months later, she began sleeping with my ex-boyfriend, to whom I had lost my virtue the year before, and with whom I had not parted on pleasant terms. As one might imagine, that roommate arrangement turned out rather disastrously. Aside from lamenting the demise of my friendship with Leah, college meant long-awaited freedom from my parents and the glorious opportunity to experience life on my own. (Read: drink lots and lots of beer, skip lots and lots of classes.) When I wasn't going to house parties, attending college football games, or acting like a poseur doofus smoking clove cigarettes in the Rathskeller of the student union, I attended class, studied enough but not too much, and managed to earn respectable but not write-home-about grades. I divided my time between studying, partying, and working to earn tuition money.

For some reason, it never really occurred to me to stop and focus on what I was going to do once college was over. Wisconsin was a very large state school, with over 40,000 students enrolled, and it wasn't as though career counselors were purposefully wandering the 933 acres of campus, hunting down random undergraduates and forcing them to face the music. They were there if you sought them out, but if you didn't, you could survive in peaceful, ignorant bliss until graduation.

In the movies, after you get your college diploma, you are handed an entry-level job in a mysterious field like marketing or banking or human resources or pharmaceutical sales, along with a cubicle that you can call your very own, a bulletin board upon which you can tack Dilbert cartoons, and a box of business cards that make you feel more important than you actually are. To this day, I wonder why it is that at no point during my four years at college did one person (be it a career counselor, professor, or parent) say to me, "You know, you're going to have to find a job and a way to pay your rent after graduation, because student loans and two-dollar all-you-can-drink parties don't go on forever, missy." Possibly they assumed that such a statement was self-evident. If so, they were mistaken.

I was barely three steps off the stage at college graduation, diploma proudly in hand, when that fact did become obvious to me. I was armed with a B.A. in psychology and philosophy, neither of which was the most practical or marketable field of expertise, and I was suddenly hit with the realization that I had no idea what to do with my life. And that I had bills to pay. And that soon I would be getting a little rumbly in the tumbly with hunger, and that even ramen noodles cost money. And that this here piece of paper that I got in the mail says that in six months they expect me to start *paying back* the student loans I took out? Don't they know I'm not even employed?

Nervously, hesitantly, I visited the university's career services center, where I met with a counselor named Delores who wore a gauzy, flowing purple tunic and chunky turquoise jewelry. Delores asked me a litany of *What Color Is Your Parachute?*–type questions about my ideal work environment and my personal communication style, sat me down to take a Myers-Briggs personality test, pronounced me a "type INTJ," and then explained that I would do well at a job that allowed me to use my "creativity and originality" within a "structured environment." The world was wide open to me, she said, and she wanted me to consider all my options. Where would I be happiest working? Might I like the climate in San Francisco? Had I ever considered working abroad or traveling? Did I prefer a bustling, big-city atmosphere or a more laid-back, small-town life? Would I prefer the predictability of working for a large corporation or the informality of a smaller business? Had I ever considered an entrepreneurial venture?

These were all questions that were lovely to ponder in the abstract, but not too practical to my real-life situation. I lived in Madison. My boyfriend, Joe, lived in Madison. We lived *together* in Madison. Neither of us had any money to move away from Madison, even if we were so inclined. And I needed a job right away. I didn't have time to spend months exploring the depths of my psyche to try and determine what sort of career would help me become completely self-actualized. All of this information seemed quite disappointing to Delores. But sometimes the truth hurts. And the truth definitely hurt me, because Madison was a college town flooded with overqualified, underemployed workers—people with master's degrees and Ph.D.s could be found tending bar and waiting tables all over the city.

As a stopgap measure, I took an eight-dollar-an-hour job stuffing envelopes at a small local nonprofit organization (a job that provided me with neither my very own cubicle nor my very own set of business cards), and considered my options as I stuffed. *Fold paper, fold paper, stuff envelope, seal.* Become an oral surgeon? No. I don't really like mouths. *Fold paper, fold paper, stuff envelope, seal.* Astronaut? Nah, you probably need to know something sciencey to do that, and I barely made it through Chemistry 101. *Fold paper, fold paper, stuff envelope, seal.* Insurance adjuster? Oh, please. *Fold paper, fold paper, stuff envelope, seal.* Philosopher? I'm qualified to do that, but I'm not seeing many "philosopher needed" ads in the paper . . . *Fold paper, fold paper, stuff envelope, seal.* Law school? Maybe I should go to law school. That's not a half-bad idea. With a law degree, maybe I could even do some good in the world!

I had always enjoyed a good argument, and the thought of becoming a lawyer had crossed my mind on a few occasions—the prospect of practicing law intrigued me. But I must admit that my decision to go to law school was made by default more than it was fueled by a raging desire to practice law. I wanted so badly to be an adult, to be a professional, to be taken seriously, but I had no idea how to go about it. With no other real clues, hints, or prospects for a professional future, law school seemed like a respectable, practical option that might actually land me a real job—one that didn't involve opening someone else's mail, learning how to operate a telephone switchboard, or standing in cushy, orthopedic shoes saying "Hi, my name is Martha, and I'll be your waitress this evening." A job with not only my own business cards and my own Dilbert-ready bulletin board, but probably even my own office (maybe with a window) and possibly even my own secretary.

"Law school opens so many doors," my uncle Mark said.

"Don't do it," my aunt Elaine, Uncle Mark's wife, said.

"If you were a lawyer, you could work to achieve social justice," said the director of the nonprofit organization I worked for.

"With a law degree, you will have infinite opportunities," proclaimed the new, no-nonsense career counselor who I had gone to see behind Delores's back.

"I have no idea what to do with my life," I responded. "Count me in!"

"I don't know what to do with my life either," Joe told me. "Let's get married. I'll stand by your side while you get your law degree, then I'll get to ride the gravy train once you're a highly paid attorney!"

"Yes!" I answered, to the world's most romantic proposal. The dual coups of marriage and law school would undoubtedly transform both of us into serious, respectable, mature adults.

The problematic part of the whole scenario was that Joe and I would be paying for the nuptials ourselves. Although our parents were happy to hear of the planned union (they found it infinitely preferable to our sinful cohabitation over the previous year) and surely would have loved to help us out financially if they could have, that just wasn't in the cards. We didn't even bother to broach the subject, as it was understood from the beginning. Chances are, if your parents don't pay for your college education, they're not paying for your wedding.

I had visions of a candlelit ceremony where I would stand, radiating a beautiful bridal glow, costumed in a flowing white silk wedding gown. In my dreams, the ceremony would be followed by a lovely reception at a lakeside hotel (with an open bar and champagne fountain), complete with a tiered cake adorned with fresh strawberries and roses, with a miniature bride and groom perched on the top. The reality was that we were stretching it to even think we could afford a wedding at the courthouse followed by a reception at the local VFW with pitchers of foamy beer, a greasy fish fry, and an Entenmann's Iced Devil's Food Cake. The disparity was troublesome, to say the least.

I didn't really need the fanciest of weddings—I'm not one of those girls who began collecting back issues of *Modern Bride* magazine at age fourteen—but I did want something memorable in its own way. It was the beginning of an exciting new adventure for Joe and me, and I wanted something that would do it justice. Ultimately, we decided that we'd either find a way to do the traditional white dress down the aisle or would do something altogether unconventional. Not that we really knew what "unconventional" would be. Vegas? A beach in Mexico? I just hoped that we'd be able to afford the wedding before gray hairs began sprouting from our heads.

The solution came via fax one day while I was at work, answering phones and stuffing yet more envelopes. An unsolicited facsimile, an advertisement, boasting of discounted airfares to locations near and far. *Incredibly* discounted airfares. Airfares that even Joe and I could begin to afford. Clutching the paper between white knuckles (because I knew that what I was about to propose was a long shot), I took the advertisement home and presented my case to Joe, using my best lawyer-to-be voice.

"Joe, you know how much I've always wanted to visit New York City, right? Well, I saw this ad today that says that we could fly there for only $120 each. Round trip. I think we should go. If we stayed with your sister and her husband, it wouldn't cost us a penny. It would be fabulous! And you know how we've been worrying about how we'll ever afford to get married? Well, I was thinking . . . why don't we get married while we're there? We talked about doing something exotic. New York is exotic, right? Maybe we could find a judge to marry us in Central Park. Central Park!"

Joe said nothing.

Nervously, I kept pitching.

"I'm thinking a sort of elopement. Tell people afterward and let the chips fall where they may. We wouldn't have to deal with the awkwardness of getting both of my parents together in the same room for our wedding or with the drama of our two families actually meeting. And, seriously, how cool would it be to say that we *eloped* in *Central Park?* Plus, it would be like a wedding and honeymoon all wrapped up in one. And all for less than $300! Or for sure for less than $500. How can we ever beat that? I know we can't really afford even that right now, but we do have credit cards we could use. In the long run, it would be way cheaper than any of our other options."

Anxiously, I awaited his response.

"Let me call my sister to make sure it's okay," Joe said. "But I'm in."

So, on a beautiful Wednesday afternoon in early September, we flew out of Madison and landed at LaGuardia Airport. I had my face pressed so tightly into the tiny airplane window, craning to see my first glimpse of New York City, that I'm surprised my nose ever recovered its natural shape. I took in every detail of the foreign-feeling taxi ride through Queens and Brooklyn, and we were in line at the City Clerk's Office at nine the next morning to get our marriage license. After a day and a half of wandering around Manhattan—me with my mouth hanging open and a tiny bit of excited, overwhelmed, New York–jealous drool dripping from my cheek the entire time—Joe and I got married in a cozy nook of Strawberry Fields in Central Park, with Joe's sister, her husband, and their nine-week-old daughter as our witnesses. I wore a short, strappy, bright red dress that I had purchased, on clearance, for $39 at The Limited. Joe wore a plaid jacket and a thin black tie that were, in retrospect, both quite regrettable.

We wandered around the park for several hours afterward, enjoying the perfect, sunny seventy-two-degree weather and eating ice-cream sandwiches purchased from a curbside vendor. That night we stayed at the now-defunct Hotel St. Moritz in a deeply discounted room overlooking Central Park. Two days later we returned to Wisconsin. Joe had to drag me back kicking and screaming. I was in love with New York. I wanted to stay.

Once we were home, I turned my attention to the law school portion of the Martha Adulthood Plan. My 3.35 undergraduate grade point average was within the realm of the acceptable, and as long as I could get a respectable score on the entrance exam and write a coherent application essay, I figured that I shouldn't have a problem getting into law school somewhere. My expectations weren't too high, and I wasn't spending too much time overanalyzing the whole situation by worrying about pesky little things like, you know, how I was going to pay for this whole endeavor or the fact that I could legitimately stand to be about $100,000 in debt if I ended up going to a private school. Those were mere quibbling details! To be worried about later! Meanwhile, this plan offered an end to the otherwise endless *fold paper, fold paper, stuff envelope, seal.*

The first step was to take the Law School Admissions Test, better known as the LSAT. The LSAT is a standardized exam designed to test students' critical and analytical thinking skills. Unlike every other college or graduate school entrance exam in existence, all of which question students' understanding of actual subjects like math or science or history, the LSAT requires absolutely no concrete knowledge of any subject matter whatsoever. It doesn't test *what you know,* it tests *the way you think.* This makes the LSAT the perfect gig for intelligent people who really don't know anything. People like me. It's nice to know that the world accommodates us, too, even if it does relegate us to a life in the law.

Under the guise of examining your logical reasoning skills, the LSAT ties your brain into intricate knots. It does so by asking questions not far removed from this:

> A man walks into a bar, and the bartender tells him that he will serve him five free beers if he can answer one question correctly. The man readily agrees. The bartender lines up eight beers on the bar: an Amstel Light, a Budweiser, a Corona, a Dixie, an El Toro, a Fosters, a Guinness, and a Heineken. He sets forth the following rules: If you drink the Amstel and the Guinness, you must also drink the Heineken. If you drink the Dixie, you may not drink the Fosters or the Guinness. If you drink the El Toro, you may not drink the Budweiser. You must drink exactly two of the three bottles of Budweiser, Corona, and Fosters. Now, you have three minutes to come up with a complete and accurate list of the five beers that you can drink to follow all of these rules. Go! (Note: you may not change your mind and ask for a shot of Jack Daniel's instead.)

Because I am the type of geek who gets an instant endorphin high when presented with a task that involves making checklists or graphs, with solving puzzles or logic games of any sort, or with answering any type of question asked in a multiple-choice format, the LSAT was my friend.

I spent several months mastering the art of working out these mind-bending problems, and each Saturday afternoon I could be found sitting at my bright blue–painted desk taking a three-hour-long sample exam, scoring my test, and then analyzing my answers. Although I had consistently been doing well on my practice exams, when test day arrived, I woke up in a clammy sweat, my stomach a bundle of clenched nerves. I was so afraid that I honestly didn't think I was going to be able to make my legs walk the mile and a half to the campus classroom where the exam was to be held. But I had no choice. I was counting on this plan to work. I forced myself to put one leg in front of the other, did some deep breathing to try and calm my nerves, and motored through the exam, which turned out to be not too terrible. Uncharacteristically, I left thinking that I hadn't done half bad, even though I hadn't been afforded the luxury of taking a Kaplan test prep class like many of the other people in the room. I had done all I could; there was nothing else to do but sit back and wait for my score.

I agonized terribly during the monthlong wait, which seemed interminable. When the results of the test finally arrived, I was speechless. I had scored a 172 out of a possible 180 points. This placed me in the 99th percentile of all test-takers nationwide—a truly stellar score. A score that, I quickly realized, was probably good enough to counteract my less-than-fabulous college grade point average and gain me admission into a better-than-average law school. My mind started racing with the possibilities. Suddenly I was catapulted into very unfamiliar territory. I was face to face with the prospect of admission to an esteemed institution instead of a continuation of my relative mediocrity. I had a brief vision of myself driving a Jaguar XJS someday instead of a used Ford Escort.

I spent the next few months in frenzied excitement, sitting with Joe on our sagging couch and poring through mountains of glossy law school brochures, each exclaiming the diversity of the student body, the breadth of the curriculum, the brilliance of the faculty, and the wholly unique experience that I could get from that school and that school alone. Phrases such as "There is no other law school that brings together such intellectual talent and commitment, from such a remarkable diversity of cultural perspectives, in such an exciting campus, so never mind the enormous price tag" and "Our commitment to rigorous and exciting legal training and to pathbreaking scholarship has no parallel, so try to ignore the fact that you will have to mortgage your entire future to attend" peppered my dreams. Needless to say, I didn't sleep well.

Law school catalogs always feature photos of people looking so fascinating, so brilliant, so intellectually desirable that even if I had been a conceptual artist hell-bent on producing postmodern sculptures made entirely out of recycled metal for a living with absolutely no interest in the law whatsoever, after an hour locked in a room with a stack of those brochures, I'm pretty sure I would have had pen to paper filling out an application. A shorthaired and severe-looking woman pictured in a lecture hall, mouth caught agape in speech, hands gesturing wildly, surely making a brilliant observation about the true meaning of Justice. A bespectacled man, older than your typical law student, photographed in animated conversation with a professor, clearly having a meaningful discussion about the intellectual pitfalls in the Supreme Court's most recent decision. A gorgeous woman with a shocking head of dark curls pictured reading a book in the law library, undoubtedly digesting legal precedent dating back hundreds of years and formulating ideas for changes in the American penal system that would make our entire society a better, happier, more peaceful place in which to live. I wanted to be one of those people.

Enjoying the opportunity that I hadn't been given when selecting an undergraduate institution, I argued the relative merits of close to a hundred different law schools with Joe. Together we distilled the information in the catalogs that I had received, then I studied the lists of law school rankings until I had them practically committed to memory. Finally, I came up with complex lists of "safety" schools, "reasonable target" schools, and "pipe dream" schools to which I might apply. The final product reflected nothing so much as my desire for the two of us to leave Wisconsin and start our lives over somewhere else. My choices were scattered liberally all across the country, with a noticeable gap in the flyover states: Harvard, New York University, the University of Southern California, Loyola, the University of Washington, Northeastern, Georgetown, Florida State University, and Columbia—my very first choice of school.

I approached college professors who were complete strangers to me, but who had at some point decided to give me good grades in my classes, and asked them to consider writing letters of recommendation attesting to my intellect, character, and overall fitness to practice law. I shed tears of frustration when attempting to write some sort of meaningful and insightful personal statement that would, in three double-spaced pages or less, provide a glimpse into my true self and demonstrate exactly why it was that Saint Peter should open the pearly gates of an elite law school for me and allow my entrance.

I filled out a financial aid application two miles long that asked me questions about how much money my parents had made at their high school jobs and whether or not I had properly invested the babysitting money I had earned when I was thirteen, and then I fervently prayed that somehow, some way, I would figure out a way to finance this whole endeavor. I knew it would involve taking out staggering amounts of student loans. But at the time it kind of felt like Monopoly money—it wasn't like the twelve actual dollars occupying my wallet at that moment. It was *theoretical* money. Plus, no one would lend me more than I would be able to afford to repay, right?

In the end, I sent out one application and one application alone. I had fallen in love with New York City on my brief marital visit, and I had taken to fantasizing about living there someday. Columbia was the best law school in New York City, and that was where I wanted to be. Even with my high LSAT scores, I didn't think my chances of admission were particularly good, but I was determined to try. And I soon found out that Columbia had an early decision program that I hoped might just be my way in. Essentially, they promised to give me an early answer (and, by implication, a potential leg up in the selection process) if I promised them my soul. If they accepted me, I promised to enroll, with-holding any other applications and forsaking all others who might say yes to me down the line. I knew it was a long shot, but I had nothing to lose. I'd get Columbia's answer in December, and if they said no, I would still have plenty of time to send in applications to my other chosen schools. If they said yes, well, I couldn't even let myself imagine what I would do if they said yes.

I waited with bated breath each day as I checked my mailbox, hoping to see a fat envelope from the admissions office. Although the envelope was thin when it arrived, it contained the magic word *Congratulations*. I was going to the Ivy League.

I had absolutely no idea what I was in for.

One

Welcome to the Dollhouse

"The smaller the mind, the greater the conceit."
—Aesop

I arrived at law school constipated with fear. I had committed the cardinal law-student-to-be mistake: watching the movie *The Paper Chase* more times than I care to count during the nine months between receiving that thin acceptance letter and actually starting law school. This was my idea of trying to "get a glimpse of law school life." Instead of doing something reasonable or constructive, like—oh, I don't know—perhaps *talking* to a law student and *asking* what school was like, I decided to put my fate in the hands of an outdated, sexist movie that features men with ridiculous hair and unforgivable sideburns and portrays a terrifying and utterly unrealistic snapshot of law school.

The movie had depicted a life fueled by fear, competition, and insanity, and by the time school started, I had worked myself up into a frenzy, thoroughly believing that my time at law school would be three years of pure horror: no time for fun, no time for laughter, no time for friendship—nothing but torturous intellectual boot camp, run by cruel professors and populated by backstabbing and neurotic fellow students, all of whom would inevitably be smarter than me. I mean, they had to be smarter than me, right? They were going to an Ivy League law school!

When I nervously walked into the law school building that first morning to attend the kickoff of orientation, I was, theoretically, a full-fledged adult. In the handful of years that I had been out of my parents' house, I had developed an impressive tolerance for alcohol and a nasty shoe-shopping habit. I had gotten married. I had managed to hold down my envelope-stuffing job for an entire year, and had even been granted some faxing, phone-answering, typing, and editing duties. I had been forward-thinking enough to get my dark brown hair cut into a questionably flattering pixie style because I knew that giant pouffy sausage bangs, although a big hit in Wisconsin, weren't going to make the grade in New York. Hell, I had my very own mounting credit card debt! And if out-of-control consumer debt doesn't definitively make you an adult, then what does? But if I was such an adult, how was it that I found myself standing in the law school lobby awkward and alone, unable to escape the overwhelming feeling that I was a freshman in high school all over again?

All around the reception area were little clusters of people chatting like old friends, smiling and laughing as though they shared inside jokes that I clearly would never be a part of. Orientation was the very first organized law school activity, so how was it possible that they were all so friendly? Did they all know each other already? That's it—they had probably all gone to Harvard and Yale and Andover and Groton together, hadn't they? I began to wonder if I was the only one there who hadn't gone to a private boarding school since the age of seven.

I examined the group of guys in front of me. It was as though they had never even bothered to change out of their prep school uniforms. They were all wearing lightly wrinkled khakis that stood in contrast to their firmly pressed pinstriped button-down oxford shirts—most of them with blue and white stripes, but a couple of the jauntier ones had opted for pink and white. And they all had ramrod-straight pearly white teeth and heads of hair that looked as if they had been stolen from unsuspecting JCPenney male models. Not that any of these guys had ever stepped foot into a JCPenney's.

There they were, chattering away about private boarding school things that I would never understand. Although I couldn't actually hear their conversation, I knew what they were saying.

"Remember that time at boarding school when we got caught conjugating Latin verbs during our designated Shakespeare study period?" asked a blue-and-white-striped one.

"Twee hee hee hee hee!" they all guffawed in unison.

"And how, at the Yacht Club regatta, you got so drunk that you puked all over Thornton Blakemore's brand-new Sperry Top-siders?" reminisced a pink-and-white guy.

"Twee hee hee hee hee!"

"And remember that asshole Emerson Deveraux III who ratted you out to Headmaster Smith during sophomore year for having a girl in your room after lights out? I heard he got dinged by Goldman Sachs for an analyst position!"

"Twee hee hee hee!"

Okay, so maybe not every single person in the lobby fit that overly starched boarding school mold. But they were all smiling, talking, mingling in groups that made them easily identifiable— right out of the halls of my high school. A group of obvious jocks over there, a group of former cheerleaders next to them, a few disaffected artist types standing over to the side. It seemed instantly obvious who the "in crowd" was destined to be—a mixed group of fresh-faced young men and women who were born in the Land of J.Crew, and who exuded the subtle confidence and aura of those who had always been popular. There were also people the likes of which my white-bread Midwestern high school had never seen. Still, it seemed as if they had all sought out their own kind: a handful of observant Jewish men wearing yarmulkes, a larger bunch of Asian students, a smaller group of African-American students, many of whom managed to already be sporting Columbia Black Law Students Association T-shirts. Even the people who looked like they had been band geeks or burnouts in high school had somehow managed to find each other and congregate in their own little clusters. Where was my cluster? Was I destined to be that weird loner Ally Sheedy chick from *The Breakfast Club? Oh God, I hope I don't end up sitting all alone at a lunch table making sandwiches out of Cap'n Crunch cereal and Pixie Stix.*

Busily flitting about were several shockingly thin women who looked as if they were dressed to attend fashion shows or openings of chic new art galleries instead of law school orientation. Are four-inch heels, tight pencil skirts, cleavage-baring spaghetti-strapped tank tops, and teensy-weensy Prada bags really appropriate attire for going to school? I felt very frumpy in my kicky little floral Gap skirt, button-down short-sleeved sweater, and flat slip-on sandals. The fashionistas clacked about the lobby in their heels, smiling and making small talk with various people, but never once did they speak to one another. They never even looked one another in the eye. Oh, sure, they'd take surreptitious glances to size up the competition when they thought they could get away with it. But despite their similar appearances, you could tell immediately that they had nothing but disdain for one another. None of them clacked in my direction. For that, I was thankful.

Where were the normal people? Where were the smiling, friendly faces pictured in the law school brochure? When the school praised the diversity of the student body, I figured that they meant "We have students from many different cultures, from all sorts of educational backgrounds, and with wide and varying experiences, all of whom you will get to meet and learn with in a collaborative environment." I didn't know that what they really meant was "We have many different kinds of off-putting, snobby, exclusionary people here, none of whom are going to be the least bit interested in speaking to people outside of their predesignated cliques." Somehow I had failed to be predesignated. Was there some sort of sign-up sheet along with my registration materials that I had missed?

Faced with this situation, I did what any hysterically unreasonable person would do: I ran into the bathroom, locked myself in a stall, and hid there for the ten minutes before the official orientation program began, biting my cuticles and contemplating how terrified I was. Columbia, with its green quads and marble-columned buildings plopped in the middle of the urban jungle, was a long way from Wisconsin. Sure, if you plugged your ears while in the middle of the campus in order to drown out the sirens, the car alarms, and the underground rattle of the subway, you could imagine that you were somewhere else entirely. A week earlier, when I had first strolled down Columbia's College Walk, paved with sextagonal stones and herringbone-patterned bricks, looking up at the weathered façade of Butler Library with the names of Homer, Herodotus, Sophocles, Plato, Aristotle, Demosthenes, Cicero, and Virgil carved into the stone, gazing at the impressive rotunda of Low Library with Columbia's trademark "Alma Mater" statue with her raised arms in front, I somehow had a hard time believing that I was indeed in New York City.

Until, that is, I exited the campus gates at 116th Street and walked out onto Broadway. All at once, I was bombarded by the competing smells escaping from Ollie's Noodle Shop and the falafel store next to it, surrounded by tiny Korean-owned bodegas on every corner, disgusted by the small hardware store that had a frighteningly thick layer of dust on every single item that had obviously been sitting in the window for years without change, perplexed by the secondhand bookstore that never appeared to have even one patron, enticed by the raucous sounds of the afternoon drinking happening at the West End bar, and irritated at the double-decker tour buses that were always stopped at the corner of Broadway and 112th street outside Tom's Restaurant, which had achieved fame by serving as the exterior of the diner on the TV show *Seinfeld*.

What had I gotten myself into? In Wisconsin, I had never even heard the word *falafel,* much less seen an entire restaurant devoted to it. In Wisconsin, people still wore acid-washed jeans. In Wisconsin, a fancy dinner consisted of bratwurst boiled in beer with a side of squeaky cheese and a warmish can of Pabst. In Wisconsin, there were no boarding schools, at least not to my knowledge. In Wisconsin, I hadn't known one person who owned four-inch heels. In Wisconsin, I felt at home. Here, I had no idea where—or if—I would ever belong.

Eventually, I sucked it up, plastered a fake smile on my face, and went back out to confront my fate. People were slowly filing into a massive lecture hall to hear the official Dean's Welcome Speech, and I joined in the fray. I was caught a bit by surprise when I first walked into the classroom. I had been picturing rich mahogany paneling, cushioned burgundy leather seats, hand-painted portraits of Supreme Court justices, and other grandiose accoutrements befitting an Ivy League school. Instead I walked into a room that had obviously been decorated in the mid-1960s, made of tiered horseshoe-shaped rows of benches—surprisingly worn-out and shabby—centering around a stage with a wall of blackboards that had been sloppily erased and a large podium covered in odd-looking vertical slats of wood. Wait. On second glance, I realized that the walls of the whole room were covered in those peculiar wooden slats, many of them chipped and warping. For $30,000 a year in tuition, you got torn upholstered benches with the stuffing popping out and peeling Formica desktops? For a fleeting moment, I felt a warm flash of superiority—most of the lecture halls at the University of Wisconsin were more regal-looking than this. The law school was in need of a major makeover.

I sat for a few minutes picking at a crack in the desktop in front of my seat in a place where the Formica was already coming loose, until a starched-looking guy with wire-rimmed glasses and a jaw shaped like an anvil took the seat beside me. I recognized him immediately. He was one of the boarding school people who had been twee-heeing in the lobby a few minutes before. (He was a pink-and-whiter.) I gave him a polite smile, we exchanged hellos, and then he immediately got down to business.

"Charles Whitmore. But you can call me 'Chaz.' I'm from Yale undergrad. Before that, Exeter. In New Hampshire. I assume you've heard of it? So, what about you? Where did you go to school?" he asked.

"The University of Wisconsin. In Madison."

"And before that?"

"Before that? Um, Grafton High School. In Grafton. Wisconsin."

There was an awkwardly long pause as his ivied brain tried to wrap itself around this piece of information. "So . . ." he trailed off, "you went to a *public school?*" By that point, his voice had morphed into an undeniable sneer.

I was rendered utterly speechless. There were actually people in the world who had the audacity to say things like that out loud? Later I thought of about twenty scathing replies that I wished I had had the wherewithal to come up with at the time (mostly along the lines of "Yes, and now you'll notice that I'm sitting right here next to you, you Boarding School Bastard"), but at the time all I could do was sit there and feel my face redden with shame. Thankfully, the dean chose that very moment to begin addressing the room. I made a mental note to make a little Chaz Whitmore-shaped voodoo doll that evening and to go straight to work with some razor-sharp pins. Then I turned my attention to the stage.

The dean was an unassuming man of average height who had a markedly disheveled appearance. He wore a pair of oversized glasses perched atop his nose, giving him an owlish look that wasn't altogether unpleasant once you got accustomed to it. He began by telling us how privileged we were to be studying at an institution with such accomplished professors, such a diverse student body, and such a rich history—all right in the middle of New York City, one of the most vibrant and exciting places on earth. He told us that Columbia Law graduates went on to become U.S. Supreme Court justices, CEOs of Fortune 500 companies, U.S. senators, drafters of constitutions of newly liberated countries, creators of legal precedent, and leaders of free nations. In three short years, we would count ourselves among this elite group of alumni.

Quickly, the dean moved on to praising the diverse back-

grounds, intellectual abilities, and impressive achievements of my
entering class, proclaiming us "the most accomplished and
promising group of students in the law school's two-hundred-
year history." So, you know, no pressure or anything. He mentioned the Olympic athlete who sat in our midst, the professional
ballet dancer, the published author, the Broadway actor, the Harvard valedictorian, and the Nobel Prize–winning neurosurgeon
(okay, that last one is a lie, but not a very far-fetched one). No
mention was made of me, the woman who stuffed a damn good
envelope, typed 60 words a minute, and knew how to send a fax
overseas. He told us that the 340 members of our entering class
had been chosen from over 6,000 applicants, and then casually
dropped in the fact that the average undergraduate grade point
average was over 3.7 and the average LSAT score was in the 97th
percentile. So much for that leg up I thought I had with my fantastic 98th percentile score. How had I ended up sitting amid
these overachievers? When the dean finished his welcome speech,
I can't say I felt particularly welcomed. It was a little more like I
had just been slyly insulted by a person expert in the techniques of
passive-aggressive subterfuge.

As we were all filing out of the lecture hall, I was feeling a bit
shell-shocked and trying to wrap my mind around all that had
just been said. *You are smart,* I told myself. *They let you in for a
reason, even if you're not exactly sure what that reason is. Just remember that you've always done reasonably well in school, and if
you apply yourself you'll do fine here, too.* If I kept repeating that to
myself over and over, maybe I would start to believe it?

There was a buzz of activity in the lobby as we all organized
ourselves into alphabetical groupings in order to receive our class
schedules. During the first year of law school, everyone would be
taking the same set of classes. We would have no choice about our
course load or who our professors would be—everything was assigned to us randomly. For each of us, the first semester would include an ungraded class in legal writing, and graded classes in
contracts, torts, and civil procedure that, along with later classes

in criminal law, constitutional law, and property, would form the basis of the foundation law school curriculum.

Anybody who had watched *The Paper Chase* as many times as I had could tell you that Contracts is supposed to be the class to fear. But that one didn't frighten me so much. After all, while I might not have known exactly how contracts worked, I at least knew what they were. But torts? What were torts? (I would soon find out that a tort is "a private or civil wrong or injury for which the court provides a remedy through an action for damages.") And civil procedure? That sounded suspiciously like a Miss Manners type of class that might be more appropriate as an offering at a Southern finishing school than as a four-credit class in the foundation law school curriculum. (It's not. It's a class that teaches you the staggeringly copious rules governing when, where, and how you can sue people.)

We were told that our class would be broken up into three sections, each with a little over a hundred people. Each section would take all of its classes together, and our sectionmates would essentially be our family for the next semester. Much like your in-laws: love them or hate them, there would be no getting away from them.

When I got to the head of the line, gave my name to the flustered woman sitting behind the registration table, and was handed my first semester schedule, I found out I was in something called "Section B." I had a brief moment of paranoia. *Wait. Are these sections assigned randomly or is this some sort of . . . of . . . sectionalized judgment of my abilities? Have I been assigned to this section because "B" is a grade that I am more than familiar with receiving? That's so rude! But hey, at least I'm not in section C, right?*

It was then, in the middle of my reverie, that I had my first encounter with Christine Hsu. A tall woman with a pleasant smile, she looked friendly enough. As we stood there with newly minted schedules in hand, she began to speak to me in a voice that was unexpectedly Valley Girl–esque, and in a way that made every sentence sound more like a question than a statement.

"I'm nervous, you know? Being here? And seeing all of these people? And actually getting our class schedules? It makes it all seem so *real?*"

Hey, someone else who's nervous! "Yeah, I know what you mean. I've been so excited about this for so long, but it seems so strange to actually be here," I said.

"Of course, the first year is really just the necessary evil of getting the basics behind us? I'm really looking forward to second and third years when I can take some clinical classes and do some pro bono work? I went to Stanford and got my degree in social work? After graduation, I'll be doing public interest law?"

Stanford. Not Ivy League, but frankly better than some of the Ivies in prestige. Still, at least she didn't mention boarding school at Choate Rosemary Hall. "Really? I did nonprofit work before coming to law school and I think I might like to continue on with that afterward," I said, wondering if I had found a kindred spirit.

She continued, "But so many people here go to work for law firms? Selling their souls for money? It's like a *testament to greed.*" When she said that last part, there was absolutely no question in her voice. Her previously pleasant eyes had turned rather feral.

"Well, different strokes for different folks, I guess," I said. Although I hoped to do some good with my law degree, the truth was, I wasn't completely sure what I wanted to do after graduation, and I hadn't ruled out the possibility of selling my soul to go work for a gigantic law firm. After all was said and done, I just wanted a job. "Plus," I added, "once you're massively indebted with law school loans, pulling down a gigantic law firm salary might not seem like such a bad option. You've got to pay the bills, right?"

She paused for a moment, seemingly unfamiliar with the concept of having to borrow money in order to finance one's education. Then she wrinkled up her nose and replied, "Yeah, I suppose some people have loans to pay back or whatever? But still, it's no excuse. *No excuse at all.*"

For the second time in less than an hour, I was stopped in my tracks. The only thing that I could think of to say was, "So, what section are you in?"

"Section C."

Ha!

As we were herded around the building for our school tour, I was fixated on one thought and one thought only: the catalog had lied. Not only about the smiling, welcoming faces, but about the building itself. I knew the law school wasn't going to be your stereotypical Ivy League edifice. It was located across Amsterdam Avenue from the main Columbia campus, a fact the school did disclose in its materials, even though the catalog was filled with photographs of the grassy quads and impressive brick-and-marble buildings of the main campus itself. Jerome Greene Hall, though, where the law school is housed, was built in the 1960s by an architect with less than classical tastes. I would later learn that students referred to the law school building as "the Toaster," and indeed it did resemble some sort of boxy metallic kitchen appliance prone to burning its contents and ejecting them prematurely. For this, I was prepared. I had seen pictures of the building's exterior.

For the interior, I wasn't prepared. The catalog photographs had featured students debating with professors, students studying in the library, professors giving animated lectures, always focusing sharply on the images of the people and blurring away whatever was in the background. There was a reason for that: the shabby lecture hall where we had the Dean's Welcome wasn't an aberration. It was par for the course. As I was led through the halls, I tried to ignore the gloomy atmosphere, and instead focused on the great legal minds who had graduated from this same institution. Franklin Delano Roosevelt. Theodore Roosevelt. Benjamin Cardozo. Ruth Bader Ginsburg. Fine, so they had attended Columbia before the law school was housed in this particular building. Still, their spirits probably still kind of lived in the halls, right? And really, no matter how depressing the edifice was, I couldn't overcome my elation at the fact that I had been accepted into their ranks.

The rest of the day was a cavalcade of lectures, instructions, and introductions of varying levels of boredom. My back stiffened by the hour as I sat through presentations by the law librarians ("We have a collection of over one million books, including at least one work published in every year since 1517, just in case you're looking for some light beach reading!"), the Information Technology Department ("Forget what the librarians told you. There are three thousand different ways you can use the computer system to do legal research—no books required!"), the Security Team ("Columbia may be located on the edge of Harlem, but you're safe here, really!"), the Student Health Service ("You had better have proof that you got a measles shot back when you were ten years old!"), the Career Services Department ("We expect you to have a job upon graduation, otherwise you're going to ruin our statistics!"), and the Financial Aid Office ("We're not just giving you this money, you know; you're going to have to *pay it back!*").

Ah, the financial aid session. This was one of the few orientation sessions that was not mandatory for all students to attend. It was only for those of us who were taking out government and/or private student loans. Conspicuously absent from this session were the illustrious Chaz Whitmore and most of the rest of his prep school ilk, the do-gooder Christine Hsu, and the clacking fashionistas. I liked the looks of the people in this room: the nonrich, the nonprivileged, the self-sufficient, the indebted. These were my kind of people.

It was there, right after I had listened to a forty-five-minute lecture on the importance of borrowing responsibly, had sworn up and down to the director of financial aid that I absolutely would not, under any circumstances whatsoever, use borrowed federal funds to finance spring break trips to Jamaica, and had signed away the rights to my firstborn child in exchange for a tuition loan, that I met Rachel. A casually dressed woman with chin-length auburn hair, a smattering of freckles, and angular features, she came up to me and said, "This whole day has been pretty intense, hasn't it?"

"Definitely," I replied.

"I don't know. I still can't quite get over the dean's speech this morning. I always thought I was smart and accomplished, but I think I'm now supposed to feel like an irredeemable loser because I wasn't a Rhodes Scholar or something."

"No kidding," I said. "I'm pretty sure the speech was supposed to be welcoming, though. See?" I asked, rifling through the stack of papers I was carrying. "It says right here on our orientation schedule: *Dean's Official Welcome.*"

"Welcome, my ass. Now I'm going to have to start wondering if they let me in as part of some bizarre psychological experiment, you know? It wouldn't be that surprising—half of the people here seem like total nutjobs. Just ten minutes ago some asshole was telling me in a reverent voice about how he went to Yale and Exeter, like I was supposed to bow down in his presence or something. Screw that. I told him that I didn't even know where Exeter *was.*"

A woman with an attitude. I liked that.

"By the way," she said, "my name is Rachel. Rachel Wolfe. And since nobody here seems to be able to utter more than two sentences without rattling off their entire résumé, I'll just tell you now and get it over with. I'm from outside of Minneapolis. I went to the University of Minnesota, and I was an English major. I came out to New York to work as a paralegal in a law firm a year ago, which basically means that I've been typing FedEx labels for a living. I don't know Latin, and I don't have a trust fund. That's why I just signed a mile-high stack of promissory notes putting me in debt up to my ass."

"Hi, I'm Martha. It's really nice to meet you. Really really nice."

And that was that. My first law school friendship. I was no longer a one-woman show.

Of course, once the alcohol started flowing, more friendships quickly followed. (If they had just served mimosas at the welcome reception, it would have made the whole ordeal much easier.) That night, the law school had organized an orientation cruise for the incoming students on a boat that would travel around lower Manhattan in New York Harbor, underneath the Brooklyn Bridge, past the lights of Wall Street, and around the Statue of Liberty. Of course, by the time we were gazing up at Lady Liberty, almost everyone was too tanked to really appreciate it. Booze on the cruise was free, and for those of us about to begin living on student budgets, a deal like that wasn't to be passed up.

I had brought Joe with me to the event, and Rachel had dragged along her live-in boyfriend, David, who was just entering law school at Fordham, and who had accompanied her to the Columbia cruise under extreme protest. David was a bit of a curmudgeon: within the first half hour of the evening, I had heard him lament the "Goddamn Yankees," "Goddamn law school" (which hadn't officially begun yet for either of us), and the "Goddamn weak drinks on this boat." I kept waiting for him to move on to more sweeping statements like "Goddamn life" or "Goddamn humanity," but thankfully we never got that far. Underneath the façade, however, David really was a nice guy, and by the end of the night I had the distinct feeling that Rachel, David, Joe, and I were going to be good friends.

After someone accidentally bumped into me, causing me to spill my beer down the front of Joe's pants, I excused myself to get a new beverage. Carefully, I made my way across the crowded deck to the bar, which was in a dim room inside the boat with a completely empty dance floor, where a mirrored disco ball hung sad and unaccompanied while the Seal song "Kiss from a Rose" echoed from the speakers. As I stood in line at the bar surveying my surroundings, a deeply tanned young woman with warm brown eyes and a head of shiny honey-blond hair smiled at me and said, tipsily, "Hi, I'm Katie. I need another beer. And, oh my God, I totally saw a dead guy yesterday morning."

"I'm Martha. And, um, you saw *what?*" She couldn't be serious, right?

"A dead guy!" Katie replied. "My mom just helped me move out here from California—that's where I'm from—and we had just finished unloading things into my dorm. Afterward, we were hungry, right? So we decided to go get brunch. We were going to the Baci Café over on Broadway, because one of my suitemates said it was good. Anyway, right in front of the restaurant was a dead guy just lying there on the sidewalk. We practically had to step over him in order to get inside! There was an ambulance there, but the ambulance guys were just kind of standing around and taking their time. Is that what New York is always like?" She seemed to sincerely think I would know the answer to her query.

"I'm not sure," I answered, hesitantly. "But I don't think so. I mean, I haven't seen any dead people yet, and I've been living on campus for over a week now." As though that made me an expert.

"Well, that's reassuring. Things can only get better from here, right?"

"Probably so. But, Katie? Why didn't you just choose another restaurant to go to when you saw the dead guy?"

She laughed sheepishly and said, "Well, I figured things like that might just be par for the course in New York. I mean, the people sitting at the outside tables not three feet away were acting like they hardly even noticed! They were just eating and smoking and drinking coffee. And I didn't want to look like the girl from California who didn't belong. So I pushed my mom into the restaurant and acted like it was no big deal. But it was *totally* a big deal."

"That makes sense," I said, understanding her desire to fit in. It was nice to meet someone else who admitted to feeling out of place.

Although I took an instant liking to Katie, just a few minutes of speaking to her made me suspect that there might be a pretty big difference between the people who had taken time off and worked (if even only for a year or two) before coming to law school and those who had plowed straight through right from college. Even a short amount of time truly out on your own, I realized, does give you a different perspective on things. I was hardly the world's most mature twenty-three-year-old, but I felt kind of old standing next to Katie. She was living in the dorms (albeit fancy dorm suites reserved exclusively for law students). I hadn't lived in a dorm since my freshman year in college. Her mother brought her out to law school. I came with my husband and my cat. She had spent the last year chairing fund-raisers for her sorority and acting as a delegate at Model United Nations conferences. I had spent the last year trying to pay my rent.

With fresh beverages in hand, Katie and I headed back outside so that I could introduce her to Rachel, David, and Joe. As we were walking, I noticed two guys following a few feet behind us.

"Do you know who they are?" I whispered.

"Yeah. The short one is Aaron, and the tall one is Wade. I'm not sure why, but they've kind of been following me around all night."

"Well, I have a guess. It might be because you're tall, blond, and gorgeous?" *And wearing a really short skirt,* I thought.

"Oh, I totally doubt that. I mean, do you see how flat my chest is? My sister just got her boobs done. Now she's sleeping with one of the Denver Broncos. They seem like nice enough guys, though."

"The Denver Broncos?"

"No. Aaron and Wade."

And, indeed, they were. Wade was an eternal frat boy from Chicago, who at the very outset expressed his intention to do as little work and have as much fun as possible over the next three years. "As long as I come out of it with a diploma, I figure I'm golden," he said, beer in hand, about four seconds after I met him. In stark contrast, Aaron was apparently making it his profession to be an eternal student. He was in his early thirties and had a Ph.D. in political science from Princeton, had studied at the London School of Economics, and had just finished a teaching stint at a university somewhere in the hinterlands of England. Unsure of what to do next, he had opted for yet more schooling.

By the time Katie, Wade, Aaron, and I had fought our way

through the crowds on the deck of the boat, the intoxication level had visibly increased, the outside temperature had noticeably decreased, and Rachel was talking to a woman named Elizabeth Lee, a very professional-looking woman who wore perfectly tailored black pants and a crisp white silk button-down shirt, which contrasted with the more casual attire that most of the other students were wearing. Her habit of talking with her hands immediately drew my attention to the immense, sparkling diamond ring that she wore on the third finger of her right hand. Each time Elizabeth gestured, the light reflected off the facets in a new direction, and I was somehow reminded of the lonely disco ball adorning the empty dance floor near the bar. Self-consciously, without even thinking, I found myself twirling my diamond engagement ring backward, so the minuscule stone faced the palm of my hand.

During a short conversation with Elizabeth, I learned that she was from Boston, where her father was a name partner in a law firm, she had gone to Penn, and she had spent the last two years working as an analyst at Smith Barney, which had left her with dark circles under her eyes from the sleep deprivation she had survived during her tenure there. Elizabeth definitely seemed to have a head for business.

"I considered going for my M.B.A., but decided on law school instead. To tell you the truth, it's really what my father wanted. I know I'll end up back in investment banking someday—I want to focus on structured finance—but he kind of insisted that I do it this way." In painstaking detail, Elizabeth went on to explain the opportunity cost of choosing law school, which takes three years, instead of business school, which only takes two years: an extra year of studying, an extra year of paying tuition, an extra year of forgoing an impressive salary. A wise businessperson, I was told, would go the business school route, invest the extra money in a moderately aggressive portfolio—or even just a CD with a decent interest rate that compounded monthly—and sail off to a heavenly future with Merrill Lynch.

Once convinced that her speech was over, I answered with a

simple "Yeah," not really understanding what she meant, and thinking that we probably didn't have much in common.

"It's weird how some people here seem to think that if you want to make money, something is inherently wrong with you. I mean, isn't that what we're here for? To train ourselves for careers? Careers where we will make money? But this afternoon at this Asian Law Students Association meeting that I went to, I overheard this woman who was ranting about how it's our duty to use the law to change society and how people who dare go into corporate law are essentially loathsome, soulless warriors for the devil. What's up with that? Since when is it wrong to want to make a living?"

"I don't know. But I think I know just the woman you're talking about."

As we all stood on the deck, watching the twinkling lights of lower Manhattan, we made a rather unlikely group. But such is the nature of friendships forged at the beginning of law school: you're thrown together, unsure of your place, and desperate to establish an overall social order and to figure out exactly where you fit. You want to know who you should look up to and who you should shun, who you should admire from afar and who you should laugh at. So, out of necessity, people at law school form friendships very quickly and under extreme duress. Without the luxury of being particularly choosy, we scan the room for others who have looks of fear in their eyes that approximate our own, we offer a hand in friendship, and we hope for the best. Because, for the most part, those friends are who you're going to be stuck with, for better or for worse. Kind of like an arranged marriage. Welcome to law school!

Two

Gunning for Glory

"Good teaching is one-fourth preparation and three-fourths theater."
—Gail Godwin

When I stepped into the lecture hall a few minutes before our very first law school class was scheduled to begin, the professor was not yet there, and the room was abuzz with an unmistakable sound: the sound of gossip. Oh, sweet gossip! I knew this place was just like high school! And because I didn't remember having done anything really embarrassing in public as of that particular moment, I was pretty sure the gossip wasn't about me. Intrigued, I trotted over to Rachel and Katie and asked, "What's going on?"

Excitedly, Katie replied, "Didn't you hear about Julia Spencer?"

"Julia Spencer? Who's that?"

"She was that curly redheaded woman who got sloppy drunk on the orientation cruise, remember?" Rachel said. "But it doesn't matter. She's gone."

"Gone? She dropped out already? But we haven't even had our first class yet!"

"No. Not dropped out. Totally better. She got into Yale!" Katie screeched.

"What?"

"Yale Law School," Katie answered. "She was on the waiting list there for months, and they called her up yesterday to say they had a spot for her after all. She packed her stuff and was out of here like forty minutes after getting the call."

"But . . . but . . . we all just packed up our lives and moved here to New York like a week ago. Then she up and moved all over again to go to New Haven?" I asked.

"Of course she did, Martha," Rachel answered. "And you can bet your sweet ass that I'd have done the same thing. Come on, it's *Yale* that we're talking about here. Seriously, somebody must have *died* in order to free up that spot, because people don't just change their minds about going to Yale."

Rachel was right. Yale was the crème de la crème. Columbia may be Ivy League, but even among the elite schools, there is a hierarchy. According to the current *U.S. News & World Report* rankings (the most widely read and respected list), Columbia Law School is the Number Four law school in the country. (Although the rankings do change a bit from year to year, they never seem to change significantly, especially among the top order of schools, which rarely shift more than one or two spots in either direction, if that.) Yale is first, Stanford second, Harvard third. Rounding out the top ten are New York University, the University of Chicago, the University of Pennsylvania, Berkeley, the University of Michigan, and the University of Virginia. Beyond that, the law schools are ranked numerically down to number one hundred (comprising the first two "tiers" of schools), at which time it seems like the ranking people got tired and threw in the towel— the rest of the seventy-some law schools out there are simply divided into "Tier Three" and "Tier Four" and listed alphabetically within those categories without any further explanation.

Anyway, I was more than happy right where I was. But apparently some people thought that, even within the top handful of schools in the country, it was worth uprooting your life at a moment's notice to move up a few notches in the hierarchy. Me? I wasn't so sure. I mean, would you really want to go through law school with everyone knowing that you were the very last person accepted? That's kind of like volunteering to be the last kid picked in gym class, isn't it? I hoped for Julia Spencer's sake that she was able to slip into Yale unnoticed, and that she wasn't forced to wear a scarlet "W" for the next three full years in order to signify that she had been admitted from the waiting list.

The gossipy buzz about Julia died down the second our professor walked into the room. It was our first official class—Contracts—and I was sitting in my seat, pen anxiously poised to paper, curious to meet the professor who would be teaching me this most fundamental of law school courses. He was middle aged, stocky, and despite his neatly combed graying hair, he looked weathered. He wore a suit and tie, and when his jacket swung open, you could see the outline of a pack of cigarettes in the breast pocket of his shirt. He stepped up to the podium, introduced himself as Professor Sidney Burrough, and unrolled the large seating chart that we had all been required to sign during orientation, choosing the seats that we would occupy for the rest of the semester, which allowed professors to note the names of the students they were speaking to if asking or answering a question. He told us that in his class we would be studying the law of economic exchanges, looking to both common law and the statutes contained in the Uniform Commercial Code to understand how contract law enables our economy to function in a reliable, efficient, welfare-maximizing manner.

After giving a lengthy speech about how the class would be run and philosophizing about the importance of having default legal rules to fill in the gaps when contractual disputes arise, Professor Burrough lifted his head and noticed that we were all in a collective frenzy, scribbling in our notebooks or typing on our laptops, trying our best to take down his every word, afraid that if we didn't, we'd be missing something critically important.

"Don't write all of this down, people!" he reprimanded. "Why must you all write and write? Stop writing. *Start absorbing.*"

Then he posed a question to the class. "Now. Say that a violin dealer offers a violin for sale, and agrees to sell it to a customer for $500. Later, before the sale is consummated, the dealer discovers that the violin is actually a rare Stradivarius worth over a million dollars, and he no longer wants to follow through with the deal.

There was an agreement between the parties. An underlying premise of the agreement has been changed. Should the contract be enforced anyway?"

Unsure whether this was a hypothetical question or if the professor actually expected an answer from someone, there was an awkward silence throughout the classroom. Finally, my friend Aaron, the perpetual student, raised his hand.

"Yes, Mister . . . Mister . . . Berger," Professor Burrough said, after consulting the seating chart and locating Aaron's name.

"Well, I would think that because the violin dealer was a professional, he should have known the value of the violin before he offered it for sale. So possibly he should bear the burden of his own mistake and be made to go through with the deal."

"An interesting point, Mr. Berger. What if, instead of a professional dealer, it was me—a man not at all knowledgeable about anything musical—who found the old violin in my grandmother's attic and then, without knowing its true value, made a deal to sell it for $500? After finding out what it's worth, should I be forced to sell for the agreed-upon price?"

"In that case, maybe not. You wouldn't have had any reason to know the real value of the instrument."

"Ah, but if I was a smart boy, I would have gotten the violin appraised before I offered it for sale."

"Well, that's true," Aaron replied.

"What if the price differential wasn't so great? What if, after making the deal, I found out that my grandmother's violin was worth $5,000 instead of $1 million? Should I be made to sell it for the $500 price?"

"Maybe in that case . . . it doesn't seem so egregious."

"You see, these are the kinds of contracts that are prevalent in our society: simple agreements, often not even in writing, where the parties don't anticipate anything unusual and don't negotiate any contractual provisions to address contingencies like this. In such cases, we need a set of rules to fill in the blanks, and to render these contracts complete. If we didn't have default rules, we would need lawyers to argue every single dispute from scratch, and the transaction costs would prevent these economic exchanges from ever happening. It could bring our entire economy to a halt."

"Professor Burrough," asked Aaron.

"Yes, Mr. Berger?"

"I understand the importance of having the rules. But what is the rule? Does the violin dealer have to sell the Stradivarius like he promised?"

"Oh, I have no idea!" he laughed. "It's just a question for thought. I expect that some courts would make him sell the violin and some wouldn't. I suppose I could go away and do some research if I knew how to use those computerized research services like Westlaw and Lexis, but I don't—even though they've both been explained to me many times. For tomorrow, read pages one to eighteen, pages thirty-eight through eighty-two, and pages eighty-nine through one-twenty-six in your casebook. I'm sure there will be some actual rules in there." And then, to signal the end of the class, he rolled up the seating chart, put it underneath his arm, stood directly beneath the big NO SMOKING sign at the side of the dais, took a cigarette from the pack in his pocket, and lit it, exhaling a furious stream of smoke.

I had gone into my first law school class with the naïve expectation that the professor was going to go up to the podium and *teach us the law of contracts.* But, it turns out, that is decidedly not the way it was to work.

Elite law schools pride themselves on the fact that they instruct students on "how to think like lawyers" instead of teaching them the actual law that they need to know in order to *be* lawyers. They focus on legal theory instead of "black letter law." Instead of standing up in front of the class and saying "In order to have a valid contract, you need (i) an offer, (ii) an acceptance, and (iii) an exchange of something of value, and I will now explain those things to you so that you, too, can understand them," the professors make you figure it out for yourself. They do this by employing the case method, where they force their students to read hundreds of judicial opinions ("cases") during the course of a semester, somehow decipher what each case is saying, and then try to piece the rules extracted from each case together to understand how they work in unison to form an entire body of law. It's not dissimilar to trying to work an eight-hundred-piece jigsaw puzzle made up of only plain white pieces.

Each day the class studies several assigned cases, trying to distill the court's logic and figure out exactly what the meaning of each decision is. This task is made all the more difficult by virtue of the fact that many of the most important decisions were written in the days before the cotton gin had been invented, making the language a little bit less than user-friendly. The professors know what the cases mean. (I'm sure that when they are granted tenure, they are given teacher's editions of the five-inch-thick casebooks that explain the exact meaning and importance of each decision.) But do they explain the meaning to the students? No. No, they don't.

Instead, they rely on a medieval torture device called the Socratic method. Rather than lecturing or explaining or teaching, professors call on students and question them at length about the meaning and implications of each of the assigned cases. Socrates' original theory was that asking his students a series of questions like this would force them to arrive at their own answers by gradually building a logical chain of reasoning. But somehow I really don't think the modern version of the Socratic method is exactly what Socrates had in mind back in the days of ancient Greece, when he was off wearing his cute little toga and questioning his students. I could be wrong, but I don't picture Socrates making his students cry. Over time, though, the Socratic method has been twisted into a process whereby venerated law professors reduce innocent law students to quivering heaps of jelly by questioning them relentlessly in front of a large class filled with their peers, most of whom are consciously suppressing the urge to squeal aloud with glee over the fact that they have been spared the terror of being selected as that day's official victim. They say that the point of the Socratic exercise is to create a dialogue between professor and student, a challenge that will draw out deeper and deeper knowledge. In reality, it is more like fraternity hazing.

The professor asks. You answer. He says, "But what about this? How do you reconcile your answer with this?" You dig deep within yourself and find a response. He then says, "Okay, so how about we twist the facts of the case around, then how would you respond?" This process is then repeated ad nauseam until, at some point, the professor has backed you into a corner and proved that you are nothing but a monumental idiot. You might be best off just acting like an idiot right off the bat when you're called on, because chances are about 99.9 percent that you will be made to look like one before the ordeal is over. I know from experience that it's best to make the process as short and sweet as possible.

Thankfully, the Socratic method has largely fallen by the wayside at many, if not most, law schools, and certainly in large part in the Ivy League. These days most professors find a tiny bit of kindness in their hearts and find some way to straddle the fence: they assign a group of people to be "on call" for each particular week (letting you know in advance that you'd damn well better do your reading), they call on people in alphabetical order (again, everyone appreciates some advance notice), or they simply rely on people to volunteer.

Every law school seems to have at least one holdout, though, one sadistic professor who feels the need to test his students' mettle and assault them full-on with the Socratic method. Why does he do this? Does he believe in his heart of hearts that it is his duty to make students sweat in order to build character? Is he clinging to the sweet, sweet memory of the generations upon generations of law students who have suffered the Socratic fate, unwilling to let the tradition die with him? Is he just plain mean? No one knows. No one asks. Everyone is too busy trying to avoid eye contact with him, lest they be the next one called upon.

My personal sadist was my Civil Procedure professor, Victor Strickland, who was a towering figure in perfect athletic shape from riding his ancient three-speed bicycle from his home to the law school each day, and without a single hair on his knobby, aging head. His booming voice and brusque manner left students shaking in their seats, and he was uniformly feared throughout the school, even by those who weren't in his class. I think people (possibly even other professors) were afraid he might stop them at random in the hall and start grilling them about the Federal Rules of Civil Procedure. "You there, the one with the brown hair, glasses, and double chin! Recite Rule 12(b)(6) and provide a concise but complete explanation! Now!" It wasn't out of the realm of possibility.

About two weeks after classes had started, I got called on by Professor Strickland. It was eight-thirty on a Wednesday morning and I was sitting innocently enough in class, having let my mind wander momentarily to the enigma that was Brian Peters, the Show Off who sat directly in front of me. Brian arrived at least ten minutes early for class each day, which gave him ample time to spread out his inch-thick stack of tabbed and cross-indexed notes, open his casebook to the day's assignment (highlighted in a systematic manner with six different colors of fluorescent ink), display his meticulously typed class outline, and arrange the supplemental Law Review articles that he found while doing unassigned research in a symmetrical arc around his seat for all to see. Brian was a quiet guy, but he was terribly intimidating in a subtle sort of way—without ever uttering a word, his proudly displayed color-coded notes and extracurricular research let everyone know exactly how ahead of the curve he was.

"Today," Professor Strickland started, "we are going to begin to explore the fascinating topic of the constitutional limits of personal jurisdiction in the federal courts. I trust that you have all done your assigned reading. Now, I would like to speak with Ms. Kimes."

He was met with a sickening silence, because my brain simply couldn't wrap itself around the fact that he was actually calling on me.

"Ms. Kimes? Has Ms. Kimes graced us with her presence in class today?" he asked impatiently, glancing down at his seating chart.

"Oh yes, yes I'm here," I stammered, in shock upon realizing that I was the one he was addressing. *Way to start off on the right foot, Martha, you dumb-ass.*

"Ms. Kimes, can you tell us the facts of *International Shoe v. Washington?*"

Stay calm. You've read this case. You may not really understand what it means, but you at least know what happened. Now open your mouth and say something marginally intelligent. "Yes?" I replied, feeling the stares of my classmates burning into the back of my head.

"Well . . . ? What were they?" he demanded, his bald pate shining underneath the fluorescent overhead lights.

Several quiet giggles emanated from around the room.

Shit. Shit shit shit. "Um, the International Shoe Company manufactured and sold footwear? The company was incorporated in the state of Delaware and was run out of Missouri? But they conducted business around the country?" *Why are you suddenly turning every sentence into a question? You're not a contestant on Jeopardy!*

I began again. "The company had twelve employees in Washington State, who displayed merchandise—shoes—and accepted orders. The company didn't have any offices in Washington, though, and it didn't enter into any actual contracts there. The State of Washington was trying to sue the company for failure to pay unemployment taxes, and brought suit in a state court in Washington."

"What was the question to be decided?"

"The issue was whether or not the International Shoe Company could be sued in a court in the State of Washington without violating the Due Process Clause of the U.S. Constitution."

"How did the Court rule?"

"The Supreme Court said that the company could be sued there."

"And can you explain the Court's reasoning?"

Crap. No, I really can't explain it, because I don't really understand it. What to do, what to do? I've got to say SOMETHING. Oh, I know! I'll just regurgitate some of the nonsensical yet important-sounding quotes from the decision that I highlighted here in my casebook. Brilliant plan! "Well, the court stated that 'Due process requires only that in order to subject a defendant to a judgment in personam, if he be not present within the territory of the forum, he have certain minimum contacts with it such that the maintenance of the suit does not offend traditional notions of fair play and substantial justice.' "

"Yes, but what does that *mean*, Ms. Kimes?" he barked.

Okay, brilliant plan foiled. "I think that it means that if a company does enough business in a particular state, then it can be sued there. That it's a matter of determining whether or not the company had the necessary minimum contacts with that state to make it fair to have to defend a lawsuit there."

"Fine. What is your opinion of the disposition of this case?"

My opinion of the case? My opinion is that it is really unfair that the case is entitled International Shoe. *This makes it sound like a sexy—or at the very least marginally interesting—case about footwear. Possibly hand-crafted French sandals or supple Italian leather loafers. But instead it turned out to be a case about some schlocky company that, according to the facts stated in the judicial opinion, only provided its salesmen with* one shoe *from each pair to display as a sales tool. My opinion is that the title of this case is misleading and that the company has a lot to learn about properly marketing shoes.*

I knew, though, that an answer like that would not go over

very well with the Sadistic Professor. The Socratic method is not the proper venue for offering truthful opinions; it is a time for trying to minimize damage. Instead I took a cleansing breath, threw my shoulders back, and said, "I think the idea of minimum contacts is a crucially important legal precedent, and I think that the case was well-reasoned and logically sound. It makes sense that if you transact business somewhere, you can reasonably expect to be able to answer for your actions in that place." *Phew.*

He paused for dramatic effect, making it clear to everyone that this was where it was going to get interesting. "Are you sure of that answer, Ms. Kimes?"

"Yes?" I squeaked, in a very unsure voice, by then fully aware that I was about to take a public beating.

"So you are saying that, even though I live in New York, if I happen to go on vacation to Boca Raton, and if I happen to buy a pair of sandals while I'm there, that a year later I should be able to be sued in a Florida court for something wholly unrelated simply because I wanted to be able to expose my toes to the fresh warm Florida air during my holiday?"

Is he trying to be funny at my expense? "Well, no. I mean, that's not what I was trying to say."

"You think that my spur-of-the-moment decision to walk into a shoe store in Boca and buy some sandals means that my cousin Samuel, who lives in Albuquerque and has never even been east of the Mississippi, should be able to sue me in a court in Florida because he thinks my failure to return any of his phone calls over the last eight years has caused him great pain and suffering? Is that what you're saying? Because that seems like the logical conclusion of the statement you made here just moments ago."

There were a few nervous titters from the far corners of the lecture hall.

Okay, so he's definitely trying to make a joke at my expense. I blinked back tears as I stammered, "No, that's not what I meant! Not at all. What I meant was . . . was . . ." And then there was nothing. Total silence. I clearly had no idea what it was that I meant. And everyone knew it. *Dear God, make this end now, please?*

I'm not sure if he took pity on me at that point or if he just gave up. It didn't matter. I was just happy to be done. "Is there anyone else who is prepared to address the issue at hand?" Professor Strickland asked.

About three milliseconds after those words had passed from his lips, a man's hand shot up into the air. A hand with long, fat fingers that looked like sausages connected to an arm that had a disturbing amount of wiry dark hair peeking out from underneath the cuff of a freshly pressed shirt. Todd Sebastian. The Gunner.

There's one in every single classroom in every single law school in every single corner of the world. Whether you're at Yale or at Southeastern Podunk Law School, walk into any random lecture hall and wait five minutes, tops—you're sure to see a student who is so enamored with the sound of his own voice in the classroom that he finds it physically impossible to keep his hand from gunning up into the air every time the professor asks a question, even if it's merely a rhetorical one. Ten minutes after school began, everyone was already sick of the Gunner.

"I am fully prepared to rise to the challenge," Todd stated, "and to address the issues that Ms. Kimes was unable to meaningfully discuss."

I can't believe that sycophantic asshole just said that!

"Although I agree with the Supreme Court's ultimate decision," he said, "I must note that I do consider its reasoning a bit pedantic. Nevertheless, I do not believe that the rationale that the Court set forth would permit your cousin to bring the suit of which you speak in a Florida court. You see, the *International Shoe* decision wouldn't allow such a case to go forward in Florida because your contacts with the state were not so continuous or systematic as to allow general jurisdiction by courts in the state, as this would offend traditional notions of fair play and justice."

Why couldn't I have said that? I could feel the silent snickering of my fellow students. I just knew that Chaz Whitmore was sitting in his seat two rows behind me and smiling a smug little smile, secure in the knowledge that my failure to perform was thoroughly attributable to my pedestrian academic background.

It wasn't that everyone was cheering the Gunner's success—they all felt as much disdain for him as I did. But witnessing another student's failure at the Socratic method was like watching a train wreck: although painful, it was impossible to look away. It was an unusual opportunity to watch another person's belittlement, an opportunity that was simultaneously horrifying, empowering, and somewhat embarrassing. Whenever a fellow student was performing well, the mixture of emotions in the room inevitably included both excitement at the possibility that one of us might actually manage to beat a professor at his own game, and resentment over the fact that the student holding his own was someone other than ourselves.

As I squirmed in my seat, Todd continued. "If anything, the decision would only allow specific jurisdiction for a cause of action arising out of the narrowly tailored activity that you conducted by purchasing your undoubtedly lovely sandals within the forum state. It's this crucial distinction between specific and general jurisdiction that is at the crux of the Court's reasoning."

As though timed perfectly to coincide with the Gunner's last word, the Sadistic Professor snapped his casebook shut, indicating that the class was over.

Afterward, Rachel ran up to me in the hall outside the classroom and said, "Martha, I know what you're thinking. But you did fine. Fine! Better than fine!"

"I sounded like I barely had command of the English language."

"No, not at all! You knew the facts of the case and you knew what the Court decided and you explained it all just fine."

"Oh, come *on*. By the end I could barely string together two coherent words."

"That's just the way it works, Martha. I mean, it's only been a couple of weeks, but it's quite clear how this whole thing goes down. No matter how much you know, how many times you read the case, how perfectly you think you have it mastered, the professor will keep going and going and going until he's succeeded in making you look like a fool. Especially Professor Strickland—he's like the Energizer Bunny. Only meaner."

"Well, what about that asshole Todd and his 'I can explain everything that Ms. *Kimes* can't! Ms. *Kimes* didn't understand the crucial *difference* between the blah and the blah.' I can't believe him!"

"Martha, we all hate him. I bet his own mother hates him. And do you notice how even Professor Strickland is starting to hate him? I mean, we're barely two whole weeks into classes and he's already stopped calling on him. Todd just raises his hand and starts talking."

She was right, of course, but that didn't stop the sting. I went home, took a long, hot shower to wash off the feeling of violation that had overcome me, and began plotting my revenge.

When Joe arrived home, I made a confession.

"Honey, there's something I have to tell you. I'm not sure exactly how you'll react, but I've got to get this off my chest. I'm thinking about becoming a murderess."

"Oh really? Exactly who is it that you plan to slay? This nasty professor you're always talking about?"

"No. Todd Sebastian—the Gunner. He made me feel about two inches tall in Civil Procedure today. And he's just so . . . so . . . *smarmy*. I bet he ate paste as a child. Yes, he definitely has the aura of a paste eater."

"Murder might be a little drastic, don't you think?"

"Drastic? You should have seen him in class! It was bad enough that I was dying at the feet of Professor Strickland, but then Todd just swooped in like a vulture waiting to feast on my bloody remains."

"You'd probably go to jail if you killed him. That might interfere with your law school plans."

"Well, I bet there's some loophole that would get me off, don't you think? Self-defense? Insanity? Defense of my own sanity?"

"I wouldn't know, Martha—you're the law student here," Joe said, rolling his eyes at me. "In any case, can we agree that it's best for you to at least hold off on the killing for a little while?"

"I guess. But in the meantime, can I leave a jar of paste on Todd's desk with an anonymous note saying 'Eat your heart out'?"

"Probably not, honey."

"Damn. Just damn."

So I didn't kill the Gunner. But I did spend a lot of time contemplating the essence of his evil. Because when it comes down to it, it's not just that the Gunner likes the sound of his own voice. It's not just that he wants to display his intelligence. The Gunner is jockeying for position, trying to win by intimidation. He's trying to make himself look smart, sure, but more than that, he's trying to make *everyone else feel dumb*. The second part is far more important than the first. The Gunner lives for the class taught by the Sadistic Professor. In that class, he's not just raising his hand to answer a question in a vacuum. He's raising his hand to answer a question that another student has demonstrated an inability to answer. It's the Law School Holy Grail: the simultaneous display of one's own superior knowledge coupled with the instillation of self-doubt and feelings of ignorance in others.

This is the nature of competition in law school, especially during the first semester when students have yet to receive grades or class standings and therefore have no objective measure by which to reassure themselves of their own intelligence or to figure out how they compare to others. Every law student has heard stories of people who rip pages out of books in the library or hide books necessary to complete assignments, simply to prevent their classmates from being able to do their work. These are the typical tales passed around when people discuss the "cutthroat competition" in certain law schools.

But the competition that I witnessed, especially during my first year, went far more to the core. It didn't just mess with my ability to do my assignments, it messed with my head. It messed with my soul. It made me question my intelligence, my ability, and my self-worth. The competition that I witnessed was that of a hypnotizing subconscious mindfuck performed by Todd Sebastian, Brian Peters, Chaz Whitmore, and the myriad others who simply couldn't manage to feel good about themselves and their own intelligence unless they made others feel inferior.

It's a mindfuck, all right, but you know what? It totally worked on me.

Three

THE LETTER OF THE LAW

"To be conscious that you are ignorant is a great step to knowledge."
—BENJAMIN DISRAELI

With my battle wounds from my tangle with the Sadistic Professor still fresh, stinging, and quite possibly infected, I moped around feeling like a total fake, a complete fraud. I was completely overwhelmed by everything laid out before me. All I could focus on was the fact that I had uprooted my life and borrowed thousands upon thousands of dollars for tuition, and all I was doing was *pretending* to be a law student. Because I didn't feel like a law student. I didn't feel like I was learning the law. Although I had been studying diligently, I couldn't get a real grasp on any of the material. I suppose that I had absorbed a few points about jurisdiction and negligence and bargained-for exchange, but I knew for a damn fact that everyone else understood those things on some cosmic and enlightened level, while I was just muddling through, trying to make it day by day.

Just as I was reaching the end of my rope, I figured out what my problem was. One late September day as Rachel and I were having lunch, I noticed an unfamiliar-looking book sticking out of her frayed canvas bag—it was taller than our casebooks, relatively thin in comparison, had a paperback cover, and bore the words *Gilbert Law Summaries: Contracts* down the spine. Curious, I looked more closely and saw another book next to the first, entitled *Calamari and Perillo on Contracts*. And right next to that one was another, bearing the title *Civil Procedure—Emmanuel Law Outline*. And next to that one was a book called *Civil Procedure: Examples and Explanations*.

"Rachel, no wonder your bag is always overflowing! What are all these books?" I asked. "None of them were on our class lists."

"Outlines? And hornbooks?" she replied incredulously, as though the answer should have been obvious to any three-year-old.

I answered with nothing but a questioning stare.

"Are you seriously trying to tell me that you don't have any commercial study aids?" she asked.

"Well, um, no. I just bought what they told me to buy."

"Martha, you need to march your ass down the street to the bookstore, *tout de suite*. This shit is like the *answer key*. Or at least it helps you make sense of all that indecipherable nonsense in the casebooks. It's like CliffsNotes for law school!"

My eyes instantly widened. "These books *help make sense of stuff*? They might *make me understand*?!?"

Before she could even answer, I was off and running, credit card in hand. One hour and over three hundred dollars later, I returned home laden with commercial outlines (truly the mother lode—they include a complete course overview, showing how each case fits into the larger picture of the class), hornbooks (which provide scholarly explanations of the fundamental rules, principles, and issues in each area of law), Nutshells (which provide general overviews of legal topics, without delving into the real nitty-gritty or analyzing the cases in detail), and various and sundry other workbooks, restatements, and commentaries that promised to offer me some sort of window onto the law—all of which I had thrown into my shopping basket willy-nilly. I felt as if I had a new lease on life.

With my newfound study aids in hand, I decided that I needed to map out a plan. Preventing any further public humiliation at the hands of my professors became priority one, and I dove in headfirst and settled in to a maniacal study routine.

During the first few weeks of classes, I had been blissfully content to simply do my assigned reading, try to understand and digest the materials, and hope that things would somehow magically sink in at some point. But it hadn't really been working. And my conversation with Rachel made me realize that it was not enough to just read the assigned cases—apparently I needed to read the assigned cases, read the hornbooks' discussion of the importance of the assigned cases, read the commercial outlines' explanation of how the assigned cases fit together with previously assigned cases to form a unified body of law, read the Nutshells' vague explanation of the assigned cases and their relevance to the subject matter at hand, and read a few other books that would offer commentary and further explanation of the assigned cases. My daily reading load had quintupled. I was studying what seemed like every waking moment.

And it wasn't just me. And, apparently, it wasn't a disease unique to Columbia law students. One afternoon, while shopping at the Apple Tree market around the corner from my apartment, I ran into David in a narrow aisle that housed an oddly assorted jumble of soft drinks, cat litter, and hand soap.

"Hey, David, doing some grocery shopping?" I asked, stating the obvious.

"Yeah. Rachel drank the last of the coffee."

"So how are classes going at Fordham? Are you settling in?"

"I'm so sick of studying," David answered. "And look at my backpack—I'm going to get a hernia before I make it the three blocks home. This thing weighs a goddamn ton."

"What do you have in there?"

"Ah, I just got back from a trip to the campus bookstore. I had to go buy Gilbert's for Contracts, and the Emmanuel outline for Torts, and some flash cards for Civ Pro—you know. I was using Rachel's, but she got sick of sharing. I'm pretty pissed. If I could have kept reading her outlines, I would have saved myself a couple hundred bucks. Goddamned expensive study aids."

"So you're using all that stuff, too?" I asked, looking for reassurance.

"Shit, yeah. I'm not sure why, though. It's supposed to make life easier, right? But instead reading all this crap just makes your work take ten times as long."

"Well, I'm glad it's not just me," I said, grabbing a bag of cat litter and a box of tissues. "Now I've got to get back to the casebooks."

But the problem was, after having read the cases and the eighteen incantations of extracurricular explanatory material, even if I felt like I might understand things on at least a basic level, my experience with Professor Strickland had taught me that understanding can take leave of you on a moment's notice once a professor calls your name. In order to be truly safe, I decided, the understanding culled from the myriad sources that I had gathered for each class needed to be reduced to writing, memorialized on a single page of paper that I could cling to with shaking hands when forced to explain the facts, reasoning, and holdings of a case in front of my classmates.

Conventional wisdom says that, at least during the first year of law school, students should prepare a "brief" for each case they are assigned to study. A typical case brief summarizes the facts of the case, sets forth the case's procedural background, identifies the specific issue that the court is addressing, and gives a concise explanation of the reasoning behind the court's decision—all on one short page.

In theory this sounds easy enough—just type up one page! In practice it's really not. Especially when you're assigned to read three or four cases for each class, and you have several classes each day. Culling a fifteen-page-long decision and deciding what is important and what is superfluous is not an easy task, even if you have study aids at your fingertips. Hell, a lot of times, simply identifying the question at the center of a case is far from simple. Is the court trying to decide if the defendant breached a contract, or if a contract even existed in the first place? Is the suit being dismissed because there wasn't a real case or controversy or was it because the plaintiff lacked standing to sue? Is the court saying that the defendant wasn't negligent or just that the plaintiff had assumed the risk of harm?

At first, it took me at least an hour to read each case, even if it was only four pages long. Every three minutes, it seemed, I was consulting *Black's Law Dictionary* to look up an unfamiliar term casually tossed in the middle of an opinion, and every fourth minute it seemed that I had to stop and go back to reread the paragraph that I had just completed, because, although my eyes had passed over the text, nothing had sunk in. Concentration is a discipline that is hard to master.

I would sit down at my desk, poised for a meaningful and productive study session, open my casebook, put on my glasses, uncap my highlighter, and begin to read. "We have held that consideration is sufficient if there is a benefit to the debtor or an inconvenience or deprivation to the creditor . . ." And before I was through the first sentence, my subconscious would hijack the minuscule portion of my brain that actually knew how to concentrate, and my mind would begin to wander. *God, my throat hurts. And my glands here in the right side of my throat feel all swollen up. I wonder if it's German measles. Wait, didn't I have a measles vaccination? Oh good Lord, I bet it's amoebic dysentery. No—a goiter! That's it! Slowly but surely, day by day, my glands will continue to swell bigger and bigger until I've got a protuberance the size of an overripe pineapple sticking out the side of my throat. Maybe I could disguise it creatively by wearing a silk scarf? I don't even know how to tie a scarf. Why couldn't I have been born French? Those French women are born with scarf-tying genes. And I bet they never get goiters, either.*

"How's the studying going, honey?" Joe would ask as he passed by my desk.

"Studying? I think I'm diseased. How am I supposed to study?"

"What?"

"Are goiters fatal?"

"Martha. I promise, you're one hundred percent goiter-free. Go back to work."

Work. Right. "We have held that consideration is sufficient if there is a benefit to the debtor or an inconvenience or deprivation to the creditor . . ." *I wonder how long it's been since I tweezed my eyebrows. Maybe I should take a short break and go do some plucking. I bet I have some hairs growing on my big toes that could be tweezed, too. Or maybe I should make an appointment to get them waxed. My eyebrows, that is, not my toes. Do they even do toe waxes? That would be weird, wouldn't it? Also, that sounds really painful.*

"Martha! I know you're not working out there," Joe would call from the bedroom. "Study!"

Study. Right. "We have held that consideration is sufficient if there is a benefit to the debtor or an inconvenience or deprivation to the creditor . . ." *What in the world is stuck between my teeth? It's not a popcorn hull—I haven't eaten any popcorn recently. All I had for dinner was a Caesar salad. Is that a crouton stuck in there? A tiny piece of anchovy? God, I love anchovies. They should put anchovies in everything. But then Joe would have to cease all ingestion of food. He hates anchovies. It must have been that strict upbringing of his. Raised in that rural Wisconsin town, where his mother only cooked bland casseroles with names like "corn noodle" and "salmon noodle" and the most exciting spice that she ever used was ketchup. It figures that he wouldn't appreciate a good brined and cured plankton-feeding fish.*

"Martha, are you working?" Joe would yell once again.

"I'm too stupid to concentrate," I would moan in reply. "Do we have any anchovies in the cupboard?"

But as painful as my new study plan was, I found that it actually seemed to work. Not too long after my dismal performance in Civil Procedure, I was shocked to find myself tentatively raising my hand in response to a question posed in class by my Torts professor. Unlike Professor Strickland, my Torts professor ran his classroom in a relatively friendly manner and generally relied on students' willingness to volunteer to speak. But when I found myself volunteering, it was as though my hand was operating independently from the rest of my body: at the same time that I felt myself raising my hand slowly into the air, I wondered what in the world had possessed me to make such a monumentally stupid move. But by then, it was too late. The professor had noticed my hand and had called my name.

We had been discussing some aspect of product liability—under what circumstances manufacturers should be responsible for producing dangerous products.

"Should the manufacturer of a handgun be liable if it produces a gun that is built in such a way that it will go off at random?" the professor asked, hypothetically.

"Of course," an enthusiastic man in the front row answered.

"Why?"

"Because that's dangerous!" the student replied.

"Well, should a dairy farm that makes butter be liable because butter causes high cholesterol and heart attacks?"

And that is when I raised my hand. And when the professor noticed. And when he looked at the seating chart, noted my name, and called on me.

"No, I don't think so," I responded.

"Why not, Ms. Kimes? The butter is dangerous, no?"

"Yes, I suppose it is."

"So how is that different from the gun?"

"Well, people who buy butter know that it's bad for them, but they want to buy it anyway. They're just getting what they bargained for. I guess the people buying the gun may know that it's dangerous under certain circumstances, but they have no idea that it could go off at random—it's not what they expected when they bought it."

And here, instead of a berating tirade, I got what was possibly one of the most wonderfully simple replies that I've ever received. "Aha!" he said. "So the butter buyers are purchasing something inherently dangerous, but they *know* in advance that it's dangerous.

And they're willing to accept that. They're *assuming the risk* of eating the butter! Very good, Ms. Kimes. *Volenti non fit injuria.* To a willing person, no injury is done."

I clung onto the words *Very good, Ms. Kimes* like an emaciated squirrel clutching the one lone acorn that will have to sustain him for the long, oppressive winter. Sure, it wasn't exactly a "You're the most brilliant student I've ever encountered, Ms. Kimes," or a "You will surely be a Supreme Court justice someday, Ms. Kimes," or even an "I promise to give you an A in my class, Ms. Kimes," but I wasn't complaining. A professor had said something good to me. Those four words had me floating on air.

Torts class did something else to me aside from buoying my confidence: as the class went on, it also sent my thoughts spiraling in the fashion of a paranoid lunatic. Torts is basically a class where you study "civil wrongs" that people commit against each other—things that are negligent and stupid but not criminally punishable—and then you analyze the parties' right to monetary compensation for the tragedies that have befallen them. These injuries run the gamut from surgical instruments accidentally left inside appendectomy patients to limbs severed in bizarre industrial accidents to maiming caused by unexpectedly exploding Coca-Cola bottles.

Studying these injuries teaches you a lot of important things. But mostly it teaches you the fact that danger lurks around every corner. After you study torts, you will never look at life the same way again. I first learned this when we began to study a famous case from the 1920s called *Palsgraf v. Long Island Railroad Company.* In that case a woman named Helen Palsgraf (who I couldn't help but picture as a kindly older woman with bluish hair, wearing a silk scarf with an overly busy design and a lapel pin far too large for her jacket) had just purchased a ticket to ride the train to Rockaway Beach (and here I picture her changing into one of those old-fashioned swimming outfits with the ruffly bloomers and a swim cap to protect her big blue hairdo while she frolicked with her grandchildren in the sand). Poor, unsuspecting, innocent

Mrs. Palsgraf was waiting on the platform for her train to arrive, anticipating her day at the beach, when injury befell her in a rather odd and unexpected way.

Suddenly, a man ran by, trying to catch a departing train that was on its way out of the station on another track. As it turns out, this was a particularly stupid man. Not only was he stupid enough to jump onto a moving locomotive, but he was stupid enough to do so while carrying a big box of fireworks. As he was jumping, he began to fall, and two railroad workers pulled him into the moving car. This caused some jostling, however, and the package of fireworks fell onto the tracks, exploding when the train ran over them. The shock of this explosion caused a scale, which was located "at the other end of the platform, many feet away" to fall, bonking poor Mrs. Palsgraf on the head and causing her injury.

Mrs. Palsgraf may have been unlucky, but she wasn't dumb, as she chose to sue the railroad for her injuries instead of the firecracker-carrying man because, well, deep pockets and all. The issue for the court to decide was whether or not Mrs. Palsgraf's injury was "reasonably foreseeable," making the railroad somehow liable for negligence due to its employees' actions in helping the firecracker-toting man onto the train.

Ultimately, the court decided that no, the railroad wasn't responsible because, really, who could have anticipated that Mrs. Palsgraf would have ended up being whacked in the head with a scale because somebody helped a guy way down at the other end of the platform jump onto a train? (Never anywhere was an explanation provided as to why a scale was hanging on the train platform in the first place, by the way.)

After spending weeks analyzing cases like these, a strange thing started happening to my brain. I absorbed the "Wow, freaky ass shit happens to people and they get hurt totally out of the blue" part, but I somehow managed to breeze on by the "and these are random anomalies that happen like, only once every 18.9 years, and even then, mostly only to people who kind of had it coming" part. And then my brain turned on me and made me into a paranoid freak. As I waited on the subway platform for a train, I found myself nervously eyeing people waiting on the other side of the platform—were any of them holding suspicious-looking boxes that could drop, explode, and cause a scale to fall on my head?

As I walked the few blocks from my apartment to school, my mind would start racing. What would happen if that flying pigeon landed on the air conditioner hanging out of the apartment window way up there right over me, and then the weight of the pigeon somehow tipped the air conditioner out of the window and sent it plummeting down toward the ground straight in my direction? And then what would happen if, as I saw the air conditioner looming down on me, I ran to get out from under it and, because I hadn't been looking where I was going, I accidentally stepped right on the tiny little teacup Yorkie that the old lady who lived down the street was taking out for a walk? What if I ended up squishing that yappy little dog right under my foot because I was running just that fast to get away from the cooling unit? What would happen then? Would I be liable for the squashing of the dog? Or would the responsibility fall to the City of New York, which should have poisoned that pigeon long ago to keep this tragedy from ever occurring in the first place?

Yes, that is a brain on torts. It ain't a pretty sight.

Even in my mentally unbalanced state, however, I was sane enough to recognize the importance of following the all-important Law School Rule: never admit to anyone how hard you're studying. The goal is to minimize the appearance of doing actual work but maximize the display of your newfound legal knowledge, making it look breezy and effortless, as though it all just comes naturally to you.

Nevertheless, I decided to break that cardinal rule and admit the fragile state of my psyche to Rachel, Katie, and Elizabeth one week when we were all out for our regular Thursday-evening margarita session. We had taken to gathering weekly at the dimly lit bar of a little Mexican restaurant on Broadway that featured brightly colored piñatas hanging from the ceiling and cheap happy-hour drink specials, and the four of us had developed a pretty tight bond as the semester went on, based primarily on alcohol and law school gossip. It was from Rachel that I learned that the Gunner was reportedly a former child actor who had appeared on *Alf* or *Full House* or some similar show when he was a kid; from Katie I learned that Chaz Whitmore was rumored to be sleeping with a woman from Section A; and from Elizabeth (who had been classmates with the woman at Penn) I learned that Chaz's paramour was admitted to Columbia off of the waiting list. Together, we had all learned that an eight-thirty a.m. Civil Procedure class can be a painful thing to attend the morning after a girls' night out.

"You guys? I think I might be losing it," I admitted, as I absent-mindedly drew designs in the frost on the outside of my margarita glass. "I just feel so overwhelmed. Like it's just too much, you know?" I couldn't believe I was saying the words aloud to someone other than Joe, admitting my failure to these new friends. "Sometimes I just freeze up and can't make myself do anything at all, because I don't even know where to begin. Why does it look so easy for everybody else?"

"Nobody said it was easy," Elizabeth answered, swirling the ice in her glass.

Although the rest of us always ordered frozen margaritas, Elizabeth insisted on getting them on the rocks. Why was that? Who would turn down a perfectly good frozen margarita at a rock-bottom happy-hour price for an inferior drink that wasn't even on special? I often didn't understand Elizabeth.

"You just do it," she continued. "I have a study schedule that I stick to. One and a half hours of studying at night for each of the classes I have the next day, and then four hours for each class over the weekend. That's it. Not a minute more."

"I know what you mean, Martha," Katie said. "And it's not even just all the work, you know? It's that there's this . . . this . . .

aura of competition in the air? It's making me totally paranoid. I'm spending way too much time comparing myself to everyone else."

"Yes!" I practically shouted, happy to know that I wasn't the only one keeping a mental scorecard of my own shortcomings.

"And let me tell you—living in the law school dorms doesn't help any," Katie added. "I swear, it's just one giant, bizarre contest with my suitemates—who can study the hardest? We're all silently keeping tabs on one another and watching how much everyone else is working. It's like if you're the first one to turn off your light and go to bed at night, you've admitted defeat or something."

I shuddered just to think of it. Hundreds of law students living in close quarters with absolutely no sane outside influence? Nothing good could come of that. At least I had Joe to counterbalance my psychoses.

"It's just as bad at my place," Rachel said. "I mean, David and I lie in bed at night dissecting minor points of the Uniform Commercial Code. It's insane, but I don't know how to stop. I'm not sure if we're supporting each other, enabling each other, or trying to one-up each other. In any case, law school is doing nothing for my love life, let me tell you."

I thought back to the night before, when Joe and I had, for the first time in ages, actually climbed into bed at the same time. I had gotten into the habit of staying up until all hours studying, and Joe usually retired by ten-thirty or eleven because he was working temp jobs, which usually required him to be in a nameless, faceless office by eight o'clock each morning. But that night I had given up on studying earlier than usual and our schedules had converged. As Joe started to subtly put the romantic moves on me, I tried to force myself to think about something other than the difference between the rules of acceptance for bilateral contracts and unilateral contracts. *Concentrate, Martha, no more thinking about law! Sex it up! Hubba hubba!* But I just couldn't do it. My head was so wrapped up in school nonsense that I just couldn't extricate myself. As I reluctantly turned Joe down, I must have accidentally muttered something legal-sounding out loud, because before I knew it, he was rolling over in bed all in a huff saying "Maybe you should be sleeping with your Contracts professor—you two would have such exciting pillow talk." So much for a smoking hot newlywed sex life.

Suddenly, our waitress set a big bowl of chips and salsa on our small table, almost knocking over my drink in the process.

"Josh came out from L.A. to visit me last weekend, and it was a total disaster," Katie was saying, and the blotches of bright red that appeared on her cheeks indicated that she was truly upset. "He wanted to go out and party, I wanted to stay in and study. He wanted to talk about sports, I wanted to talk about law school. We settled for talking about the O.J. trial while he was sneaking glances at *Sports Center,* and then I dragged him to Monday's Civil Procedure class, just so he could experience Professor Strickland in person. We had a big fight before he left—it was awful. He said I had *changed,* and the way he said it, it was really terrible. We didn't even have time for makeup sex before he left. Which might be good, because I'm still kind of mad. He just doesn't understand how it is here."

Hesitantly, Elizabeth said, "You guys? Don't take this the wrong way, okay? But you all need to chill out a little bit. I do plenty of work, too, but it's just a matter of keeping it all in perspective."

"Oh yeah? When's the last time *you* got lucky?" shot Rachel.

Elizabeth had no reply.

"God, we're pathetic," I moaned. "How about we all do a shot of tequila and pretend we're sex kittens instead of law students?"

The next day I thought back to what Katie's boyfriend, Josh, had said to her. He was right: law school was changing us in sometimes subtle, sometimes profound ways. It started with little things, like the way writing case briefs was becoming second nature to me. And the fact that I was getting to know my way around the law school library like it was the back of my hand. And when I got called on by Professor Burrough in Contracts class, I actually put in a semi-decent showing. And I continued to volunteer answers every once in a while in Torts, because I had learned that raising my hand wasn't going to cue the apocalypse. And the new legal language that surrounded me was actually sinking in, and I couldn't help myself from employing it. Who was I turning into? This wasn't the me I used to know. I was reluctant to admit it, but it turned out that I was really excited about what I was learning. The Law was actually kind of interesting. Sometimes even fascinating—albeit hard to understand.

By the end of the first semester I had become thoroughly steeped in the language called Legalese—it's all I had been reading, hearing, and learning to speak for months. So used to this bizarre new lexicon, I wouldn't have been surprised if, on a random Tuesday afternoon, I had walked up to the guy behind the counter at the Hamilton Deli next door to the law school and, instead of saying "I'd like a meatball sub with a Coke, to go," I had found myself regurgitating the phrase "For good and valuable consideration, the receipt and sufficiency of which is hereby acknowledged, I do hereby agree to purchase, and the Deli does hereby agree to sell to me, one sandwich, the contents of which are expressly agreed between the Parties to contain a minimum of five fully-cooked meatballs, at least six fluid ounces of tomato-based sauce, a sprinkling of Parmesan cheese (which the Deli represents and warrants to be freshly grated), all of which said foodstuffs are to be contained within a somewhat-freshly baked sandwich roll, heated to a minimum of 230 degrees Fahrenheit, and wrapped tightly in nonstick tinfoil, accompanied by a 24-ounce carbonated Coca-Cola brand beverage, to be packaged in a container allowing egress from the Deli for external consumption."

But, on a more basic level, I realized that law school wasn't just teaching me to alter my manner of speaking and to pepper my sentences with a few Latin phrases here and there. It wasn't just educating me about *quasi in rem* jurisdiction and the requirements to form legally binding contracts. It was training me to fundamentally alter the way I thought.

A few days earlier, as a way of praising a student's performance in Contracts class, Professor Burrough had remarked, "Yes! Don't you see? You're becoming corrupt and cynical because you've caught my spirit!" Although this was meant as a joke, it was born of a nugget of absolute truth. We were being taught to become cynics. To become skeptical. To second-guess everything we were told. To peel back the layers of every statement, looking for a loophole or hidden trap. To analyze every word to death. To distrust people. To become the kind of people other people hate. Indeed, we were learning to think like lawyers.

One early November evening I returned home from the library to find the one-drop beat of a Bob Marley song vibrating from the stereo, a vase of flowers on the table, and a beaming smile on Joe's face.

"I got the job!" he exclaimed.

"I knew you'd get it—congratulations!" The temp work that Joe had been doing for the past months was wearing thin both on his nerves and on our bank account. "Actual salaried employment! I am so proud of you!" I shouted, as I jumped onto him and gave him a giant hug.

"Whoa there, Betty," he said, as I realized that I had jumped a bit too forcefully, and had almost toppled us both. "It doesn't pay all that much more than most of the temp jobs have, but it's a great career move. I'll have benefits. And hey, you can't beat the commute."

"So what's your exact title going to be?" I asked.

"Development Associate."

"Development Associate. That sounds so professional! Joe, this is the best thing ever. Change your clothes—we're going out to celebrate."

Joe had found a position doing fund-raising work at Columbia Business School, which was all of two blocks from our apartment. It didn't pay fabulously, but it was a job. A good job. A job on a career track. Celebration was definitely in order. We were going out on the town.

An hour later, we were wandering up and down Avenue A trying to find the restaurant I had chosen—a chic East Village restaurant where two Midwestern dorks like us had absolutely no business being. Fifteen minutes of wandering later, we finally found it—there was no discernible sign outside, just the letter *A* painted discreetly upon the front door, which was about ten steps down below street level. A hostess, who was dressed from head to toe in black, led us through the crowded restaurant to a laughably small banquette table near the back, which was separated by only about three inches on either side from the patrons at the tables next to us.

Instead of congratulating Joe, reading the menu, or salivating over the thought of a frisée salad with goat cheese and a champagne vinaigrette, I found myself digging into my purse and pulling out the ticket that the coat check woman had given me after I handed her our jackets minutes before. For some reason, I felt absolutely compelled to scrutinize the fine print on the back of that ticket. It stated, in a font so minuscule that it was barely perceptible to the naked eye: "The restaurant is not liable for loss of personal property for any sum exceeding two hundred dollars, unless such value in excess of two hundred dollars shall be stated upon delivery and a written receipt, stating such value, shall be issued, but the restaurant in no event shall be liable beyond three hundred dollars, unless such loss occurs through its fault or negligence."

I didn't know exactly what that meant, but it sounded suspicious to me. "I don't like the sound of this one bit," I stated emphatically to Joe, who was busy reading the wine list.

"What?" he replied, lost in concentration among a long list of pinot grigios and sauvignon blancs.

"They're trying to limit their liability for losing my coat to two hundred dollars. Or maybe three hundred dollars. I don't understand it completely. But it doesn't matter—that coat is priceless!" I said, possibly a little bit louder than I should have.

That's when our neighbors began stealing furtive glances in our direction.

But indeed the jacket was priceless in its own way: it was a family heirloom. It was made of dark brown leather, scuffed up in just the right places, and all-around hip-looking in a retro sort of way, and I had stolen it from the back of Joe's closet back in college and claimed it as my own. At the time, Joe told me that his brother had shot a deer years and years before while hunting, and that his family had eaten the meat and had the hide made into a jacket. Now, knowing that this coat was made from a deer that Joe's brother had killed wasn't exactly my idea of heaven—hunting just ain't my bag—but I really really liked this coat. So I took the story in stride and tried to tell myself that it was cool to be wearing a coat made from a poor defenseless animal killed by my then-boyfriend's brother. That Joe's family was like the Native Americans, who didn't let any single part of the buffalo go to waste after a hunt. And that's a point of pride, right?

Just before law school, my lofty illusions were shot to hell when Joe's older brother saw me wearing the jacket and said, "Oh, I remember that coat!" And then he began to recount the story about how my outergarment had hailed from roadkill.

As the story unfolded, I learned that not only had Joe been raised by a lovely but stoic mother who cooked a lot of casseroles and used a lot of ketchup, but that his father had once been an assistant game warden in their small Wisconsin town. Part of his job was to "address the situation" when someone hit a deer with their car, which apparently meant hauling the carcass to the town dump. In my crash-course in roadkill etiquette, I was told that no one would ever take the meat from a roadkill deer, not even in Joe's family. But I was also told that it was perfectly kosher to take the *hide* of a deer that has become roadkill, because deer hides have all sorts of different uses. One of which is to make jackets. Jackets that someday unsuspecting girls may end up wearing.

So ultimately I wasn't lying when I hissed to Joe in the Avenue A restaurant that the jacket really, truly, was irreplaceable. My newly legalized mind didn't know what to do when faced with a disclaimer of liability over the loss of a priceless redneck heirloom. Although the language on the back of the coat check ticket was clearly boilerplate nonsense, I felt powerless to let it go. Before I knew it, I found myself emboldened by the pinot grigio (the cheapest bottle on the list), ranting to Joe, and threatening to march straight up to the coat check and inform the anorexic-looking attendant that I wanted her to return my jacket, pronto.

Joe looked at me as though I had suggested that we begin practicing Santería and perform a ritual chicken sacrifice right in the middle of the restaurant. "Eat your stupid grilled shrimp in mango-tamarind sauce. We're celebrating! Next month, we might actually be able to pay for this dinner," he replied, forcing a forkful of food into my mouth in an attempt to shut me up.

"Mmmmm. But still . . . it's unfair. But yum . . . this shrimp is fantastic." I smiled at him and said, "And congratulations again on the new job, honey. I'm really proud of you."

After that, the dinner improved. On the way out, Joe insisted on reclaiming our coats himself, leaving an overly large tip in the jar, and shoving me out the door before I could open my mouth. Happily, the jacket kept me nice and toasty warm as we trekked to the subway and returned to campus, where I was secure in the knowledge that I was definitely the only girl at Columbia wearing a roadkill carcass.

Four

FEAR AND LOATHING

"If you have wine today, get drunk today; worry about tomorrow's worries tomorrow."
—CHINESE PROVERB

As Thanksgiving neared, I could hear the thunder rumbling in the distance, but I had no clue how violent the storm would become once it actually descended. With the end of the semester in sight, all minds were focused on the fact that final exams—the results of which would comprise our entire semester's grades—would soon be upon us, and I don't think there was a person in the entire first year law school class who wasn't wrought with fear over the upcoming test of our collective mettle.

Without the money (or, frankly, the inclination) to return to Wisconsin for the holiday, Joe and I made plans with Rachel and David to have a Thanksgiving feast together, and I promised not to let myself truly panic about exams until after our day of celebration was over. The four of us had come up with two simple rules for the holiday: ridiculous amounts of wine were to be consumed by all, and not one word about the law was to be uttered by anyone. Our apartment, the site of the Thanksgiving celebration, was declared a Law School-Free Zone. The plan was that Rachel and I would cook while David and Joe watched football, we would all feast on turkey and the accoutrements, then the men would be relegated to kitchen clean-up duty while the women retired to watch *Grease*, which conveniently happened to be both my and Rachel's favorite movie.

I temporarily pushed my studying aside and spent far too many hours poring over recipe books, all of which mistakenly assumed that I had at least a cursory understanding of cooking. Even though I had a frightfully small amount of culinary experience, I had ridiculously high aspirations, and I envisioned a truly elegant holiday fête à la Martha Stewart. With this in mind, I went to the store and returned with an armful of cooking magazines: *Gourmet, Food & Wine, Bon Appétit, Cook's Illustrated*—I bought them all, and together they promised me complete meal plans for seven different types of Thanksgiving feasts (Classic, Southern, New England Style, Southwestern, Pan-Asian, Rustic Italian, and Basque). I sat lost in thought, flipping through the glossy pages, imagining a dinner highlighted by savory turkey breast roulade with porcini mushrooms and pancetta or a plum-glazed roast turkey with spinach, bacon, and cashew stuffing, and of the turkey sandwiches with black olive and fig vinaigrette that I would make from the leftovers the next day (not to mention the leftover turkey, tortellini, and watercress soup that I would cook).

But as I sat there mentally making my shopping list, I realized that my student loan-financed bank account didn't really allow for a Thanksgiving dinner that included 187 ingredients, including roasted chestnuts, achiote paste, densely marbled Roquefort cheese, shaved black truffles, and fresh lemongrass. Also, there was the fact that our apartment's pressboard IKEA furniture wasn't exactly fresh off the pages of *House Beautiful* magazine. Reluctantly, I realized that although I might have been a Martha, I wasn't destined to be Martha Stewart.

Eventually I embraced my humble roots and settled on a menu that included roasted Butterball turkey, Stove Top stuffing, green bean casserole made with cream of mushroom soup and a can of fried onions, store-bought pecan pie, and, just to add a little panache, roasted spaghetti squash in a brown sugar and butter sauce. And many, many bottles of cheap wine. I imagined the lavish Thanksgiving dinner that was probably going to be served to Chaz Whitmore on a silver platter by a maid in a crisply pressed uniform at his family's Nantucket mansion and felt a slight pang of jealousy and regret, until I realized that it was highly unlikely that the people at his Thanksgiving table were going to drink as much wine as the people at my table (even if mine was cheap wine). And they definitely weren't going to be drunkenly watching *Grease.*

Although I had come to my senses a bit and realized that my fantasies about an exotic Thanksgiving feast weren't within my means, it turned out that I hadn't been thinking very far ahead as far as logistics went. Joe and I had gotten pretty lucky in the Columbia housing lottery, but our apartment wasn't exactly what you would call grand or palatial. Still, we weren't complaining. While some students had been relegated to the law school dorms, we lucked out and got assigned to a decently sized one-bedroom apartment on 119th Street with three whole closets and shining wooden parquet floors. There are advantages to getting married young: at least at Columbia, you get a "get out of the dorms free" card and are sent straight to the head of the graduate student apartment line. Sure, the kitchen was really a converted closet, the hot water never really got hot, and you needed to keep the windows open all winter because the radiator only ran in overdrive, but it was in a doorman building and it was only three blocks from the law school. All in all, I felt as if we'd done pretty well. Unlike Rachel and David, who had gotten stuck in a dingy sixth-floor railroad apartment with a view out over the housing projects, in a building with an elevator so iffy that I willingly walked the five flights of stairs up to their apartment whenever I went to visit.

Our apartment was decently sized but not exactly decently furnished. As I planned Thanksgiving dinner, I realized that Joe and I had only two chairs at our kitchen table, plus one rolling office chair that I used at my desk. So in order to accommodate four people at our wobbly pressboard table, I was forced to turn to my next-door neighbors—whose apartment always emanated a strange odor vaguely reminiscent of boiled cabbage and burned

Tater Tots—in order to borrow a folding chair from them. Then, there was the matter of cookware. More specifically, the matter that Joe and I had almost none. But between our own meager supply of saucepans, Rachel and David's similarly paltry cache of pots, and a disposable aluminum roasting pan purchased at Key Foods, we cobbled together an adequate, although somewhat less than ideal, set of cookery. The fact that my kitchen was so small that only one grown adult at a time could fit inside it was an obstacle that couldn't be easily overcome.

Somehow, though, Rachel and I managed to tag-team in the kitchen, pulling the gizzards and various other mysterious bagged remains from the inside of the turkey and discarding them with disgust, preparing the boxed stuffing and figuring out which turkey orifice to place it in, and glopping cream of mushroom soup onto frozen green beans in order to make the casserole that both of our mothers had tortured us with over many, many years of Thanksgivings. We had broken out the wine at the exact same time that we broke out the vacuum-wrapped turkey, and by the time we got to the spaghetti squash, we both realized that neither of us had the slightest clue as to how to cook it—together we looked at each other, looked at the squash, and started to giggle. The panache part of the meal plan just wasn't going to happen.

Okay, so we could much more easily have eaten the exact same (although likely better and probably less expensive) Thanksgiving feast that we concocted had we gone to the diner down the street. But both Rachel and I were proud of the meal we had made, and that pop-out thermometer on the Butterball turkey didn't do us wrong. It was juicy and moist along with the Stove Top stuffing and the jarred turkey gravy that I had purchased. Plus, there was all the wine. The lack of law school talk was just the proverbial gravy on the Thanksgiving turkey.

When the meal was over, Rachel and I retreated to the living room, popped our movie into the VCR, and warmed up our singing voices. (Every true *Grease* fan knows that singing along to the tune of "Summer Nights" with John Travolta and Olivia

Newton-John is the highlight of the viewing experience.) With wine glasses in hand, Rachel sang the part of Danny, and I was Sandy. "Summer lovin', had me a blast," she half-sang, half-shouted in a fake baritone. "Summer lovin', happened so fast," I answered in my embarrassingly warbly voice. And then, together in perfectly horrible unison, we kept on going until the boys forcibly shut us up.

For the sake of the neighbors, who could probably hear every note through the paper-thin walls, Joe and David put a quick stop to our singing. The four of us lounged around, drank yet more wine, picked at gloppy pecan pie, and remembered Thanksgivings past, family fights over the dinner table, and that one great-aunt everyone seems to have who manages to get sauced each holiday and always insists on pinching everyone's cheeks.

Soon, though, despite our best efforts to steer clear of law school conversation, David's peculiar obsession won out.

"C'mon, Martha, you know you want to," he begged, nodding toward the first-year law school facebook that sat on my desk across the room.

"David, we all *promised*. No law talk today."

"It's not law talk. It's a *fascinating puzzle of human drama!*" he pleaded, giving me his best drunken puppy-dog eyes.

"Oh, come on, honey. It's been forever since we watched David do this," said Joe.

"Fine. Go get the damn book," I relented, to the sound of Rachel and Joe's laughter.

David was undeniably obsessed with the Columbia Law School facebook. During orientation, all 340 first-year students had been forced to stand against a blank white wall in the lobby and have our pictures snapped, mug-shot style, and these pictures had been assembled into a booklet with our names, hometowns, and undergraduate colleges listed underneath each photo. David was a law student at Fordham, which is a very well respected Manhattan law school, but it is ranked number thirty-two compared to Columbia's number four. I suspect that this twenty-eight-place distinction between himself and his girlfriend had left David with a bit of an inferiority complex, and it had definitely given him a strange fascination with the students who went to Columbia. In this vein, he had committed each detail of the facebook to memory. He took great pleasure in being quizzed on his memorization skills.

I opened the book up to a random page, and selected a picture of one of my classmates. "Miranda Hutchinson," I called out.

"Oh, I know this one!" he yelled. "She's from Franklin Square, New York, and she went to Brown undergrad. And she's not particularly photogenic, I might add."

"Anthony Perino," I quizzed.

"From Brookline, Massachusetts. Went to Yale. And was wearing *a tie* in his photo. Who wears a goddamn tie to orientation?"

Rachel grabbed the facebook from my hands. "David, you are such a freak. How do you remember all these people?"

"I study the book while I'm on the toilet," he replied, as though it was the most natural answer on earth.

"Whatever, freak. You'll never get this one. Lisa Chao."

"Ah, don't think you can fool me that easily, sweetums. She's from Beijing, China, but she studied at the Sorbonne. And she's a hottie, at that."

"Touché."

It went on like this for quite a while, all of us taking turns and David only on rare occasions asking for a hint ("Just tell me what state he's from, and then I'll remember the rest"), until I developed a bit of a stomachache, which I initially attributed to a little too much pecan pie. But then, as it got later, my guts started to rumble. And then rumble some more. By the time we had finished the facebook game, I started to wonder if I might be getting sick.

"I'm not feeling all too good," I said, weakly.

"Did you wash your hands with really hot, soapy water every time you touched the turkey while you were preparing it?" Joe asked.

"Well, I know that I washed my hands really well *before* I touched the turkey. Afterward, I'm not so sure about."

"But Martha, don't you know that raw turkey has like a thousand different kinds of bacteria? *E. coli* and salmonella and listeria and all sorts of bad shit," said Rachel.

Apparently I didn't know. And, apparently, I hadn't been fastidious enough when stuffing the uncooked bird, and some sort of turkey-borne food poisoning had befallen me. I sprinted off to the bathroom, pleading gastronomic distress, when David called out after me, "Martha, are you sure you don't want to take the facebook in there with you?"

I woke up the next morning, stomach still tied up in salmonella-induced knots, head pounding with leftover wine residue, and faced reality. There was no escaping the fact that my first law school exam was just around the corner. There were three more weeks of classes, followed by a two-week "study period" over the holidays, then exams were upon us. The mere thought made my soul feel every bit as awful as the then-current state of my body.

The thing about law school exams is that they're a one-shot deal. There are no midterms, no quizzes, no points for in-class participation (much to the dismay of the Gunner). Just one four-hour exam that tests the sum total of everything you've learned during the entire semester. And the results matter . . . a lot. First-year grades play a terribly important role in deciding who will have the honor of making Law Review, who will get selected for prestigious judicial clerkships after graduation, and what high-paying law firm job offers students will receive. And you go into the all-important exams basically blind—you've received absolutely no feedback as to your abilities or comprehension of the subject before the big test. There's nothing to do besides cross your fingers, hold your breath, say a prayer, and hope for the best. Well, either that or curl up and cry. And it's hard to write in a exam booklet when you're in the fetal position.

The more I thought about it, the worse I felt, and it wasn't just the food poisoning and leftover red wine tannins talking. I realized that for all the time I had studied throughout the semester, I had mostly just been worrying about day-to-day survival, and had managed to shrug aside the big picture. I had a giant pile of briefs for the assigned cases for each of my classes, but I had, for the most part, let them slip from my memory the instant that class was over and my chance of being called on had passed. I had no sort of synthesis, no greater understanding of torts, contracts, or civil procedure, no real clue as to how everything fit together. And that's what I would need for exams. The tests were not simply going to ask me to regurgitate the holdings of various cases. They would assess my ability to understand the underlying principles and extrapolate those principles to new circumstances. They were going to be in-depth essay exams designed to test my facility at spotting issues and my knowledge of the entire body of law that I had studied over the course of the semester. They would be asking me to synthesize all the concepts I had learned (or was supposed to have learned) and apply them to new and novel situations designed specifically to test my mastery of the laws and the policies behind them.

In my Contracts exam, for example, I knew that I wouldn't be asked to recite the facts of *Lucy v. Zehmer* or answer true or false to the sentence "Under the Uniform Commercial Code, an acceptance that adds terms to the offer is valid." Instead, I would be presented with a complicated set of facts, and would need to ask a long litany of questions before I could even begin to formulate my answer: Is there a valid contract? Was there an offer with valid and certain terms that was properly communicated? Was the offer accepted in a proper manner? Was the consideration binding or illusory? Absent actual consideration, was there promissory estoppel or detrimental reliance? Are there any defenses to formation? If there is a valid contract, what are the terms? Were the terms of the contract performed? Was there satisfaction or excuse of all conditions precedent, concurrent, and subsequent? Was the contract discharged by rescission, accord and satisfaction, nova-tion, impossibility, illegality, or frustration of purpose? If there was a breach, what are the appropriate remedies (expectation damages, consequential damages, liquidated damages, or specific performance)?

I didn't really begin to understand what most of these ques-tions meant, much less think that I could ever commit them to memory and apply them to a strange fact pattern in a very limited amount of time. The idea that I was going to have to somehow, within the next five weeks, find it within myself to gain some comprehensive understanding and knowledge of the bodies of law regarding contracts, torts, and civil procedure was enough to send me into an uncontrollable panic.

And it wasn't just me. It seemed as though the anxiety was contagious. As soon as we returned to school after Thanksgiving, everyone was instantly in a state of emergency, no matter their level of preparedness. As a group, our class looked horrible—none of us were sleeping, we all had bags under our eyes, and we had taken to rolling out of bed, throwing on baseball caps and dirty sweatpants, and crawling to our nine a.m. classes in a di-sheveled and unkempt state—even the fashionistas had given up. The line at the coffee counter was three times longer than usual, and the number of smokers huddled outside the front doors of the building had grown from a small group of puffing stragglers to a veritable herd of nicotine-sucking students (me included—I had started smoking again, despite the fact that I had quit two years before). There were rumors of infighting and threats of ex-pulsion from study groups for failure to perform. Sometimes you could hear muffled sobs emanating from study carrels in the li-brary.

Just before the end of the semester, professors began holding official review sessions to go over the important concepts from the class and to answer students' questions. These sessions often seemed to cover topics never before mentioned in class or on the syllabus. Invariably, there were students who would raise their hands and ask questions about tiny, picky, remote, tangential issues that did nothing but freak everyone else out about the fact that they, too, hadn't thought far enough ahead to worry about those topics. When you're at a place where you're still trying to figure out what the term *res judicata* even vaguely means, it doesn't calm your soul a lot to listen as the student sitting in front of you asks the professor, "It's my understanding that the concept of mutuality as to collateral estoppel, which originally began as the equivalent to the privity requirement in the res judicata context, is one that has really eroded over the years. Can you go over the rationale behind this gradual change of policy?"

Those review sessions didn't do a lot to calm the panic. As I sat in the library listening to the students around me review issues that I hadn't even begun to cover yet ("So, under the UCC damages rules, if the seller breaches and also keeps the goods, the buyer's recovery could be *either* the market price at the time of the discovery of the breach minus the original contract price *or* the replacement price minus the contract price, right?"), I decided that I would be better off huddled alone at home, away from the rest of humanity, where my only competition would be myself.

I packed up my things, trudged home, and holed up at my desk among my giant stack of commercial outlines and hornbooks and class notes and case briefs and casebooks and restatements and multicolored highlighters. I warned Joe that he shouldn't bother me if he knew what was good for him. In order to keep a wide berth, he started working late and spending his free time playing racquetball at the campus gym with my classmate Wade, who for some reason hadn't bought into the final exam frenzy. When Joe did come home and tiptoe past me toward the bedroom, all I could manage was a stressed-out nod in his direction and a reminder to please be quiet, because I had work to do. I barely left the apartment, except to attend my final handful of classes, and even then I would immediately rush back to study in seclusion. It was oddly reminiscent of *The Paper Chase*, where

Hart and Ford ran off to a hotel, isolated themselves completely, and went all wiggy in preparation for their first exams.

I started, basically, from the beginning. I concentrated on one subject at a time until I reached the point where I absolutely, positively couldn't stand to read even one more word about torts, and then I'd start all over with contracts. And then with civil procedure. Subject by subject, I reread my briefs of each case, reread the hornbooks and commercial outlines, reread my class notes, and then re-reread all of them until I felt I understood everything. I wrote my own outlines, organizing the different topics in a logical flow and setting out the policies behind the cases and concepts. I condensed my outlines into mini-outlines that included only the really important stuff. I drew flow charts with complicated lines and arrows connecting various topics and showing how the different concepts worked together. I made gigantic bulleted lists, laying out the steps of analysis that I would need to go through on exam questions. Finally, using all the materials I had at my disposal, I took sample exams from previous years that the professors had made available. Then I freaked the hell out when I compared the answers I had come up with to the model answers the professors had provided. I realized how much more there was to learn, and I started back to read everything once again.

In the meantime, I wasn't exactly eating or sleeping. I was, however, drinking about five pots of coffee per day and smoking like a fiend. My appetite was nonexistent—I was too wired from the caffeine and the nicotine and the overwhelming worry—and the mere thought of food disgusted me. In a small concession to health and physical well-being, I took to drinking a Chocolate Royale–flavored SlimFast shake or two every day and popping a multivitamin along with my morning pot of coffee. My weight dwindled. When I finally reached my absolute studying limit at two or so each morning and decided to step away from the books, I would find myself unable to sleep—clearly, the half-life of caffeine is longer than thirty minutes—so I would have a glass or two of wine and try to unwind while watching *Insomniac Music Theater* on VH1. After about an hour of that, I would drag myself to bed and lie there awake, trying to find sleep, but instead unconsciously reciting various mnemonic devices designed to help me memorize essential elements of the law:

> What is the test for justiciability? ***CRAMPS.*** The issue must be *C*oncrete, *R*ipe, *A*dversarial, not *M*oot, not a *P*olitical question, and there must be *S*tanding.

> What is the sequence of pleadings filed in a civil case? ***CARAT.*** *C*omplaint, *A*nswer, *R*eply to counterclaim, *A*nswer to cross-claim, *T*hird-party complaint/answer.

> What are the defenses to formation of a contract? ***MUDIFIS.*** *M*istake, *U*nconscionability, *D*uress, *I*llegality, *F*raud, *I*ncapacity, *S*tatute of frauds. (Yes, I know that "mudifis" isn't really a word. But at that point I was beyond caring.)

When I was finally able to get the damn mnemonics out of my head, I would begin to regret watching *Insomniac Music Theater,* because invariably the lyrics to Beck's song "Loser" (which VH1 played every single night) would haunt me over and over and over and over until, finally, I would just get back up and start studying again. "Soy un perdedor, I'm a loser baby . . ."

Of course, right in the middle of this craziness fell the winter holidays. I do believe that the Grinch himself must have been in charge of the decision to give first-year law students a couple of weeks over our winter "break" to study for exams (upper-class students took their exams right after classes ended, before the holiday break began) because, as I can personally attest, lying awake at night plagued by pure, unmitigated fear doesn't exactly put one in the holiday spirit. Nevertheless, I had planned long in advance to knock off the books to attend a New Year's Eve party at Wade's apartment. I couldn't fathom how he had time to plan a giant party—and he had promised that it would be the Place To Be that night—because he was in the same boat as I was. Wade was probably worse off, actually, because he hadn't spent much time studying during the semester. While everyone else was staying up until all hours of the night trying to understand the difference between actual and proximate cause, he was playing racquetball with my husband and bragging about how little work he had been putting in.

On December 31, with my Civil Procedure exam just four days away and so much left to learn, I just couldn't do it. By my calculations, there were less than eighty full hours of studying time left, and I couldn't imagine wasting a precious few of them attending a party instead of memorizing the rules regarding compulsory joinder of parties. Several hours before the bash was to have begun, I called Wade to offer my regrets. The conversation wasn't a good one.

"Sorry, I don't think I'm going to be able to come to the party tonight after all," I said.

"What? Are you kidding me? What's *your* excuse?" he practically shouted at me.

"I'm sorry, Wade, but my excuse is that I am on the verge of having a complete and total mental breakdown? That I still have over three hundred fifty unread pages of Wright and Kane's hornbook and that, even with the help of Glannon's Civil Procedure guide, I don't think there's any way I will *ever* understand the rules about ancillary jurisdiction?"

Then there was an interminable pause. When he finally did speak, I was surprised to hear neither an angry nor a sympathetic response. Instead, he answered me with a voice of pure desperation, saying, "But Martha, so many other people have already canceled. At this point, I need you for the numbers."

So at least I knew my friendship was truly valued. On the other hand, I did get some measure of comfort from the fact that I wasn't the only one who had reneged on party plans because of severe emotional distress. I don't think there were very many first-year law students among us happily ringing in the year 1995.

"I'm going to turn on some football for a little while," Joe said the next afternoon, flopping down in front of the TV and preparing to watch some college bowl game. Although he wasn't a heavy man by any means, our aging futon couch creaked as he sat.

I hesitated, then said, "Well, the thing is . . ."

"Don't tell me. You need to study."

"Yeah, I do. You know that my first exam is in three days."

"Of course I know. How could I forget?"

"Do you think you could go into the bedroom to watch?" I asked, apologetically. My desk, my computer, my giant stacks of books, and my small writing table were in a little nook just off our living room, and I found it absolutely impossible to concentrate when the TV was on.

"Martha, the bedroom is four feet away from your desk. Even when I watch television in there with the door closed, you ask me to turn it down."

"I'm sorry," I answered, nervously lighting a cigarette. "I just have trouble concentrating." I knew that my holing up in our apartment to study curtailed his activities around the house, but I wasn't trying to be unreasonable. I was just trying to catch up. And to be completely honest, the idea of Joe getting to sit back and relax while I was spending eighteen hours a day poring over my books struck me as a little bit unfair.

"I understand. I do. But all I want to do is watch some football. For an hour. Maybe not even that. Is that too much to ask? Can't you study at the library?" he asked, his voice betraying the pent-up frustration he had obviously been feeling.

"But I don't have my computer there. My outlines are all on the computer," I reasoned. "And I hate lugging all of these books around." I exhaled smoke toward our open living room window.

If I had to spend every waking moment studying, shouldn't I get to do it in the place where I was comfortable?

Joe sighed and said, "Don't take this the wrong way, but I swear, lately I feel like I've been exiled from my own home. I am never alone here—do you realize that? *You never leave.* I go to work in the morning and there you are, sitting at your desk. I come home at night and there you are, like you never moved. I go to bed at night and you're in the exact same spot. I've got to tiptoe around you every weekend because you can't be disturbed. I'm sorry that you have a concentration problem. I'm sorry that you're so stressed out about exams. And I do realize how important they are. I'm not unsympathetic. But you're not the only one who counts around here. *It's not actually all about you.*"

Shit. That hurt. But he had a point. I had made myself, both literally and figuratively, the center of everything. I had imposed my law school aspirations as the core of our collective focus. I had placed my desk right in the center of our small apartment. I had moved us both across the country, and wouldn't even let him watch an hour of football. Law school had taken up so much of my time and attention that I'd scarcely been paying attention to my own husband. God, I felt two inches tall.

"Joe? You're right," I said, with tears threatening to escape from my eyes. "I'm sorry. I'm not actually a crazy person—I just play one in law school. I'll go to the library. I'll be back tonight. Enjoy yourself. Watch football. Take a nap. Dance naked around the apartment. I love you." I packed up my books, headed out, and vowed to try to be less self-centered—as soon as exams were over.

I arrived for my Civil Procedure exam twenty minutes early and surveyed the room, which was an eerie mix of calm and chaos. A woman in the front was cracking her knuckles while she frenetically paged through her outline, seemingly operating under the impression that a few final minutes of studying were actually going to make a meaningful difference in her performance. A guy about five seats to my left was sitting as still as death, hands folded, staring straight ahead, in what appeared to be a catatonic state. Several small groups of people were huddled together, hissing last-minute reminders and sending whispered murmurs about *in personam jurisdiction* and *forum non conveniens* floating about the room. A man near the back seemed to have an entire breakfast buffet laid out before him, and was causing the whole room to smell like greasy sausage. One woman, who I didn't recall ever having seen in class before, had a giant array of pens, pencils, pencil sharpeners (yes, sharpeners—plural), erasers, Kleenex, paper clips, and tape flags arranged in neat rows on the desk in front of her, and sitting right in the middle of all of it, apparently as some sort of talisman or good-luck charm, were three of those frightening miniature troll dolls with soulless black eyes and neon orange hair.

My friends and I had all selected seats scattered about the room: I was a near-the-back type of girl, Elizabeth was right up front, Katie seemed to have some superstitious belief that she needed to be sitting on the left edge, and Rachel the right. Aaron was two seats to the right of me, and Wade was somewhere in the middle. With the exception of Wade (who refused to make eye contact with any of us, because, as it turned out, we had *all* blown off his party), we waved to each other, smiled nervously, and then set about our various preexam routines.

I reached into my backpack and felt around until I found the one thing that gave me some comfort: my trusty, lucky pencil. That pencil—your basic Woodbine number two with a little pink eraser at the end—had seen me through years of tests, and the myth of the pencil had slowly grown and grown, until it took on larger-than-life proportions. It started during my junior year of college, when I had used the pencil on a midterm exam in a statistics class, upon which I miraculously scored 100 percent. The longer the luck lasted, the more my belief in the power of the pencil deepened. As the pencil grew shorter, I began to conserve its power, and I only used it on exams of great import. I used it when

I took my LSAT, upon which I had scored so well, so a superstitious person could reasonably argue that I was in attendance at Columbia Law School thanks to that lucky pencil! Feeling the familiar stub in my hand brought me no small measure of comfort as I sat there waiting for my Civil Procedure exam to begin. I knew that I wouldn't be able to use it on my actual test (it being the type of exam that called for pen and ink), but I had every intention of rubbing it all over my exam answer book in order to infuse it with some of the pencil's lucky essence.

I tried my best to keep calm, to take a few deep cleansing breaths, to clear my mind of all external distractions. To get myself into a place where I could just concentrate and give the exam my best effort the second we were given the go-ahead to open the booklets we had been handed. The Xanax I had taken that morning was doing its job, and I felt as if I was keeping it together pretty well, all in all.

Then, out of nowhere, I felt my chest constrict and my ears begin to burn. I was struck with the realization that every single thing I ever knew about civil procedure had escaped from my brain. I couldn't move, I couldn't breathe. According to the clock, there were less than three minutes before our exam would begin, and my mind was blank. I was frozen, I didn't know what to do. I glanced down at the floor. To my backpack, which was sitting unzipped, brimming with the casebooks and outlines and notes I wouldn't be allowed to use during the Sadistic Professor's closed-book exam. Desperately, I grabbed my outline and opened it up to a random page. Just laying my eyes on the words *International Shoe* and *minimum contacts* flipped a switch in my brain. Triggered by the visceral memory of my humiliation months before at the hands of Professor Strickland, everything instantly fell back into place.

The proctor finally said "You may open your exam booklets now," and then four hours later, he said "You must immediately put down your pens and close your exam booklets." The exam was atrocious. It was four hours of frenzied issue spotting, writing, crossing out rethought sentences and paragraphs, rewriting, trying to ignore the Beck song that was playing over and over inside my head, and then looking at the clock only to realize that there were four minutes left and I had eighteen more important points that I needed to cover. All of my well-laid plans to budget my exam time, to leave myself room to go back and reread and edit my answers, were shot to hell. I was finishing an exam that consisted of only two questions to begin with, and I was leaving one of those questions only partially answered. I began frantically writing in abbreviations and fragmented sentences, just to try to get as much down as I could in those last few precious minutes. I was in the middle of a sentence when the proctor issued his final proclamation, and once he spoke, that was that. I closed my exam booklet, passed it to the outside aisle, and stumbled out into the hall.

I stood in the hallway reeling, exhausted, trying to wrap my mind around the great failure that had just transpired, and the Gunner must have been able to smell my fear. He had been hovering like a vulture outside the classroom door, and as I tried to decide whether to wait for Rachel, run home to eat consolatory ice cream, or spontaneously burst into tears in front of all my classmates, he made a beeline straight toward me.

"So, Martha, what did you think?" Todd asked, with an obnoxious smirk on his face.

"Well, erm. Um. Hard. Yeah. Bad." I couldn't even pretend that it was anything other than horrible.

"Yes, it was rather challenging. But parts of the exam were so obvious—anyone who didn't argue that the plaintiffs in the class action suit should be able to invoke offensive collateral estoppel had to be out of their mind, right?"

"Umm. Well. Yeah. Right," I said, with tiny droplets of sweat forming on my brow. *Yeah, I remember writing something about collateral estoppel. And I know I'm not a math whiz, but there's at least a fifty-fifty chance that I said that the plaintiffs should be able to invoke that, isn't there? Maybe this didn't go as badly as I thought.*

"I especially liked the way Strickland snuck that little point about ancillary jurisdiction in there—that really turned out to be so crucial to crafting an answer that expressed a holistic understanding of the issues in the second question, don't you think?" he asked, the smirk growing exponentially wider.

"Hrmm. Erm. Right. Right." *Ancillary jurisdiction? I didn't notice anything about ancillary jurisdiction. I certainly didn't* WRITE *anything about ancillary jurisdiction in my answer.*

"Martha? Martha? Why, I didn't say anything to upset you, did I?" he was asking in a disingenuously coy voice, as I turned and rushed away. Before I had even rounded the corner, I saw him making a beeline toward his next victim.

I plugged along through my two remaining exams, both of which seemed far easier than my Civil Procedure test, and, shockingly enough, I was able to learn from my previous mistake and pace myself in a way that enabled me to actually answer all the questions. Hell, I even managed to walk out of my Contracts exam with a bit of a spring in my step, thinking I had turned in a pretty solid performance.

And ultimately I learned a valuable lesson from my run-in with the Gunner: never, *never,* NEVER talk to anyone about the specifics of your exams after you're finished. There seem to be two camps on this issue: the talkers and the nontalkers. After that first day, I was firmly in the nontalker camp. Oh, sure, in speaking with my close friends I found nothing wrong with a "So, what did you think?" or a "Wow, that was a tough one!" or even a "Boy, who would have thought this entire exam would have been based on the text of William Shakespeare's last will and testament—I couldn't have come up with an exam idea weirder than that if I was in the middle of a nasty fever-induced hallucination." But anything more detailed than that was strictly verboten as far as I was concerned.

Besides, after the exams were over, who had time to talk about them? It was time to stop talking and start worrying about grades.

Five

THE AGONY AND THE ECSTASY

"To the uneducated, an A is just three sticks."
—A. A. MILNE

I never studied the intricacies of matrimonial law, so I'm not really an expert on the subject. But I know in my heart of hearts that there are certain things that really should be grounds for an instantaneous divorce, no questions asked. This was one of those things.

"Martha, seriously, they're just grades," Joe said to me, just as I was about to hit the high point of the latest in a string of panic attacks that I had suffered in the four weeks since final exams were over.

"What?" I replied, incredulously. "Just grades?"

"Yes, I mean, I know they're important. I do. But I wish you could calm down a little bit. I hate to see you like this—you're making yourself crazy. Don't take this the wrong way, but I think you're kind of losing perspective."

"*Losing perspective?* Do you know how much these grades mean? *Everything* is riding on my first-year grades—whether or not I'll make Law Review, what kind of job I'll be able to get—everything." Was he really that clueless?

"Martha, if you keep stressing like this, you're going to be dead before you graduate. Believe it or not, and as unlikely as it might seem at this particular point, I would kind of miss you if you were departed." He hesitated, then added, "But just in case, before you die, we really need to talk about this $450 phone bill."

"Joe, I already said that I was sorry about that. Did you really have to bring it up again right now? I've got other things on my mind."

"Seriously, Martha. We're on a tight budget. We just can't afford stuff like this. That's half of a month's rent."

Okay, so maybe Joe had a point. Instead of letting out a sigh of relief after exams were over and relaxing a little bit, I had spent every waking moment obsessing about my performance, rehashing and re-rehashing the exam questions in my mind. And maybe Joe was justified in being a tiny bit fed up with my obsessive mood swings and the way I would be asking him one minute, "If they kick me out of school, can we still stay living here in New York?" and then two minutes later I would be saying, "You know, I think my first Torts essay was tight. Seriously tight. I might not have done half bad."

And maybe I *had* run up a $450 phone bill. But this was early 1995, long before there was such a thing as a cable internet connection. We were talking dial-up, and I considered myself lucky to have even that. Grades were going to be reported on the law school's computer network, which I could access from the school computers or from my very own living room via a newfangled thing called the internet. Oh sure, each time I dialed into the network from home the outgoing call cost me seven cents. But it was just seven cents! Seven cents was nothing, nothing at all! Until you multiplied it by about seventy times a day, added in countless hour-long teary long-distance phone calls to far-away friends, and taxed it all at $8\frac{1}{2}$ percent. That's how I ended up with a $450 phone bill before my very first grade had even been reported.

But how was I to resist? Classes had started back up a week after our first semester finals were over, and we all knew that it would be at least several more weeks before we learned any of the results. Nevertheless, each day, there would be whispers in the halls:

"Rumor has it that Feldberg is really quick grading his exams—one year he had grades posted after only a week and a half." *Ooh! Even though I didn't have Professor Feldberg, it has been a full week since I took my first exam. I'd better go check for grades!*

"Jennifer's roommate Cassandra's boyfriend, Noah, has a second cousin who says that he knows a guy who went and talked to Professor Strickland's secretary yesterday, and she said that he said that he might have his grades in within the next week or so." *Within the next week or so? One day later is within a week or so— I'd better go check for grades!*

"Section C already has two of their three grades reported!" *What did they do to deserve their grades already? Assholes. Still, I'd better go check.*

Finally, after what seemed like an eternity, my first two grades—from Contracts and Torts—were reported on the same day. The results were not good. After all the anticipation, after all the worry, I had received Bs on both of them. And those were the exams I thought I had done well on. God help me when my Civil Procedure grade finally came out.

Despite all the manic worrying about failure that I had done in the previous weeks, I realized that I never truly thought that would happen—nobody actually flunks out of Columbia Law School. (Once in a while someone may quit, but no one really fails.) In my heart of hearts I had been harboring more than a glimmer of hope that I would do superbly, surprising everyone by the broad insight, pointed knowledge, and sweeping understanding of the law that I had gained during my first semester. That possibly my Torts professor would be so impressed with my performance that he might use my exam as the model answer he would hand out to students in future years. There was a tiny but ridiculously real part of myself that had believed that was an actual possibility. Maybe a bigger part of myself than the one that thought I might receive two Bs.

And to those of you who might be thinking, "Whining bitch with her two Bs—there's nothing wrong with a damn B," I will reply, "You have *so* never been to Columbia Law School." It's hard to overstate the importance of first-year grades in law school, and it is likewise hard to explain the humiliation of getting two Bs as your very first grades.

Because at that point, for all intents and purposes, there was no grade worse than a B, unless you failed altogether. The scale allowed for no B-minuses, no Cs, no Ds. The only real options were A, B+, B, or The Unspeakable. That year, Columbia was in the process of transitioning from an old grading system to a new one. Previously, the grading choices had been E, VG, G, and P—code for "Excellent," "Very Good," "Good," and "Pass," although no one *ever* received a "P" unless they turned in a completely blank exam or something equally tragic, and no one I knew had ever met or heard of a person who had received a "P." The new system was going to be a more customary one, with grades A through F, complete with pluses and minuses. But that first semester, the administration had decided to allow the professors to keep grading according to their old E, VG, and G scale, and that they would simply translate these grades to A, B+, and B, respectively, when they were reported to us. (Apparently, the professors don't take well to sudden change.)

Yes, I was living in an era of extreme grade inflation, and B was really as bad as it got. And these grades counted. They counted for *everything*. Not only were they of the utmost importance when it came to searching for jobs and applying to law journals, but they were also the culmination of the hardest, most stressful five months of my life. Somehow those grades were more than just letters, they were official, school-sanctioned assessments of my merit as a human being. And what they had shown was that I had been right all along, that I was just a fish out of water, in over my head, and that I had absolutely no business being at Columbia in the first place.

I was thoroughly overcome with disappointment, rage, and a devastating feeling of hopelessness. I felt paralyzed, utterly humiliated, and totally ashamed of myself. No matter what lengths Joe went to in trying, I could not be cheered up. I skipped classes for days, wallowing in self-pity, lying in my bed talking to my cat about the complete lack of talent, intelligence, and ability that resided within me, while Joe came home during his lunch hour, made me Lipton Cup-a-Soup, and begged me to rejoin the living.

On the fourth day of my moping, I finally answered a call from Rachel. She had been leaving messages and more messages on my answering machine ("Martha, grades are out—call me!" "Martha, are you there? Call me?" "Martha, where the hell are you? Fucking call me already." "Martha, *you were called on today in Property class, and you weren't there to answer. Call me. NOW!*"). Finally, I gave in and picked up the ringing phone.

"Hello?" I croaked.

"Martha! Where the hell have you been?" Rachel barked.

"Got two Bs dropping out of school clearly not smart at all unworthy of this esteemed institution would belong better at one of those Sally Struthers paralegal correspondence schools better to just cut my losses and quit now but thanks for having been my friend," I muttered, and then promptly hung up.

Five seconds later, the phone rang again.

"Whaaaaaaaaaaaaaattttttttt?" I answered, stretching the word out into at least six syllables.

"Get a grip. So you got two Bs? You're not quitting school."

"Rachel, seriously. I'm devastated. I killed myself studying for *this*? I feel like a total loser." Hoping for some commiseration, I asked, "So what did you get?"

"Well . . . ," her voice trailed off, "I've gotten As so far, but whatever."

As. Rachel has gotten As. Meaning more than one A. God. She's my best friend, I can't let myself hate her. Yes. Keep repeating that. She's my best friend, I can't let myself hate her . . . Can't let myself hate her . . . "Oh. That's great! Congrats!" I said, in what I hoped wasn't an overly fake-sounding tone of excitement.

"It's no big deal. It's all just luck. Do you really think there's any logical correlation whatsoever between exam performance and intelligence? Between what you scribble into an exam book on one random afternoon and what you actually know or understand about an entire body of law? I mean, what if you had a really bad stomachache on exam day, and you blew your test because all you could concentrate on for the entire four hours was trying not to hurl? Or what if your dog had just died the day before and you just sat there silently weeping inside for the entire exam period? Bad things can happen. How does that measure true knowledge?"

Rachel had a point. "So, say for example, if you had a really horrible song from *Insomniac Music Theater* that was haunting your thoughts during the entire exam, forcing out all recollection of the mnemonic devices that you had tried so hard to commit to memory?" I asked. "You mean, if that happened, it might just mean that you had a bad day or two, and not that you're stupid and worthless altogether?"

"Of course, Martha. Look, we'll all go out this weekend and you and David can have a pity party together—he's not happy with his grades either. Oh, also? Professor Strickland's grades came out this morning. I've got to go—call me later!"

"*What?!?!?*" I screamed, before Rachel could hang up the phone. "Civil Procedure grades are out?" In the heat of my moping, I had completely forgotten to keep obsessively checking for my one remaining grade. "Should I check? I need to check. I should check. I can't check!" There wasn't even any real point. I had clearly proven myself to be a B student, 100 percent through and through. Bottom of the barrel. But still I thought . . . I should probably check. "Should I? Check?"

"Oh, Martha. Shut the hell up and *check already*. Call me back."

I knew she was right. Although I wasn't looking forward to it, it had to be done. My other two professors had left me beaten and bloody, up against the ropes, and I was just waiting for Professor Strickland to swoop in and deliver the knockout punch. Three Bs truly would be the end of the world. And I knew for a fact that if there was one class that I had definitely bombed, it was Civil Procedure. If Torts and Contracts had been Bs, this one was sure to be worse. Was it possible that I might turn out to be that one person who comes along every 6.9 years and is actually given a C? Or even a failing grade?

I wished I had some strong libations that I could use to steel my nerves before spending my final seven cents dialing in for grades. But I wasn't a daytime drinker, and my liquor cabinet was empty except for the dregs of some remaining Thanksgiving wine that had surely turned bad. So I said a silent prayer, booted up the computer, and waited for that awful dial-up-modem-connecting noise to stop, indicating a successful connection. I logged on to the law school network, reluctantly clicked onto the "View Reported Grades" button, and waited. And waited. And waited. (Dial-up can choose to be very slow at very important times.) Then I let out a blood-curdling shriek so loud that it probably could have been heard all the way to Brooklyn. I debated who to call first, Joe or Rachel, but Rachel won out. There are some things that a fellow law student can understand better than a husband can.

When she answered the phone, I couldn't find the right words. I could barely find *any* words. I could barely find my breath. So I just started screaming. "Rachel! Rachel!!!!! *Rachellllllllll!*"

"So?" she asked.

"An A. An A! A real live A. And from the Sadistic Professor, no less! Holy *shit!* Surely getting an A from Professor Strickland counts like eighteen times more than getting a B from either of my other professors, right?"

"Absolutely, Martha. Absolutely. And you knew all along that you were going to kick ass in Civil Procedure, right?"

"Right! Of course! I knew all along!"

Once the shock wore off a little bit, I felt like a soap-opera accident victim who had just recovered from an extended case of amnesia. I tore off the rancid pair of pajamas I'd been wearing for days, made myself a triple-strong pot of coffee, and took a nice hot shower. Then I practically skipped the three blocks down Amsterdam Avenue from my apartment to the law school, beaming from ear to ear. *Bs in Torts and Contracts? So* what! *Everyone knows Civil Procedure is the hardest class of the first year. And everyone knows that, after a semester's worth of fear instilled by the Sadistic Professor, receiving praise from him counts, like, twenty-five-fold!* It was like having been in an abusive relationship—once you kick a puppy enough times, if you finally hold out your hand and deign to give him the tiniest scratch behind the ear, he will be giddy beyond his wildest dreams. Right then, I was that puppy.

I pranced to the offices of each of my professors (bounding up the five flights of stairs to the faculty offices because, really, why waste that limitless energetic joy on an elevator ride) to pick up my graded exam books, along with the model answers they passed out, showing us what our ideal responses should have looked like if we had been given seventeen days to prepare them instead of merely four hours, and if we had been recognized experts in those fields of legal discipline instead of merely first-year law students.

I collected my exams, carried them to the library, and sat back in a comfy chair to take a look. It took about six total minutes and one cursory flip through each of my exams before I realized the absurdity of the entire situation. In each of my answer books I had started out with an impressive and tidy penmanship, writing well-thought-out and meaningful sentences that seemed to have earned me no credit whatsoever. By the end of each test, I had been reduced to scrawling illegibly in the margins, writing nonsensical sentence fragments and jotting down questions that I didn't even provide answers to, but somehow earning points for merely spotting the issues.

As God is my witness, I wrote the following sentences verbatim in an answer to one of the questions on my Torts exam (and this was supposedly during the "coherent" initial part of my essay):

> The plaintiff contracted to assume the risk, and this
> was an unreasonable assumption on his part. It was as
> though he was performing an "ultrahazardous activity"
> in relation to himself—he would always be in danger,
> and this assumption of risk is a sort of strict liability on
> him.

It does not take a professor, a lawyer, or even a marginally intelligent person to realize that this statement makes absolutely no sense whatsoever. You know how you read that and it makes your eyes glaze over and you think "Damn, I don't understand at all what that means?" It's not because it's high and lofty technical legal-speak that makes sense only to people in the upper echelon of intelligence. No. *No one* understands what that means. "An ultrahazardous activity in relation to himself?" Was I on drugs? And my exam was overflowing with sentences like that. No wonder I got a B. It's a miracle I had passed at all.

I had started the first essay of my Civil Procedure exam with a nice, sensible, grammatically correct paragraph that read:

> One fact that is quite favorable to the defendants in
> this case is that judges are often reluctant to grant mo-
> tions for summary judgment, as is allowed by Rule 56
> of the Federal Rules of Civil Procedure. Such judg-
> ments go straight to the merits of the case and mean
> that no jury could reasonably find for the opposing
> party. This is a fairly extreme measure, and most judges
> would rather give a case to the jury and reserve the
> right to grant a judgment notwithstanding the verdict
> later, as per Rule 50.

This paragraph earned me no recognition whatsoever. Yet later in the same exam, in the second question that I had only halfway answered, I had scribbled the following jibberish in penmanship that I'm surprised even I could decipher:

> Best claim for in personam is against RI. They con-
> tracted with Jackson and shipped to Bklyn he compen-
> sated them though. Did they advertise in
> NY—purposeful availment?

That nonsensical crap earned me a marking of "+2" in the margin of my exam book.

Later I had scrawled a sentence (if you can call it that) that read: "NY long arm would give competence because of 302a1 contracting to supply goods to state jurisdiction maybe competence yes." That earned me a "+5."

Bizarre questions I had jotted down during those last three frantic minutes without even answering earned me credit: "Rule 4f: Does this comply with Hague? If not service improper." That was worth 5 points in the margin. "Can a lawyer ethically represent all Ds together?" Again, 5 points. "Do not need personal jrsdictn over all Ps because ability to opt out replaces min contacts." Five more points.

Those inane scribbles made up almost half of the entire forty-seven points that I received total on my Civil Procedure exam, which earned me the one and only A of my whole first semester. That right there is some fucked-up shit, folks.

If anyone harbored any illusions about grades being kept secret, they were sadly mistaken. Within hours after grades were reported, rumors were floating about over who had straight As, who had straight Bs, and who had scored somewhere in between. I swear, someone in the dorms had to have been keeping some sort of complex Excel spreadsheet, because there were over three hundred of us first-year students, and it seemed like everyone knew everything about one another's performance. I had divulged my marks only to Rachel, but my guess is that she told Katie, and Katie, gossip-hound that she was, passed my information on to the rest of the world. That's just the way things

IVY BRIEFS

worked. Keeping secrets is a logical impossibility in law school, at least when it comes to grades. And if you think keeping quiet is going to get you anywhere, you're wrong. People will just speculate, and they won't be generous, believe me. Everyone figures that if you're not talking, you've got something to hide. Better to let it be known that you got one shining A and two horrible Bs, because if you say nothing, people will assume that there was no A in the equation.

My guess is that is how plenty of the "straight B" people were plugged into the magic spreadsheet. For the most part, I bet they were just the people who weren't talking, so, whether it was out of spite or cynicism or something in between, they were plugged in as "people too embarrassed to admit their grades, so let's just assume they got straight Bs." Soon, that became the accepted truth. And on the opposite end of the spectrum were the people who reportedly got all As. Although straight-A students certainly existed (Rachel included), let's just say I'm betting that there were a lot more self-proclaimed "straight-A students" walking the halls than there were people who actually had straight As reported on their official transcripts.

And amid all of the buzzing and rumors, there was a subtle but palpable change going on. Unexpectedly, certain people who had always seemed so brilliant in class and in their study groups, but who hadn't lived up to their shining-star status once grades came out, found themselves knocked down more than a few pegs on the law school totem pole. Others, who had always been quiet in class, had earned stellar marks, and people began to look upon them with a new respect—it turned out that they were quiet but brilliant, not stupid with nothing intelligent to say. Certain students took to strolling the halls with puffed-up chests and condescending grins on their faces, somehow restraining themselves from saying out loud, "Yes, I did better than you did, but I'll still grace you with my presence." I had never been in a study group to begin with, so I couldn't say for sure, but there were rumors of groupings and regroupings, of close-knit clusters being torn apart, of previously valued members being thrown to the wayside and forcibly ejected because of one too many Bs.

In February, the Sadistic Professor threw a party for our class. The Public Interest Law Foundation—the law school do-gooder society—held a big fund-raiser every year, convincing professors, law firms, companies, and whoever else they could rope into it to donate items that would be put up for a silent auction. It was an annual tradition that Professor Strickland would host a party at his home for a group of a hundred or so students. Each year, the section of students who had suffered through his tutelage would pool their money into a group bid, win the auction, and attend the party. My year was no exception.

When Rachel, Katie, Elizabeth, and I walked up to the door of the Sadistic Professor's home, we stood there with our mouths agape. No, we weren't on Park Avenue, but we were on the steps of the most palatial home any of us could probably have ever imagined seeing. We pressed the doorbell, and were surprised to see the Lordship himself answer the door, and not some uniformed butler or French maid or something. Professor Strickland ushered us inside, offered us drinks, and acted surprisingly warm, welcoming, and friendly. It was more than a little bit disconcerting. He took our entire class on a tour of his home, telling us fascinating and extraordinary tales of where he had collected his exotic furnishings and regaling us with stories about how he had rented out his home to be used as a set for Woody Allen's most recent movie. Much like my own abode—very sought after theatrically.

His wife could not have been more different from him. Whereas Professor Strickland was a bona fide giant, she was quite miniature. Where it took about seven months to get past his brusque exterior and see the glimmer of warmth inside, she oozed kindness from the outset. Where, with his shining bald head and overbearing features, no one would be bestowing any "sexiest man of the year" awards on him, she looked as if she had once been a beauty queen. And the party seemed as mismatched as the couple did. A luxurious, opulent home filled with scruffy, poorly dressed law students who were trying to be on their best behavior. Flowing champagne served alongside Domino's cheese pizza. An erstwhile evil professor who seemed to have transformed into a real live human being with a home and a family and, just possibly, a personality that might even have a pleasant side.

Maybe it was the fact that he had given me an A, and all the champagne I had been drinking. Okay, fine—*for sure* it was the fact that he had given me an A (and all the champagne that I had been drinking). Nevertheless, two months removed from his class, while standing in his luxurious living room enjoying my champagne buzz, I found myself looking upon the Sadistic Professor with a kind heart. He was so gracious and charming! And look at his adorable wife! Sure, he had been tough. Yes, he had demanded the best of us. Indeed, sometimes the intense fear we felt while sitting in his class was overpowering. But he had been rather entertaining (well, that is, when he was making the class laugh at other people's expense and not at my own). And you know what? No one ever skipped their Civil Procedure reading. No one ever blew that class off. No one ever gave it less than 100 percent. I might have questioned his methods, but in the end, Professor Strickland got his job done. Possibly there had been a method to his madness all along. And he was throwing us a party! In my mind, he was transforming from Sadistic to Sweet.

And you know what else was sweet? *The champagne.* Although my tastes might have been maturing in the direction of the Veuve Clicquot, my student budget was still squarely within the realm of the Miller Lite, so it was nice to have a chance to imbibe a bit of the bubbly.

"Oh my God, you guys, look at these hand-carved stair railings! And this authentic medieval suit of armor! I feel like I'm in a museum," I said.

"Did you see the family portraits that were hanging upstairs?" Elizabeth asked. "Strickland has kids! I mean, adult kids, but still, kids. Can you believe it?"

"I heard that he used to be on the Olympic diving team," Katie announced.

"What?" I almost screamed. "Please tell me there aren't any pictures of him in a Speedo upstairs."

"No, but I heard that, too," Rachel said. "He is a pretty athletic-looking guy, especially for his age."

"Yeah, he is. But still, the thought of Strickland in a Speedo? Ick."

I was soon feeling as bubbly as the champagne itself. Before I knew it, I was positively effervescent. I was talking and laughing with classmates I disliked, congratulating near strangers on their good grades, and telling everyone within earshot that I had loved Civil Procedure class from the very beginning.

"Zach, I hear you put in quite a showing in Contracts, bravo!" I trilled.

"Well, Emily, I always had a particular interest in Civil Procedure. Really, it's just a fascinating topic, don't you think?" I asked with inexplicable zeal.

"Rebecca, did you know that Strickland teaches an Advanced Civ Pro class? I'm thinking of signing up for that next year!" I said, expressing what was a totally genuine at-the-moment intention.

And then, champagne flute in hand, I turned my sights on Professor Strickland. I staked him out, strategically waited for a gap in his conversation with another student, then stumbled my way over to stake my claim.

"I just wanted to thank you again for having us all over to your lovely home thissss evening," I slurred a little bit.

"It's always a pleasure," he replied, with a sincere voice. "Your class was filled with bright, engaging, promising students."

"I'm not sure, but I think some of them might not have appreciated you as much as you appreciated them. *Hiccup.* But not me.

I loved you from the verrrry beginning. You were always my faaaaaaaavorite professssor."

"And forgive me for having forgotten, but your name is?" he asked, suspiciously.

Thank the good Lord above that Rachel swooped in at that very second and grabbed me by the arm. "Thanks again for having us over, Professor Strickland. You were so generous to invite us all," she cooed, while giving me the stinkeye.

"You gave me an A, you know!" I shouted to him, as Rachel dragged me toward the door. "I especially liked the way you snuck that little point about ancillary jurissssdiction in the exam! *Hiccup!*"

Yes, it was definitely time to go home.

Six

THE POINT IS MOOT

*"Winning may not be everything, but losing has little
to recommend it."*

—DIANNE FEINSTEIN

Even aside from the $450 phone bill, the nervous breakdown over
grades, the missed classes, and the raging two-day champagne
hangover that I had after the Sadistic Professor's party, second semester was a disaster from the get-go. They had switched us
around. Section B was no more! We were merely a shell of our
former glory, such as it was. About half of our former section remained, and the rest was a sea of unfamiliar faces. Thankfully,
Rachel was still there, although Elizabeth and Katie weren't—our
time together was going to be reduced to extracurricular frater-
nization. Not so thankfully, the Gunner was still there, too.

For entertainment value, I appreciated the new cast of characters that had been added into our section. My personal favorite
was a woman named Talia Young, who spoke up on a very regular
basis in classes, always asking the most fantastically peculiar questions of the professors ("So, hypothetically, if I were a subtenant
of land in feudal England, and I assigned my subtenancy to a vas-
sal—instead of subleasing it, that is—would I still be in privity of
contract with the actual landowner?"). The class was always
buzzing with muffled snickers when she came up with these gems,
but I don't think anyone really knew if her questions were serious
(in which case she was crazier than a shithouse rat) or if she was

just looking to get a rise out of the professor and entertain the class.

Christine Hsu, the self-righteous do-gooder I had met during orientation, had joined us, along with a whole gaggle of like-minded left-wing feminists who felt the need to expound upon the evils of Corporate America and our White Patrician Society at every turn. These women proved to be perfect fodder for Timothy Frankel, outspoken conservative and member of the student Federalist Society, who took great pleasure in publicly egging them on in class.

Second semester was a bizarre mix of classes. At most other law schools, my first-year curriculum would have been rounded out during the second semester with classes in constitutional law, criminal law, and property. Instead, at Columbia, I would be taking Criminal Law, Property, and two rather esoteric and mysterious-sounding classes called Foundations of the Regulatory State and Perspectives on Legal Thought, with the important foundation class of Constitutional Law pushed off until my second year.

The course description for our Regulatory State class spoke of "market failures and externalities" and "command and control regulation" and "distributive consequences"—none of which made any sense to me. In its idealized version, I believe that it was supposed to resemble some sort of class on law and economics, but the professor I had been assigned seemed to spend most of his time lecturing about the importance of labor unions. Rumor had it that he gave out As as if they grew on trees, so I didn't feel inclined to complain too much.

Perspectives on Legal Thought was basically a legal philosophy class, which should have been a slam dunk for me, seeing as how I had been a philosophy major in college. But for some reason, although I had once been able to wrap my mind around Plato and Aristotle, metaphysics and epistemology, ontology and axiology, I just couldn't comprehend or manage to care about formalism, legal realism, positivism, pragmatism, or constitutionalism. It was pure agony to go to class, mitigated somewhat by the fact that our professor never ever called on students, but then increased tenfold by the vortex of discomfort created each day when he would pose a question to the class based on our assigned reading, wait for someone to volunteer an answer, and receive vapid stares of boredom from a hundred fifty students. Hell, even the Gunner rarely spoke in that class.

Property class is universally hated by every law student in existence, and for good reason. My professor was a short, older, nice but vaguely creepy man who never, ever took his hands out of his pants pockets. He taught us about innumerable useless things, including the difference between "shifting" executory interests and "springing" executory interests, the subtle distinction between vested remainders subject to partial divestment and vested remainders subject to complete defeasance, and the critical importance of easements and equitable servitudes. Rumor had it that he had married one of his former students years before. I suspect that he used to teach something interesting, but then got demoted to teaching Property as a punishment for his indiscretion.

Although my first semester had been dreadfully hard and markedly stressful, at least it had been interesting. I couldn't really say that much for my classes second semester. Criminal Law was the one saving grace. It was a fascinating topic, and I had a little bit of a nonsexual girl crush on my professor—she was young and warm and funny and endlessly interesting. She had a cutesy way of starting class each day by saying, "Today is Tuesday" (or whatever the day was) "and this is Criminal Law," as if to make sure that none of us had accidentally boarded the wrong plane. Professor Robinson had been an accomplished prosecutor at the U.S. Attorney's Office for years before turning to academia, and she was always regaling us with stories about indicting ex-dictators of small countries for money-laundering, convicting mafia warlords of racketeering, and offering immunity to cornered gang members in exchange for their testimony and subsequent entrance into the witness protection program. It was all quite fascinating, and it gave me actual fodder for conversation when people asked me about law school. I wanted to be like her when I grew up. Except for the part about having to be a law professor.

Second semester had caught me by surprise with a sudden quickening of the pace. The professors were moving along at warp speed—it was as though they had been treating us with kid gloves the first semester, even though at the time I thought they had been using us as punching bags. And we were also being bombarded from every direction with additional extracurricular demands, leaving far, far less time to study than I had been used to.

First, there was the not-so-small matter of Moot Court—a rite of passage for all first-year law students. Moot Court was an incredibly time-intensive exercise for which we would receive no credit or grade, but which was a required part of the first-year curriculum. Essentially, it was pretend lawyering. Students were paired up into teams, with two teams of two people each arguing opposite sides of a hypothetical appellate court case invented by a second-year law student who was specially selected to be a "Moot Court Editor," and whose qualifications consisted of having survived the Moot Court process the previous year and expressing some level of interest in ushering a slew of first-year students through. (I speak from experience, because the next year, I was to become one of the Moot Court Editors.) It was the job of the Editor to help us understand the issues involved in the case, assist us in formulating the necessary legal research, and edit various drafts of the briefs that we had to write arguing our positions.

Rachel and I instantly paired up to work as a team. In our introductory meeting with Ryan McAuliffe, our Editor, we were handed a half-inch thick "Record" of the case and were given an explanation of how the whole process would work. Everything we would need to get us started was in the Record—all the facts and supporting evidence, the procedural background, and judicial opinions from the trial and appellate courts that had already considered the case (which we would be pretending to argue on appeal to the U.S. Supreme Court). For the next six weeks we would be doing research on the issues presented, drafting briefs supporting our position, preparing oral arguments that we would present to mock judges, and meeting regularly with Ryan, who would guide us along and assess our progress.

Rachel and I agreed that Moot Court sounded like it might be fun. A chance to try our hands at bona fide fictitious lawyering! Excitedly, the two of us took our materials, walked the six blocks to her apartment building, braved the rickety elevator, settled into the couch, and decided to map out a plan of action.

"Well, I guess the first thing to do is to read through all this stuff and see what this case is all about, right?" I asked.

"Sounds good. Let's do it."

Two minutes later, I said, "Rachel, I have a question."

"Already?"

"Am I getting something wrong, or did Ryan actually make up a case about a guy who hanged himself and then choose to give the guy the illustrious name of 'James Dangle'?"

"Yes. Yes, I think he did," Rachel answered. "A subtle guy, that Ryan."

"Yeah, subtle."

Our pretend case did indeed involve the widow of a man named "James Dangle," who had hanged himself under suspicious circumstances in his home on a military base located in the imaginary state of Kent. The issues that we had to research and argue were whether or not a claim by Lieutenant Dangle's wife was barred by a judicial exception to the Federal Tort Claims Act, making the U.S. government immune to liability for his death, and, if not, whether the military personnel who responded to an emergency call from his wife had been negligent in failing to properly rescue him before he died.

A few minutes later, Rachel asked a question of her own. "Do you realize that this half-inch-thick stack of materials contains a jillion graphic details about this guy's suicide and pages and pages of indecipherable medical terminology? About how 'there was saliva hanging from his mouth and his face was expressionless' and how 'review of the cutaneous surface and skeletal structure revealed no focused information' and how 'lab data revealed that BUN and creatinine were low, although patient had high CK, and sputum culture grew staph'? I don't know about you, but I chose to go to law school instead of medical school for a reason."

"It's Thursday and it's already five o'clock," I said. "We've got to go meet Katie and Elizabeth for drinks soon, anyway. Let's worry about sputum and creatinine tomorrow."

Rachel and I were both hell-bent on winning. Moot Court was the first head-to-head competition we would have in our legal careers, and we were both determined to emerge victorious. We had never even met our opponents, but we both felt the indescribable urge to crush them like ripe grapes waiting to be made into cheap chardonnay. After we split the issues up, Rachel and I spent the next month doing an obscene amount of hours of meticulous legal research. We searched for cases near and far that might support our arguments in some small way. We looked for scholarly articles, for professional writings, for any materials that might bolster our line of reasoning. We each crafted artful, thirty-page-long briefs that argued our position, meeting with Ryan on a regular basis to discuss the progress of Mrs. Dangle's case. (Our meetings were usually on Friday mornings, and Ryan was often visibly hungover. He was also particularly fond of praising the curative powers of Chocolate Yoo-Hoo when it came time to free yourself from the ugly grip of alcohol's unpleasant remains.)

A week before the mock trial was to occur, we received copies of our opponents' briefs. To say they were less than impressive was an understatement.

"Rachel? Have you had a chance to read these?" I asked.

"This is really embarrassing," she said.

"Are these guys mentally deficient in some way? Who are they? We *are* at Columbia Law School, right? Where admission is supposed to be somewhat competitive?"

"Well, you wouldn't know that from reading this crap," Rachel answered.

"No, you wouldn't. I think we might have this one in the bag. Or wait—" I said suspiciously, "maybe they have some sort of secret plan when it comes to oral arguments?"

"It could be so. We need to prepare."

No, we wouldn't go quietly into the night. So after writing and rewriting and re-rewriting our briefs, we turned to focus on our upcoming arguments. I was a hesitant, nervous, cowardly public speaker at best. The mere thought of standing up in front of our opponents in the case, the panel of three Columbia Law alumni who would serve as judges, and whatever spectators happened to wander into the room during our presentation (and it was rumored that there were always student spectators, using their free time to bask in the glory of other students' public embarrassment) sent shivers of terror down my spine. Rachel was far more confident than I was, having been a member of her college debate team.

When the big night came, we finally met our opponents, Eddie and Dylan, for the first time. They were both in Section A, and neither Rachel nor I had ever met either of them. They looked rather like twins: both were short, dark, and intimidating, with piercing blue eyes and overly gelled hair. If this competition was going to be based on height, Rachel and I would be the clear winners, but if it was going to be based on quantity of hair products used, we were sure to lose. If it was to be based on merit, we would just have to wait and see.

Rachel argued the first half of our case. She was poised, impressive, and convincing. The brief that she wrote was well-researched and well-written, and both the explanations that she gave to supplement her writing and the answers she extemporaneously added in response to the judges' questions sounded absolutely natural and off-the-cuff. In short, not only did Rachel know how to write it, she knew how to sell it.

I sat in the horseshoe-shaped lecture hall, worrying about how

I would possibly live up to her performance, more than a little bit terrified while I waited for my turn to begin. *Forget winning—how in the world am I going to manage to croak out the words necessary to even scrape by at this task?*

Rachel's opponent, Eddie, was a disaster. Where she had been able to instantly recall nitpicky facts from the cases she had cited in order to bolster tiny nuances of her argument and to tie her position into a larger philosophical scheme of how our system of justice should operate, Eddie seemed to spend a lot of time saying things like "Well, um, I guess. There's this one case that says this guy shouldn't be guilty. Or liable. Or whatever."

When it was my turn to go up to the podium, my knees were wobbling with fear. I was panicked, wondering what exactly might come out of my mouth once I let myself speak. I was wearing a crisp black suit (because we were indeed taking this pretend lawyering thing to the *n*th degree), and I had begun to sweat through my freshly dry-cleaned white blouse. Nervously, I looked down at my notes, took a deep breath, and began reading my prepared speech. Before I was through with the second sentence, one of the judges interrupted me with a question.

"Ms. Kimes, let's get to the real issue at hand here. How can Mrs. Dangle's case possibly be allowed to go forward? The military police had no common law duty to rescue Mr. Dangle, so by definition, their actions cannot be deemed negligent. If there was no duty, how could there possibly be a violation of duty?"

Realizing that I would not be allowed to simply rattle off a rehearsed speech for my entire allotted twenty minutes, I took a deep breath and said, "Well, Your Honor, I respectfully disagree with your underlying premise. Although there is no doctrine that would create a duty for a random individual to come to Lieutenant Dangle's rescue, by virtue of the nature of the military policemen's jobs, they had a special duty to intervene. Several states have recognized this and held that police officers do have a common law duty to rescue because of their unique role in society. In particular, I would point you to the *Lee v. State* and *Munroe v. City Council* cases that I cited in my brief."

The judge nodded. I continued.

"And, even barring a general duty of police officers to rescue, the affirmative actions of these particular officers in taking control of the crime scene and reassuring Mrs. Dangle that they would attend to the situation required them to make reasonable attempts to save Lieutenant Dangle's life." I pointed my finger and tapped the podium for effect.

Another judge cut in, asking, "Even so, wouldn't the intervening act of Lieutenant Dangle's suicide attempt be viewed as a superseding act that would relieve the government of any liability here?"

"No, Your Honor," I answered. "This very issue was recently addressed in *McLaughlin v. Sullivan*—a case that presented facts quite similar to those at issue here—and the court firmly stated that an intervening act of attempted suicide should not bar action being brought to benefit the victim."

And on it went.

Before I knew it, my time was up, and I returned to my seat. How had that happened? How had I performed so well? Me—the girl terrified of public speaking. Me—the girl afraid to open her mouth and utter a word in front of strangers. I swear, I nailed every question I was asked. Somehow I was able to persuasively discuss the merits of my position, fielding impromptu questions from the judges with a grace and poise I was shocked to find residing within myself.

Still, there was a chance I could be outshined by my opponent, Dylan, who was taking his turn at the podium. But when he opened his mouth to speak, he was even more uninspiring than his teammate Eddie had been. When asked questions by the judges, he stuttered, stammered, and punted the ball. He seemed lost, unprepared, and altogether clueless. On more than one occasion, he answered a judge's question by saying, "Yeah, well, I don't really know the answer to that one." Instead of making me feel victorious, it actually made me feel kind of embarrassed for him. I sat squirming in my seat for most of his oral argument, praying that this whole thing would draw to a quick close, because I was beginning to feel pretty uncomfortable.

When the entire ordeal finally ended, Rachel and I got our wish: we were declared the winners. She was cited for having written Best Brief out of the four of us, and I was pronounced as having given the Best Oral Argument out of the group. Somehow I had pulled an unknown ace out of my sleeve.

After the judges had left the room, Rachel and I stood around with our chests puffed up with pride, congratulating ourselves on our well-won victory.

"You did write a really awesome brief," I said.

"Thanks. I can't believe the way you were so *on* during that oral argument," Rachel added.

"We kicked ass!" I rejoiced.

"No doubt about that!" she answered.

And then we heard them.

In the back of the room, Eddie laughingly said, "Dude, we sucked *ass!*"

Snickering, Dylan responded, "Do they give out awards for Best Blowoff or Tried the Least? Because we would *so* win those!"

"Beers are on me, you loser!" Eddie exclaimed.

They were fully aware that they had bombed. And they exhibited absolutely no embarrassment or regret whatsoever. Rachel and I had tortured ourselves writing our briefs and had chewed our fingernails down to the quicks with nerves before the oral argument; Eddie and Dylan had done the absolute bare minimum they could to get by. And in the end, the experience would be reflected the same way on all of our transcripts: "Ungraded Credit for L6679 Foundation Year Moot Court." Suddenly, our hard-earned victory began to seem rather hollow.

Like a one-two punch, as soon as Moot Court was over, I was notified by e-mail that I still needed to attend to getting a summer job—something I had given little thought to, because I just hadn't had time. I didn't exactly expect job offers to mysteriously fall into my lap like manna from the heavens without any effort on my part, but I hadn't spent a lot of time worrying about finding employment. There were too many other things to worry about.

To: All First-Year CLS Students
From: Amanda Wainwright, Director of Career Services
Subject: Brown Bag Lunch
For those of you who have not yet secured summer legal employment, please join us in Room B of Jerome Greene Hall at 12:00 on February 19 for a brown-bag lunch discussion about job possibilities during your 1L summer. We will discuss job search strategies, résumé and cover letter preparation, and interview training. On behalf of the entire Career Services Office, we look forward to seeing you there.
Sincerely,
Amanda Wainwright
Director of Career Services

Apparently, it was time to start worrying.

To: Rachel Wolfe; Katie McKenna; Elizabeth Lee
From: Martha Kimes
Subject: Fw: Brown Bag Lunch
Are you guys going to this? Am I a moron because I haven't been trying to get a summer job yet? It's only February! Maybe I kind of hoped that I could just walk out into the street in the middle of May, yell "I'm a Columbia Law student and I need a summer internship," and hope to have opportunities dumped at my feet?

> **To:** Martha Kimes
> **From:** Rachel Wolfe
> **cc:** Katie McKenna; Elizabeth Lee
> **Subject:** Re: Fw: Brown Bag Lunch
> I just found out that I got awarded a Human Rights
> Fellowship that will pay me a stipend over the sum-
> mer!

> **To:** Martha Kimes
> **From:** Elizabeth Lee
> **cc:** Rachel Wolfe; Katie McKenna
> **Subject:** Re: Fw: Brown Bag Lunch
> I'm going to be working at my dad's law firm in
> Boston this summer.

> **To:** Martha Kimes
> **From:** Katie McKenna
> **cc:** Rachel Wolfe; Elizabeth Lee
> **Subject:** Re: Fw: Brown Bag Lunch
> omigod! i'm totally packing my brown bag lunch as
> I type! does it actually need to be in a brown bag?

All those fantasies that I had entertained about my attendance at an Ivy League law school instantly erasing any future employment concerns? Not so much. Because although I didn't need to spend too much time worrying about my long-term career prospects (according to Career Services, 97 percent of Columbia Law students graduate with permanent employment secured), I soon realized that getting work during my first-year summer wasn't going to be a slam dunk.

Basically, at the brown bag lunch, I learned the following: (1) large New York law firms didn't hire first-year students unless they were the offspring of currently sitting U.S. vice presidents (or higher-ranking U.S. officials), so we shouldn't even bother trying; (2) smaller New York law firms rarely hired first-years, but we could feel free to send them our résumés if we wanted to waste our time and postage money that way; (3) out-of-state law firms hired Columbia first-years with a much higher frequency, so if we were at all inclined to send résumés out to firms in our hometowns, that would be a good idea; (4) there were various public service and human rights organizations that might hire us, but they wouldn't pay us; (5) we might want to also consider looking into unpaid internships working for federal judges, which, although not financially lucrative, would look very good on our résumés; and (6) it would really benefit us if a friend of the family was a partner in a law firm or a senator or a benefactor of a major charity who could put in a good word for us, because otherwise we were pretty much on our own. I left with a sinking feeling in my stomach that I might spend yet another summer stuffing envelopes. Stuffing them with legal-type materials, hopefully, but stuffing them nonetheless.

I had hoped to spend the summer doing public-interest work at some sort of nonprofit organization to figure out if that was, indeed, what I wanted to do in the long run. My ideal would have been a gig at the ACLU or at the Planned Parenthood Federation of America—something that would have been meaningful and important to me personally. Learning that such a job would neither be easy to come by nor would pay me even a nominal salary was disheartening.

I decided to hedge my bets, and littered what seemed to be every small law firm, medium-size firm, federal judge, and nonprofit organization in the city (well, at least the nonprofits that didn't cause me great political offense) with my unimpressive résumé in hopes of getting some sort of summer job. And then I waited. And waited. I received surprisingly few rejection letters in the mail. It was as though I had sent my résumés off into a galaxy far, far away, never to be heard of again.

I began to worry. No one seemed interested. No one! Not even the low-paying or—God help me—the nonpaying jobs! *Oh, God, am I going to end up as the one person in our entire class*

*who has to spend the summer waiting tables? Or folding sweaters
at the Gap? I really, really don't want to have to be a grocery
stocker at D'Agostino's. Please, oh please, let me get a job. Any job.*
After the waiting had passed the point of interminable, I finally
got a call.

I immediately called Joe to report the good news. "I got an interview!" I sang, interrupting him from an important meeting at
work. "An interview!"

"Wonderful! Where?"

"At the Center for Women's Research. It's downtown near
Union Square."

"I've never heard of it. What do they do?" he asked.

"Well, I'm not really sure. I just found their name in a binder
at Career Services. I think they do research? On legal issues affect-
ing women?"

"Would it pay?"

"I don't think so," I said. "At this point, I don't even care. Right
now, money is a secondary issue. I just need a summer job on my
résumé."

When I arrived at the loftlike office, I was surprised to see
three of my classmates clad in navy business suits, leather briefcases and portfolios in hand, sitting in the reception area.

"Hi, Sarah," I said to a woman in my section. "Are you here to
interview for the summer internship?"

"Yeah," Sarah said, dejectedly. "And so is she," she added, nodding toward a woman named Gwen, who smiled tentatively in my
direction. "Her, too," she said, pointing toward a classmate across
the room who I recognized but didn't know.

"Is this just a giant cattle call?" I asked, confused.

"I think so. Keshia Glasser from our section just left ten minutes ago. It seems like they're interviewing every single person
who sent in a résumé."

"Great," I said, my excitement dissipating by the second.

I went in and did my best to wow my interviewer—an overweight, bearish woman who wore bright red glasses and who

deigned to give me all of six minutes of her time. I regaled her with tales of my previous nonprofit experience and my dedication to whatever the organization's cause was. A week later, I got a form letter telling me I didn't get the job.

Reluctantly, I toyed with the idea of trying to go back to Wisconsin for the summer to work in a firm there. Although my chances probably would have been pretty decent at getting an actual paying position, the very thought made me want to hyperventilate. A one-step-forward, two-steps-back kind of thing. Plus, Joe had a job and a life in New York. I wasn't going to spend the summer without him, and he couldn't just uproot himself yet again to follow me around. No, whatever I was going to do, I was determined to do it in New York.

A month later, when I was about to give up all hope, I got a call. And an interview. And, after all that panicking, a job as an unpaid summer intern working for a federal judge in the U.S. District Court for the Southern District of New York. A prestigious job. A coveted job. A job that sounded too fabulous for words.

The job at the Center for Women's Research? That went to Rachel. Katie decided to go back to California, where she was able to find an unpaid position working for the Legal Aid Society. And Elizabeth was going off to work for her father for the summer.

In early March things started to get interesting.

As Rachel, Elizabeth, and I lazily sat around over happy-hour drinks, Katie pushed open the door to the restaurant, letting in a furious gust of cold wind. She scurried in, wearing a pleated micro-miniskirt paired with kneesocks, black patent Mary Janes, and a tight cardigan sweater. The forty-degree weather outside was no match for Katie's fashion sense. A tiny black backpack, the type that was all the rage at the time, served as her handbag. She looked like a twenty-two-year-old Catholic schoolgirl whose wardrobe had shrunk in the wash.

Katie sat down, tucking her skirt beneath her, summoned a

drink from our waitress, and then gushed, "Oh my God, you guys—I wish you were still in my section. The drama is unbelievable!"

"You have drama?" I asked, intrigued. "We've got no drama," I said, looking to Rachel for reinforcement.

Rachel nodded her head and quickly added, "Yeah, it's been almost two months since that time Timothy Frankel made Christine Hsu cry in Perspectives class. Which was kind of awesome, by the way."

It had been kind of awesome. Timothy was being a giant asshole and baiting her, but Christine had overreacted in a monumental fashion. The entire class had been trying to suppress its amusement. I wasn't entirely unsympathetic—I, myself, had certainly wanted to cry in class on more than one occasion. But I had managed to keep my composure, instinctively knowing that crying would just draw attention to the fact that I was a woman in what was still a man's world, despite the fact that fully half of the law students were female.

"My section is pretty dull, too," Elizabeth added.

"Okay, so on Monday? In *my* Perspectives class? There was an incident of epic proportions," announced Katie. She took a slow sip of her drink to draw out the suspense, and then continued. "Do you guys know Beth Arnold? The woman with her nose pierced and all of those tattoos?"

"I know who she is," Elizabeth said, with a wincing expression. "I don't know how she'll ever get a job looking like that." She had a point. The tattoos extended all the way down Beth's arms. She was doomed to a life of long-sleeved shirts if she had any sort of professional aspirations.

"Well," said Katie, "she talks a lot in class, you know? And it's always just this rambling PC shit. I mean, I'm all for political correctness and whatever, but after a while it's just, like, enough already. Anyway," she continued, "so yesterday Beth was disagreeing with something Professor Russo had said and she was throwing around all these statistics about gender biases in the criminal justice system and Professor Russo *laughed in her face.* And not in a friendly sort of way. Like, in a really awful, nasty sort of way. He just totally berated her in front of the whole class. He said that she was a 'disruptive influence.' "

"Wow," said Rachel. "Even Professor Strickland wouldn't have done anything like that."

"I know!" replied Katie. "I mean, Russo has always been kind of a dick. He totally gets off on playing devil's advocate and creating controversy wherever he goes. And he clearly thinks his shit doesn't stink just because he's been on Oprah *and* Geraldo in the past month talking about the O.J. trial. But he totally took it too far this time. I think he knows it, too, because last night, he sent an email to our whole class apologizing for having 'acted inappropriately.' But this isn't going to go down quietly, I can tell you. People are *pissed.*"

"Sounds like Beth should have been in my section," Elizabeth said. "She would love Professor Fox. All she wants to talk about is race, gender, and the law. But she's so busy penning articles for *The Nation* magazine that she can't be bothered to come to class half the time."

"I'm telling you guys, nothing good is going to come of this. Nothing good at all," Katie warned.

She was right. Although Professor Russo had sent an email to the class apologizing for his actions, he had another conflict with Beth later the same week. That's when some students started calling for his head. People were up in arms. Walking down the halls, I overheard everyone arguing about it—even people who weren't in Russo's class.

"How are we supposed to learn in this environment?" a heavy-set woman whined. "I mean, Russo is just so belittling. I know he likes to think of himself as provocative, but he's created a hostile learning environment."

A man to her right, poised with Zippo in hand to step outside and light a cigarette in the smoking area, said, "Oh, please. It's intellectual discourse. People who can't take confrontation don't belong in law school. He's challenging us. That's his job. That's what makes him a good professor."

"Well, I'm in a different section," added a guy who was dressed in an oversized Pittsburgh Steelers jersey, "but all I know is that if the administration decides to let students switch out of his class, then I want to be able to switch to a different class, too. I'm sick of listening to Professor Fox's liberal rhetoric. Shit."

Eventually, the Academic Services Office caved in to student outcry and created an additional section of the Perspectives on Legal Thought class, to be taught by a new professor, in the middle of the semester. This was truly an unprecedented move in Columbia Law School history. Students in Professor Russo's section were given the choice of staying or defecting. Those who transferred to the newly created section would start fresh, and end up taking a final exam based on only half a semester's worth of class—a damn tempting offer. Yet one would be rather naïve not to at least wonder if the students who stayed in his class might be rewarded grade-wise for their loyalty. All in all, from an outsider's perspective, it didn't sound like such a bad dilemma to be in. Especially because the whole thing made for very good gossip.

I, for one, know that I would have paid to have been allowed to transfer from my boring professor's section to Professor Russo's section, just for the entertainment value.

Aah, controversy and polemics! Throw a little paranoia and intense competition into the mix and you're all set. And those things were quickly added (not that they hadn't already been there to begin with) in spades when we first-year students were invited to a late spring informational meeting about the *Columbia Law Review.*

The Law Review was one of the school's many student-run academic journals, but in many ways it was the only one that mattered. Columbia had eleven other legal journals that second- and third-year students could participate in besides Law Review, most of which were topical journals that published scholarly articles on subjects like international law, environmental law, human rights law, and business law. But they were not the same beast—there was Law Review, and then there was everything else. Oh, sure, it was generally accepted and understood which of the other journals were second-tier (about four different journals, each of which claimed to be "the next best after Law Review"), which journals were third-tier, and which journals you could just walk up and join on a whim because you wanted the word *journal* to appear on your transcript.

But *everyone* knew about the mystique of the Law Review—it truly was the one definitive thing that separated the "haves" from the "have nots." Membership was the pinnacle of law school achievement, and if, at the end of three years, you wanted a concise summary of your entire worth as a student, it could be summed up as either: Made Law Review or Didn't Make Law Review. Twenty years after graduation, no one is going to still be bragging about the A they received in Civil Procedure (well, nobody except me), but people who make Law Review will keep talking about it until the day they die.

Everyone knew who the Law Review members were—the second- and third-year students who were on Law Review were like law school demigods, and first-year students would often start talking in hushed whispers when one of them passed by in the hallway. We all sat in the lecture hall waiting for the informational meeting to begin, gazing adoringly at the various members of the Law Review on the dais, fantasizing that someday we, too, might be among their ranks. Of course, ever since our first semester grades were reported and passed through the rumor mill, there had been widespread speculation over who was likely to make it. But at the meeting, the powers that be assured us that there was a chance for even those of us who hadn't made perfect grades.

We were informed that, during the summer, forty-five members of our class would be selected to serve on the staff of the Law Review the next year. The majority—about 60 percent of the slots—would be filled based on a combination of our first-year grades and our performance in a writing competition. The writing competition would be distributed to us on the last day of the second-semester final exam period, and we would each have one week to write a ten-page response to the assignment presented to us. (So much for thinking that school would be over at the end of final exams.) But a small number of the Law Review spots—about 25 percent in all—would be awarded based on the response to the writing competition alone, without any consideration of grades. An even smaller handful of spots would be awarded taking into consideration a personal statement that would help the Law Review to seek "racial and gender diversity, as well as diversity of sexual orientation, class, educational and professional backgrounds, and academic interests" in its staff members.

Those chosen would be expected to report for Law Review duty on August 1, working full-time on the journal for the month until school started. After that, staff members would be expected to contribute at least forty hours a week throughout the school year, in addition to their regular law school coursework. At the end of that year, the Law Review staff members would be elected to editorial positions for their third year, and they would then get to help choose the next crop of students who would serve as new second-year staff members.

After the prepared lecture wrapped up, there was an informal question-and-answer session.

"Um, will being on Law Review help us get jobs?" asked a timid-sounding girl in the back of the room who, from the sound of it, had experienced as much difficulty and frustration as I had in finding a first-year summer job.

"Well," responded one of the demigods, "with a degree from a school like Columbia, you'll have no problem getting a job with a law firm. But if you're aiming to get a Supreme Court clerkship, to be a federal judge someday, or to become a law school professor somewhere other than the University of Southeastern Nowhere, then you really need to be on Law Review. It opens a lot of doors."

"Why should we work the equivalent of a full-time job for free?" someone asked in a smart-ass voice.

"Because, simply put, there is nothing better that you could possibly have on your résumé than the words *Columbia Law Review*."

"I can think of two things that would be better," whispered someone right behind me. "*Yale Law Journal* and *Harvard Law Review*." I suppressed a giggle.

"Okay, but what do you actually do when you're on Law Review?" asked a guy who was much braver than I. Because although every single one of us understood the magnitude of importance that making Law Review held, I don't really think any of us understood what the staffers actually did.

"Well, during your second year, you spend most of your time editing and cite-checking articles, along with researching and writing a scholarly article of your own, which, if you're lucky, we may choose to publish during your third year. As a third-year editor, you are more intimately involved with selection of published articles, supervision of second-year staff members, and helping to shape the overall editorial vision of the journal. It's hard work, and very intellectually rigorous. That's why we choose only the best."

As the meeting was winding down, I was waiting for the Gunner to stand up and announce to the Law Review members on the stage "I look forward to working with you in the fall." I was surprised when he was able to restrain himself. But I *know* he was thinking about saying it. It was written all over his face.

Seven

GOTCHA!

"I have never made but one prayer to God, a very short one: 'O Lord, make my enemies ridiculous.' And God granted it."

—VOLTAIRE

With Moot Court completed, an unpaid summer internship in hand, and visions of Law Review dancing in my head, I realized that, although it seemed like the semester had just begun, exams were pretty much right around the corner. And I hadn't buckled down and kept up with my class outlines. There had simply been too much else to do. I had been running around like a maniac all semester just trying to do damage control. I hoped that I wasn't alone in my predicament.

I was well prepared only in my Criminal Law class, where my interest in the subject and my adoration of Professor Robinson had motivated me to keep up with my reading and to craft a well-put-together outline. Property was a bust—I considered myself to be ahead of the game simply because I had usually managed to show up for that unbearable class each day. I had purchased a Gilbert's commercial outline for the subject and was planning to sleep with it under my pillow in hopes of creating some sort of osmosis effect. Frankly, I had no idea where I stood in my Regulatory State class or my Perspectives class—both were so peculiar that they were virtually impossible to study for. Certainly there were no study aids to be purchased for those off-the-wall courses, so I was on my own.

I started back up on the four hours of sleep per night coupled with four pots of coffee during the day plan that I had followed while studying the previous semester, but this time I was wise enough to leave out the *Insomniac Music Theater.* I definitely felt the pressure of the upcoming tests, but I knew that the stress would not begin to be what I had felt the first semester. I had survived it before, so I knew it was humanly possible. Also, with everything that had been going on, I just hadn't had the time to devote to obsessive worrying about exams beginning months in advance. I was too busy worrying about whether I would make Law Review.

I had a sneaking suspicion that my only chance at getting onto the Law Review staff was by acing the writing competition—my first semester Bs likely putting me out of the running for the spots that depended on grades. But still, I wasn't willing to admit defeat. I would have happily killed my own mother for a spot on the Law Review. (Well, at the very least, I would have given it serious consideration.) It was time to put my nose to the grindstone.

Early on in the semester, our Regulatory State professor had announced that he would be affording us the luxury of a take-home exam. It's difficult to accurately impart how wonderful that news was to hear. A take-home exam! Now, there are some demented people who seem to ascribe to the philosophy that take-home exams are even worse than in-class exams, because you feel compelled to stay awake for the entire twenty-four (or, sometimes, forty-eight) hours that you have to complete them. To them I say, *oh, please.* In the grand scheme of things, what's so bad about missing a night or two of slumber? You *must* be kidding.

Given a choice between these two options, which would you take?

In-Class Exam

1. Hardly sleep for weeks on end while fanatically preparing, outlining, and committing to memory every tiny detail of information that has been imparted upon you over the course of the entire semester because you have no idea

what you will be tested on. Convince yourself that if you omit the tiniest detail from your outline, that will surely end up being the one specific point upon which the entire exam will hinge.

2. Panic excessively, effectively cutting several months off your expected life span. Consider that you might need to start taking blood pressure medication.

3. Sit for a four-hour exam period in a classroom where the fear and tension can be smelled from at least three miles away. Although you really need to go pee during the test, just hold it in because getting up to go to the restroom would waste about two minutes of your precious time.

4. Write maniacally until your hand is cramped up into a painfully misshapen clawlike formation and it is physically impossible to write even one more letter on the blue-lined page of your exam book.

5. Realize in the end that your answers are probably incorrect, but you have no time to go back and fix them because the proctor is going to call "time" in three minutes.

6. Go home. Weep uncontrollably.

Take-Home Exam

1. Hear that you will be getting take-home exam. Rejoice.

2. Immediately cease all further work for that class and laugh at the idea of making an outline or committing any material to memory, because you know that you will have access to all your books, notes, and study aids when completing the exam.

3. Pick up the exam questions at the assigned time, then sprint home and change into your most comfortable pajamas.

4. Stay awake for twenty-four hours poring over the small handful of materials that you actually need to read, analyze,

and make sense of in order to answer the questions given to you. Ignore the sizable remainder of reading material assigned during the semester, which has proved wholly irrelevant to the exam.

5. On your computer, type responses to the exam questions, using as many direct quotes from the professor as possible that you have hand-picked from your class notes. Appreciate lack of maniacal-writing-induced debilitating claw-cramped hand.

6. Because you are given more than four short hours to put together coherent answers, you have time to go back and edit your work until it actually makes sense.

7. Print out and turn in exam.

8. Go home and eat ice cream. Add tequila as necessary.

I know what my pick would be.

I sailed through that take-home Regulatory State exam, bull-shitted my way through my Perspectives exam, and suffered through my Property exam. I was appreciative of the fact, however, that my Property professor had presented us with a question about land use regulations, choosing to name one of the parties "Sparrow" and another "Hawk." (As a general rule, professors like to try to prove themselves clever in their choice of exam questions.) This reminded me of the ample amounts of class time that he had spent discussing his avid bird-watching hobby and made me remember to toss in some references to my love of marsh birds and the necessity of protecting our nation's wetlands in order to maintain their shrinking habitat. I may not have truly understood the difference between assignments and subleases, but I figured that a few references to my fondness for all things avian might just give me a tiny leg up.

My last exam of my first year at Columbia Law School was Criminal Law. It was held in the same lecture hall where the dean had welcomed our incoming class eight months earlier.

On that sunny May morning I walked into the room, in which I had spent countless hours by that point, with my head held high. Only one exam stood between me and the official end of the school year. And luckily it was the one test I was confident I was prepared for. I understood the nuanced differences between solicitation, conspiracy, and attempt. I had mastered the rules of accomplice liability. The felony murder rule? I was all over that. Besides, Professor Robinson was so fabulous that I was certain she would be charitable when crafting her exam questions.

Oh God, I was so wrong. My amazing, funny, and enlightening professor, who I had been so infatuated with all semester, turned out to be a total hard-ass when it came to exam time. She presented us with four questions (the norm was generally two, or possibly three), and included a twenty-nine-page supplementary judicial opinion that we were to read and use in formulating one of our answers. And she only gave us three and a half hours to complete the test. *How could I have ever liked this woman? Sure, she acted all nice in class and told those fascinating stories about prosecuting mafia warlords and convicting corrupt politicians, but when it comes down to the nitty-gritty, she's trying to torture us! Can't you be prosecuted for torture? You would think that she, of all people, would know that!*

There wasn't much time to concentrate on anything but answering the exam. I put pen to paper and filled up nine exam booklets, most of which were dedicated to answering a six-page-long question that set forth countless botched, bungled, and butchered crimes and asked us to discuss what charges could be brought against all the people involved, who had been given cartoonish names like "Alexandria Atrocious," "Beatrice Beaufort," "Cornelius Comfit," and "Donna Dastardly."

When our time was up, I walked out of the exam with an otherworldly feeling of weightlessness, of freedom. I was done. *Finished with my first year at Columbia Law School.* The next time I walked into a classroom, I would be an upperclassman. Upper-

classwoman? Whatever—this was no time for semantics. I didn't
even care how I'd done. All that mattered was that I was through.
Finished. I had survived. There was just one remaining piece of
business to take care of.

I looked around, scanning the faces congregated in the hallway outside the exam room until I found my mark: the Gunner,
hovering on the sidelines, waiting to pounce at the first sign of
weakness.

"Hi Todd," I beamed, as I walked up to him. "That was some
exam, huh?"

"Indeed," he replied, with that trademark smirk. "I'm glad I
spent so much time studying the subtle differences between the different insanity defenses. Really, the choice between the M'Naghten
rule and the Durham test turned out to be *so important* to that first
question. Don't you agree, Martha?"

"Riiiiiight," I answered. (It wasn't important in the least, and
this time I knew it.) "But," I replied with a smirk of my own, "you
know what I'm really glad about? The fact that I read the Second
Circuit opinion that just came out last week about defendants' liability for the death of co-felons as a result of resistance by the
victim. I mean, without having read that case, someone probably
would have jumped to the conclusion that the fact pattern in that
third question amounted to felony murder when, in light of that
opinion, it *so obviously* didn't! And that would just wreck your
whole exam, you know?"

A flash of worry passed over the Gunner's eyes, and he hesitated
just a moment too long before collecting himself and answering,
"Oh, yes! Of course! The Second Circuit case! Har har har!" Todd
wasn't going to be winning an Academy Award anytime soon.

"Well then, I've got to be going. Time to go pick up my copy of
the Law Review competition and go catch some celebratory
drinks with my friends!" I trilled, and I headed off in Rachel's direction. "Have a great summer, Todd!"

"Yeah, um, you, too, Martha," he replied, with the worry still
visible in his eyes, his face noticeably paled.

"Gotcha!" I squealed to myself. There *totally* was no such Second Circuit case.

Rachel, Katie, Elizabeth, and I weren't the only ones with post-exam celebration on our minds. It was only two in the afternoon, and our usual hangout was not yet open, so we had instead chosen to gather at the West End for some drinking and decompressing. Considering the fact that it was early on a Wednesday afternoon, the bar was crowded, and it was all with first-year law students. The bartender was taken by surprise and seemed quite overwhelmed—he couldn't begin to pour as quickly as we all could order. Within half an hour, he had called in reinforcements.

As the four of us sat reveling in the fact that we had finally finished our first year of law school, talk soon turned to the inevitable: Law Review.

"Do you think any of us will make it?" I asked. The exact same conversation was surely taking place at every other table in the bar.

Elizabeth pointed directly at Rachel, her diamond ring piercing the air, and said, "You've got a really good shot with your first-semester grades."

Rachel shrugged and said, "Well, you do, too." The bar was getting uncomfortably warm, and she pushed the sleeves of her maroon-and-white-striped rugby shirt up to her elbows.

Katie and I both glanced at each other kind of uncomfortably. Nobody was suggesting that either of us were shoo-ins.

"What if the Gunner makes it?" I asked.

"That would certainly cement his concept of his own brilliance, wouldn't it?" said Elizabeth.

"The problem is, you know he probably will," I added. "He supposedly had awesome grades first semester, and I hate to say it, but, as revolting as he is, he's smart."

"Yeah, I think most people are betting he'll make it," Rachel said.

"What about Chaz Whitmore?" I asked, inadvertently rolling my eyes.

Elizabeth let out a little huff and said, "I've never understood what you have against Chaz. He's not a bad guy."

That cemented it. Although I liked Elizabeth on certain levels, I doubted I would ever really understand her. Her family probably summered with the Whitmores out on the Vineyard or something. And I wasn't going to explain—just as I often didn't understand her, Elizabeth wouldn't have understood me. It was best to just let it go.

"You guys, do we have to talk about Law Review?" asked Katie. "I just want to pretend for a couple of hours that we don't all have to go home and face that writing competition."

"Pretend all you want, Katie, but I'm leaving here in half an hour, going to the library, and getting started," Rachel said. "I'm hoping this beer will spark my creativity."

"Me, too," added Elizabeth.

"Not me," I replied. "I'm officially on vacation until tomorrow morning. After I have another drink, I'm going shoe shopping."

As Rachel and Elizabeth trudged back to the library to begin poring over the two-inch-thick stack of materials that we had been given for the Law Review writing competition, and as Katie went back to her dorm to continue partying with other first-year revelers, I hopped on the subway to go down to SoHo to treat myself to a pair of shoes that I had wanted forever. They were funky and ridiculously expensive (for my student budget, anyway), but if surviving my first year of law school didn't merit a little splurge, I wasn't sure what would.

I approached reverently, opened the heavy door of the John Fluevog store on Prince Street, and walked into the tiny shop filled with funkadelic shoes. The store was empty save for me, two other women to whom I paid no real attention, and an over-the-top flamboyant sales clerk who kept making these bizarre bug-eyes at me and then slyly nodding his head in the direction of my two fellow shoppers. *What's with the sideways nodding? Is it a ner-*

vous tic? Is he trying to tell me to leave? What? He thinks I'm not worthy of being in his hipster shoe store? But after his eyes bugged almost completely out of his head and he continued to not-so-subtly gesture at the two women sitting in overstuffed purple velvet chairs trying on piles of shoes, I finally looked at them more closely. And then I realized.

Oh my God. OH MY GOD. OHMYGOD! Madonna! Less than three feet away from me! I am standing three feet away from Madonna! Madonna is sitting three feet away from me! We are breathing the same air. It's quite possible that at this very moment, I'm inhaling oxygen particles that she exhaled mere moments ago! Or vice versa! And she's only wearing socks! I'm looking at Madonna's socks! (Which were white and kind of ratty, in case you're curious.) I tried to act casual, refrain from staring, and stifle the all-encompassing urge I felt to begin singing "Like a Virgin" at the top of my lungs.

Instead, I played it cool. I found the shoes I wanted, asked the sales guy if I could see them in a size 7½ while the two of us both exchanged "Can you believe that's *Madonna?!?*" stares, and sat down to wait. I imagined that if I was Madonna, with all the money in the world, I would buy every pair of shoes in the store. And never have to take out student loans. I kept sneaking sideways glances, and then it hit me. *Wait. You know what? Madonna is wearing cutoff army pants and a faded red do-rag around her head, and I'm thinking that she's not seen the inside of a shower in three days, at least. I am sitting here, a giant dork from Wisconsin smacked down in the middle of SoHo next to one of the most famous women in the world, and I look better than she does! Hot damn!*

And then it got even better. I tried on the shoes and walked around the store to test them in action. Madonna's shopping companion looked at me, turned to the Material Girl, and said, "See? Those shoes are cute on her. But you couldn't pull them off. Your feet are too big." *Oh my God! I can pull off shoes that Madonna can't? Not only do I look better than she does right now, but I seem to have inherently better feet as well. I am floating on air.* Even though those shoes were rather uncomfortable and far too wide, I bought them so quickly that the clerk barely had time to swipe my credit card. Then I floated back to the subway to go home and relate the story to Joe.

I was barely through the front door of our apartment when I started yelling, "Madonna! Madonna! I was shopping with Madonna!"

"What? What are you talking about? And why do you smell like a brewery?" Joe asked.

"I went to buy this new pair of shoes and Madonna was there! I saw her socks! And I have better feet than she does!"

"What in God's name were you doing shopping at a store that Madonna patronizes? How much did those shoes cost, anyway?"

Boys can be such idiots.

"Let me give you a tour of the courthouse," Amy said, after she had showed me to my desk and introduced me around Judge Lovell's chambers. "When you interviewed with Judge Lovell back in the spring, we were still in the old building. We just moved here last month. This building is so much nicer."

"It even smells new," I said. And indeed the slight chemical smell of new carpet permeated the shining new office.

"Well, the old courthouse was so classic and beautiful from the outside, with the stone pillars and the wide steps and all," Amy added. "But our chambers were old and small, the air-conditioning in the library only worked sporadically, and some of the courtrooms were in desperate need of repair. This building may not be as attractive from the outside," she said about the more modern-looking new Federal Courthouse, "but the inside is unbelievable."

Amy, one of Judge Lovell's two regular law clerks, was right. As she led me through the plushly carpeted halls, showed me the trellised roof deck, ushered me through the well-appointed cafeteria, gave me a tour of the sprawling library, and opened the doors into Judge Lovell's enormous, opulent courtroom, it was obvious that no expense had been spared when the new Federal Courthouse was constructed.

As she showed me around, Amy gave me a bit of background. She had graduated from Harvard Law School two years before, and that summer was the end of her two-year clerkship with Judge Lovell. In September, she was headed to the litigation department of a prestigious New York City law firm, where she would be paid a handsome bonus in recognition of her clerkship. Sam, the other regular clerk, had graduated from NYU the year before, and he was halfway through his tenure with the judge.

"You're really lucky to have ended up with an internship with Judge Lovell," Amy said. "He's such a wonderful, kindhearted man. He'll give you real responsibility and you'll have a great summer. Some of the other judges around here? They treat their interns like secretaries. Nothing but photocopying all day. Then again, some of the judges around here are crazy. That's what you get with lifetime judicial appointments. But that's a story for another day, I guess."

"Oh, sure," I said, wishing that Amy would just spill the crazy judge stories right that second.

"Sam and I will take you out to lunch soon. We'll fill you in on all of the behind-the-scenes stories about the courthouse. Meanwhile, let's get back to chambers, and I'll tell you about your actual job."

Back in the office, Amy said to me, "A big part of what Sam and I both do here is to review motions made by parties to the various cases assigned to Judge Lovell's docket. Generally, they're motions to dismiss, motions for summary judgment, and habeas corpus petitions. We review the parties' briefs, read the cases cited by each side to support their positions, then do legal research of our own on the issues presented to see if there is any authority that the parties conveniently failed to mention to us. Based on the weight of the case law, we decide which side should prevail, and draft opinions explaining the decision. Judge Lovell reviews them, and usually signs off."

"So you make the judge's decisions for him?" I asked, naïvely.

"Not really. I mean, we do research, make recommendations, and draft opinions. It's pretty standard practice. Of course, Judge Lovell makes the ultimate decisions, and he's free to disagree with us. Several times, he's asked me to completely rewrite things."

"Oh. Wow. Okay."

"Anyway," Amy said, "that's pretty much what you'll be doing this summer."

"I'm going to be drafting judicial opinions?" I asked.

"Yeah, isn't it great? Like I said, a lot of judges don't give their summer interns anywhere near this sort of authority. It's fabulous experience."

"Yes. Fabulous!" I replied, secretly worried about the level of responsibility that was being conferred upon me.

Wheeling around in her swivel chair, Amy said, "I'm just going to give you this motion that's sitting on top of the pile. Let's see . . . it looks like some sort of contract dispute, and the defendant is moving to dismiss for lack of personal jurisdiction under New York's long-arm statute. Do you remember your Civil Procedure?"

"Oh, sure. Minimum contacts and all that. *International Shoe!*" Who knew that I'd be thankful for the things the Sadistic Professor taught me?

"Anyway, I'm just over there across the room—ask me or Sam if you have any questions at all."

"Great. Thanks, Amy."

That night I went home and panicked.

"Joe, Judge Lovell's clerk has me drafting judicial opinions. Let me be very clear: *I am in no way qualified to draft judicial opinions.* Where do I get off acting like a pretend judge? I'm not even a second-year law student yet!"

"They wouldn't give you the responsibility if they didn't think you could handle it, Martha. Besides, there's someone there to supervise you, isn't there?"

"Yes, but that's beside the point. *I'm* supposed to be making decisions here? What is wrong with this picture?"

"It sounds like a great experience for you. Stop freaking out."

"Joe, don't you realize? I'm supposed to draft the type of opinions that I have spent the last year reading in my casebooks. Theoretically, someday, somewhere, some poor, unsuspecting law student could end up studying the stuff I am now being entrusted to write! That is a terrifying thought."

"Okay, you're right. That is terrifying."

I wasn't sure if Joe's concession made me happy or not. "Thank you. Thank you very much."

Beginning the next morning, I read the defendant's motion. I read the plaintiff's and the defendant's briefs. I read each case cited by the parties. I did my own supplementary research, and tried to ignore Professor Strickland's voice, which kept echoing through the back of my head. I carefully considered everything I had read and decided that, all told, the defendant's motion shouldn't be granted until an evidentiary hearing was held, because there were too many facts in dispute. I drafted an opinion to that effect, trying my best to mimic the style in which Judge Lovell's opinions were usually written. At the end of the week, I gave my draft to Amy and hoped that she wouldn't laugh in my face or point out some glaring error that I had accidentally made.

A few days later, Judge Lovell sat me down to review the draft opinion with me.

"Martha, you've done a wonderful job," he said from behind his oak-paneled desk, which sat before a giant window with a sweeping view north to midtown Manhattan. A pair of peregrine falcons, which had nested high atop the courthouse, slowly soared back and forth past his twenty-second-floor window. "I agree with your assessment, and I want to tell you that this opinion was very well drafted. There are a few small things I'd like you to tweak, though—let's take a look at them. But this is excellent work. Excellent."

I couldn't believe it.

Jubilantly, I went back and edited the points that Judge Lovell wanted clarified, modified the sections of the opinion that needed some work, and gave him my final product the next day, which he read and signed off on with a flourished hand.

Later that week, I had lunch with Amy and Sam at a hole-in-the-wall Thai restaurant popular among the courthouse set. As we sat wedged into a tiny table in a room that smelled of coconut milk and chili paste, eating chicken satay and pad thai, I got the inside scoop. I learned which judges were well-respected and which were widely considered to be intellectually lacking. I learned which clerks were sleeping together and which were on the verge of being fired. I learned which judge was a raging alcoholic and which one was so old and incapacitated that he made his clerks help him to the bathroom. I learned about the special hidden tables in the courthouse library where certain clerks went to steal secret afternoon naps.

In early July, Judge Lovell began presiding over a trial in his courtroom. He invited me to spend as much or as little time as I wished observing the proceedings. Over the next weeks, I alternated between drafting more opinions for his review and sitting in his richly appointed courtroom, watching the jury selection, opening and closing arguments, witness examinations and cross-examinations. I was able to join Judge Lovell in his chambers along with Amy and Sam while he had conferences with the attorneys, and after each day's proceedings, I got to hear his gently worded opinions about the shortcomings of the two attorneys (and it was apparent even to an untrained eye such as mine that there were plenty of shortcomings about which to opine). The case itself wasn't fascinating—it was a dispute over a construction contract, and while watching, I became far too familiar with such terms as "girder trusses" and "collar beams" and "reflective insulation." Nevertheless, the insight that Judge Lovell gave me that summer was worth more than any paycheck.

I left at the beginning of August with a letter of recommendation in my hand that was likewise invaluable. It read as follows:

UNITED STATES DISTRICT COURT
CHAMBERS OF JUDGE BRYSON J. LOVELL
UNITED STATES COURTHOUSE
500 PEARL STREET
NEW YORK, NY 10007

To Whom It May Concern:

Martha Kimes worked in my Chambers during the months of June and July, 1995. During this relatively brief period of time, she drafted eight or nine opinions of consistently high quality.

It is important for your own evaluation of Ms. Kimes to know that in my Chambers, student law clerks report directly to me and I edit their drafts, rather than having the editing process go through the regular clerks. This gives me an opportunity to spend more time with the student clerks, and also to be sure that what I am reading is the student clerk's work product and not a revision authorized by a more senior law clerk.

Accordingly, I am in a position to say that we gave Ms. Kimes a considerable variety of opinions to draft, some of them relatively complex, one of them involving an important Seventh Amendment question of right to jury trial not yet decided by the Second Circuit. Ms. Kimes is an excellent legal researcher, understands and identifies the issues, and writes a lucid and well-organized legal prose. She proved capable of producing drafts which became opinions of the Court with relatively minor revisions. The quality of her work made it difficult for me to believe that she has completed only one year at the Law School, but of course that is the fact.

I recommend Ms. Kimes strongly and without reservation. If you require any further information from me, please feel free to contact me by telephone.

Very truly yours,

Bryson J. Lovell

Bryson J. Lovell
United States District Judge

Joe had to talk me out of sleeping with that recommendation letter under my pillow.

Despite the fact that I had just about killed myself at the beginning of the summer completing the Law Review writing competition, and then rewriting it over and over again in an effort to make mine the most fantastic writing specimen ever completed, I didn't receive an offer to join the Law Review staff. I was disappointed, but not terribly surprised.

The news quickly followed the release of our second-semester grades. Each day after work that summer, I took the subway from the courthouse back up to 116th Street, ran home, and instantly logged on to the computer to check my grades. I don't know whether I had actually gained a tiny bit of restraint, or whether it was just due to the fact that I was out of the house at work all day without access to the law school's online grading system, but, unlike the previous go-around, there was no $450 phone bill forthcoming. I would check first thing in the morning and then once or twice each night (hey, it was possible that some grade could get released at nine p.m., right?), and go on about my business.

When the grades were reported, I was baffled: I received notification that I had made honors. I was named a Harlan Fiske Stone Scholar for the 1994-1995 academic year. How had that happened? For my second semester, I had received a B in Criminal Law (naturally, I did poorly in the one class that I had consistently studied for all semester long), an undeserved B+ in Property, an

A- on my Foundations of the Regulatory State take-home exam, a B in Perspectives on Legal Thought, and Ungraded Credit for Foundation Year Moot Court. Along with my first semester marks, which had sent me into a spiral of despair, *these grades* earned me honors? That meant my grades were better than average? I just didn't get it. All along I had compared my performance to everyone else's and thought I had done worse than most. But that couldn't have been the case if I had made honors. Yes, there were definitely people who had been lying about their grades.

Still, none of it was enough to get me onto the Law Review. I found out by default that I hadn't made it when I got Rachel's call.

"Martha, I can't believe it," she said, with an unusual shakiness in her voice.

"What? What's going on?" I asked.

"Law Review. I got an offer to join Law Review."

"Oh my God! Congratulations! Wait . . . how did you find out?" I asked.

"They called me this morning to tell me. Elizabeth made it, too. Do you think I should accept? I have two days to decide."

They called Rachel this morning? And Elizabeth? They haven't called me. Although no one has told me "no" yet, I'm smart enough to do the math. They're going to be demigods. I shall remain a mere mortal.

At first I concentrated on trying to sound happy for Rachel instead of disappointed for myself, until I realized the absolute stupidity of the question that I had just been asked. "What? Should you *accept*? What the hell kind of question is that?"

"It's going to be a lot of work, you know? I'm not even sure if I want this," Rachel replied.

"So you're going to slave away for a year at school, slave away doing the writing competition, then get offered what amounts to the highest honor you could possibly receive at law school, and you're going to say 'no' because it means some more slaving away? And you'll go down in Columbia Law School history as the only person ever to have turned down an offer to join Law Review? Are you *insane?* I am *so* done with this conversation. Well, I'll be done as soon as you tell me whether or not the Gunner made it. Please tell me that the Gunner didn't make it?"

"Yeah. Yeah, he did."

Rachel spent the next two days acting as though she wasn't sure what she should do and then, of course, she joined Law Review. Sadly, that was the beginning of the end for Rachel and me.

Eight

WILL WORK FOR FOOD

"All I ask is the chance to prove that money can't make me happy."
—SPIKE MILLIGAN

When I returned to school in the fall, the halls were alive with the sound of money. It was law firm interviewing season and the race was on. I was crouched with my feet in the starting blocks, ready to wield my résumé and recommendation letter from Judge Lovell, shouting "Hire me!" upon a moment's notice. Provided, that is, that doing so didn't interfere with my newfound hobby of obsessively fantasizing about my bright and lucrative law firm future. If you looked closely enough, you would have been able to see tiny neon green dollar signs glowing in the pupils of my eyes.

Along with the rest of my classmates, I was about to embark upon the process of interviewing for jobs at large, prestigious law firms, hoping to secure a position as a summer associate after the second year of law school was over (with the hope that the summer job would turn into an offer of permanent employment upon graduation). Columbia had an elaborate on-campus interviewing program, and over seven hundred interviewers from hundreds of law firms from across the country would be descending upon the school during the week before classes began to conduct over fourteen thousand job interviews in total. Whereas big law firms resolutely shun first-year law students, they are *dying* to hire second-year students. Indeed, the entire recruiting program at most prestigious law firms is based on hiring law students to work during the summer after their second year at law school, wooing and impressing them over the summer, and then signing them on to return after graduation. They all have a ridiculous turnover rate, and depend on a large crop of young attorneys to pour in each year to replenish their diminishing armies.

With surprisingly little hesitation, I abandoned any previous aspirations that I once held about doing public interest work as soon as I began to comprehend exactly how much money I could make going to work for a large New York law firm. I was swept up in the buzz and, with visions of a penthouse apartment, a chauffeured Lincoln Town Car, and a summer home in the Hamptons dancing in my head, I dove in headfirst. Armed with nothing but a dog-eared copy of *The Insider's Guide to Law Firms,* law firm rankings from *American Lawyer* and the *National Law Journal,* and a handful of word-of-mouth tidbits passed down from the law clerks I had spent the past few months working with, I had morphed into an instant expert on the nature, practice, and culture of each of the top fifty or so firms in New York City, even though I had never so much as set foot inside a law firm of any kind.

And let there be no doubt about it: except for a precious few holdouts, the vast majority of my classmates and I were all going to be working at prestigious mega law firms. No matter what our original designs had been, we had quickly learned that it's just (and here you must stick your nose up into the air, jut out your chin, and don an affected East Coast accent) "the way things are done." There was not a person in my class, nor can I imagine that there have ever been more than a small handful of ostracized students in the entire history of Columbia Law School, who wanted to go hang their own small-town shingles and spend their time drafting wills for the local oldsters and defending their hometown drunks against DUI charges. We were most definitely not aspiring to have our photographs plastered on the sides of city buses next to pictures of menacing-looking eagles and the words "Injured in an auto accident? Call us!" Sure, slaving away defending soulless corporations might not have been our ultimate goal, but almost all of us would be doing it for at least a few years, even if we had to rationalize it as "good training" for our future careers in government, academia, or public service. There were a handful of public interest holdouts, to be sure, but they were the truly hardcore. Even Christine Hsu, oh she of the ersatz law firm disdain, was suddenly on board with the law firm idea.

The school was abuzz with anticipatory interviewing chatter. We were all reverberating with newly discovered caches of law firm gossip and questionably true information. And then each of us took our halfway reliable information, subtly distorted and exaggerated it, and passed it on to others—it was like a law school version of the telephone game. No matter where you turned, you would inevitably overhear some version of the following conversation:

"I can't wait to interview with Black, White and Gray. They've got such a diverse practice not only in complex commercial litigation but also in structured finance, capital markets, and international trade regulation!"

"Oh, I know. Plus I hear they've got a cookie lady who comes by the associates' offices every afternoon at three to deliver specially ground Peruvian coffee and the very freshest of baked goods. Rumor has it they actually own a coffee plantation in South America and have the beans roasted on site and hand-delivered to the firm each Sunday afternoon by a mustachioed man on a donkey."

"Isn't that fabulous? So much better than the atmosphere at Butcher, Baker and Candlestickmaker. I hear they won't even let the lawyers eat or drink in their offices! People say they monitor the attorneys' office trash cans each night looking for telltale crumbs and empty soda cans. Some guy got fired there a few years back because he couldn't control his Starbucks addiction and got caught one too many times sipping away at his desk."

"*Yes*—I heard that, too! But aside from that, BB and C is supposed to have a very collegial environment. The partners aren't screamers, and it's not at all a sweatshop like so many of the other firms. I mean, the billable-hour requirements at Washington and Jefferson are just outrageous! It's frowned upon there if you go to the bathroom more than three times in a day, because it cuts too far into your billing. So you'd better just learn to hold it in, I guess. There, they don't even pay bonuses to associates unless they bill at least twenty-seven hundred hours per year. And I hear that every single one of those hours is pure and absolute bladder-bursting misery."

"I know. And the office situation at Washington and Jefferson sounds just unbearable, too. They're so crowded that you're sure to be stuck sharing an office for at least two years. I mean, really, I don't care if they do have their very own sushi chef in the firm cafeteria, it's just a deplorable way to treat your associates."

"I know! The horror!"

The horror, indeed. My task was to digest all of this newfound information and to put together a ranked list of the firms with which I hoped to interview. This list would be passed on to the law school's Career Services Office, which would perform some sort of law firm lottery and then return an interview schedule to me, informing me of the firms I was to meet with during on-campus interview week. In this respect, the job-hunting process at elite law schools is a unique beast. Nowhere else on earth will you find the interviewees with the upper hand over the interviewers. In the bizarre alternate universe that is Ivy League Law, the students get to pick the firms with which they want to interview instead of the firms getting to pick the students that they want to meet. Kind of a sick and twisted way to go about it, but I wasn't complaining. I was on the good end of the deal. I was one of the lucky ones.

We would be devoting the entire week before classes began to on-campus interviewing: five full days of screening interviews, with each interview lasting about twenty minutes. It was a lot like speed-dating, except we were searching for high-paying jobs instead of true love. After the on-campus interviews were over, the firms were finally in charge—if they liked us, they would offer us opportunities to come visit the firm's offices for more extensive "callback" interviews. If we made the cut after that, summer job offers would be extended to us.

Possibly the most bizarre thing about the process was the fact that, because the interviews took place at the beginning of the second year of school, we were being judged solely on our first-year performance. Based upon our first-year grades, our résumés, and our interviewing skills, we would be offered summer associate positions, and the expectation was that we would likely be extended offers to return for permanent employment after graduation. Sure, the firms would ask to see a copy of our final transcript to make sure we had indeed graduated, but it was only the first-year grades that made any difference in their hiring decisions. This is why people are so neurotic during the first year—they know it is the only year that really counts. After that, we were pretty much free to screw up.

Deciding which firms I was interested in wasn't a matter of money, as all of the best law firms paid virtually identical starting salaries. (At the time, the starting salary was $87,000 plus bonuses; as of this writing, the number has been raised to $145,000 plus bonuses.) It was mostly a matter of prestige—everyone knew which places were top tier—with a small spattering of concern about "firm atmosphere" and practice areas thrown in for good measure. Some firms had particularly strong litigation practices, others were renowned for their expertise in mergers and acquisitions. Some were known for their culture of partners screaming at and otherwise taking pride in abusing their associates, other firms had "kinder and gentler" reputations. Wherever I ended up, I'd be doted upon during my summer associate tenure, then would be relegated to doing total grunt work for the first few years, during which the expectation would be that I would spend all my waking hours at the office in order to bill at least twenty-two hundred hours of my time each year to the firm's clients. I would be paid disgustingly well for it, so I wasn't in any position to complain.

When I did finally come up with my official list, it was a work of such heartbreaking beauty that it brought a small tear to my eye. On one typed, single-spaced page of paper, I had placed the names of fifty of the largest, most powerful law firms in the country, with billions upon billions of dollars of combined gross annual revenues. The money positively oozed off the page. I could picture myself in a sharply tailored suit and new Charles David heels, striding confidently toward my corner office where I would do whatever sorts of important and influential things lawyers actually did in order to earn those ridiculous sums of money. My list contained the names of ten firms that I would have sacrificed anything—even my Madonna shoes—to work for, thirty firms that were of varying degrees of prestige but not quite as desirable for one reason or another, and a handful of so-so places thrown in for good measure in case I didn't get any better offers. It's important to keep your bases covered.

I had spent days painstakingly weighing the pros and cons of each and every big firm in New York City and had come up with a list so perfect, so brilliant, that I was sure, had this been a graded assignment, I would have broken the curve. I suppose I shouldn't have been surprised when I found out that my list was exactly the same as that of every single one of my classmates—everyone was gunning for jobs at the same top ten or fifteen firms, although our specific preferences might have been a bit varied in order. Because, in the end, after all of the weighing, the agonizing, the considering and reconsidering, the firm rankings reigned supreme. You couldn't blame us, really—blindly heeding the rankings like sheep being led off to slaughter was all we knew. That's how we'd all ended up at Columbia in the first place.

After I received my interview schedule from the Career Services Office (thirty-five firms total, seven interviews a day for five straight days), I knew that it was time to prepare. In an attempt to shake things up a little bit and take a detour from my normal modus operandi of sitting at my desk and shaking with terror, I decided to be proactive and upbeat. The woman in the apartment across the hall from me, who was a Ph.D. student in biomedical engineering with an unusual fondness for crystals and Tarot cards, convinced me of the merits of taking a new-agey approach toward interview preparation, and she saddled me with a CD of soft music with harps and sitars. I dimmed the lights in my apartment, turned on the music, closed my eyes, and sat cross-legged on a pillow in the middle of my living room floor, practicing deep breathing techniques and trying my hand at visualizing my way to a cushy job offer. If I was able to picture the perfect interview in my head, surely it would come to be!

So there I sat, with my eyes closed, my legs crossed, and the tips of my thumbs forming perfectly serene circles with the tips of my middle fingers (and really, how can you properly meditate unless your legs are crossed and your fingers are encircled?), imagining interviews that were filled with witty repartee, where I had the perfect answers to the tough, meaningful questions that the Career Services Office had told us to prepare for, where the interviewers offered statements like "Martha, you are the absolutely perfect job candidate. It's people like you who make me believe there truly is a God."

The problem is, sitting like that really isn't very comfortable. Aside from the finger cramps that quickly set in, my concentration on the perfect interview visualization was frequently interrupted with the need to concentrate on keeping my ass from tipping off the overly stuffed pillow upon which I was precariously perched. I considered just sitting on the floor, but thought the pillow was probably an integral part of the whole experience, so I remained there, teetering away. In that position, I meditated my ass off.

Determined not to provide an honest answer like "shoe shopping!" when asked "What is your biggest weakness?" I developed stock answers that I kept at my fingertips, ready to respond with a smile when asked to describe my proudest accomplishment. (I might not have been the sharpest tool in the shed, but I knew that "getting accepted to this law school where I have no rightful place" probably wasn't the smartest way to reply.) From atop that pillow I prepared myself to discuss the highlights of every job I had since I was fifteen years old. Babysitting a flock of drooling young babies taught me the value of hard work and the many practical uses a creative young girl can make of a disposable diaper! By working as a waitress at Pizza Hut during high school I learned how to prioritize tasks in a high-pressure environment and I mastered the art of self-discipline when faced with an endless supply of free cheesy bread! Stuffing envelopes for months and months after college honed my attention to detail and made me realize the virtue of patience when faced with mind-numbing monotony! From my judicial internship, not only had I learned the inner workings of a courtroom, but I had also mastered all sorts of useful construction terminology! I was as prepared as I was ever going to be.

Or so I thought. On the first day of interviews, I donned my black suit, loaded up on Xanax for good measure, and went on my merry way. I was relieved that my first on-campus interview was with a firm I wasn't very interested in anyway. It was a second-rate firm that specialized in something bizarre like maritime law, and I welcomed the opportunity to warm up my interviewing muscles when the stakes weren't high. As I walked into the interview, I was expecting to meet a middle-aged man in a crisp suit and expertly knotted tie who would be cordial but not overly friendly, and who would not waste precious time with small talk before getting down to the nitty-gritty and asking those tough interview questions that separate the wheat from the chaff.

Instead, I was faced with a rotund, sweaty man who couldn't have been a day over thirty, and who had decided to shed both his jacket and his shoes, possibly in an effort to quell his profuse perspiration. *Um, okay. No shoes? No problem! Just try not to stare at his socks.* He greeted me with a weak handshake, glanced over my résumé, and opened his mouth to speak. *Stay calm and confident, Martha! Answer his questions directly and thoughtfully! Knock 'em dead! You're prepared for whatever he might ask!*

"You know, I went to law school here," he said, "and my class-mates were all a bunch of asswipes. The professors, too. Ah, well, screw 'em all, that's what I say."

Oh. Okaaaaaaaaay. That's not really a question. How does one respond to vitriol in an interview? I know, I'll give off a little laugh in hopes that he was just joking! I'll show that I'm lighthearted and humorous! "Hee hee hee!"

My laughter was met with total silence on his part.

Okay, not a joke. Just a crazy person interviewing me. Try again. "Wow, it seems like your experience was quite different from mine. I've really enjoyed my time here so far. The opportunities for learning are unparalleled, and I look forward to two more years of rigorous mental exercise."

"Yeah, I guess. What other firms have you interviewed with?"

"Well, this is the very first interview slot," I replied. "Yours is the first firm that I've spoken to so far."

"Oh, yeah. Okay. Well, I'm sure you'll meet a bunch of assholes from a bunch of other firms over the next few days. And really, think about that. Who a firm chooses to send to interview law students says a lot about the place. They send their best and brightest, and if those people are assholes, just wait until you get inside and meet the rest—they're guaranteed to be ten times worse."

Holy crap. This lunatic is the best and brightest at his firm? Am I allowed to walk out of an interview? Because any marginal interest that I ever had in his firm has gone straight out the window.

The following eighteen minutes went downhill from there. It wasn't an interview, it was a monologue. When the allotted time was over, my "interviewer" still hadn't asked me one question, and he was firmly in the middle of a tirade that he had launched upon me, explaining in a very loud, berating voice why his firm was undoubtedly better than any and all others (although the rankings certainly belied that assertion). I kept interrupting, stating apologetically that I simply had to be going—I had another interview scheduled in three minutes on the other side of the building. He ignored me and continued his rant. Finally, with no other option available, I got up and slowly walked toward the door, a fake smile plastered across my face. He got up, shoeless, and followed me, still spewing. I apologized again, shook his hand, and said that although it had been a unique pleasure to speak with him, I really, truly just had to be on my way. And then I started scurrying down the hall, desperate both to get to my next interview and to get away from him. He was literally shouting down the hallway after me as I was leaving. The last words I remember hearing were "and *that* is why you'd be making a mistake if you decided to work anywhere other than here!"

Thankfully, all the other people I met with seemed shockingly sane by comparison. None of them cursed at me even once, and each and every one of them kept their shoes firmly on their feet. But no one really asked me any questions that mattered, it was mostly just small talk. "How do you like Columbia?" "What's been your favorite subject in school so far?" "What do you like best about New York?" "What sort of law do you hope to practice?" And they didn't seem to listen much while I gave my answers (which were admittedly pat and probably not terribly interesting). Instead they nodded their heads and feigned interest while their eyes scanned over my résumé and transcript, looking to see where I had gone to college and analyzing my first-year law school grades.

It quickly became apparent that the point of the on-campus interview process was for the firms' representatives to look at your first-year transcript to see if you made their grade requirements, and to give you a once-over to make sure you didn't have two heads. (Law firms, much like law schools, may say they don't have grade cutoffs, but everyone knows they're lying.) Assuming you were of the one-headed variety and didn't actually do something so stupid as to purposefully insult your interviewer or make some sort of perverse sexual reference during your allotted twenty minutes, if your grades fit the bill, you would receive a callback interview.

On the first night of on-campus interviewing, I established what would become my routine for the week: I would run home after my final interview and sit by the phone, biting my nails, drinking cheap chablis, and willing the phone to ring with an invitation for a callback interview. Rumor had it that, although you were far more likely to receive a call from a member of a firm's legal recruiting department during regular business hours offering to schedule a callback interview, some firms had nightly powwows to discuss the day's candidates and some attorneys who had interviewed students would phone the same evening to extend a callback offer, or possibly an invitation to a dinner or cocktail party being hosted by the firm for its most favored candidates.

So there I sat that first night. And sat. And sat some more. In silence, without any ringing phones at all. And it was then that I learned the true meaning of the term *wild mood swings. Why isn't the phone ringing? I'm not good enough! They saw right through me! I'll be lucky to even get a job at some third-rate firm! How am I ever going to pay back these mounting student loans if I can't get a job?*

"Ring! Ring! Ring!" chirped the telephone, after what seemed like hours of silence.

Yes! Forget all that negative thinking! I am capable! And shining with a vibrant personality! I made honors last year! Let the callback invitations begin! "Hello?" I answered with anticipation.

"Hey Martha, it's Elizabeth. How are your interviews going?"

Okay, not a callback. But at least I have good friends who care about me, and that counts for something, right? "Okay, I guess. It's so hard to tell."

"You haven't gotten any callbacks yet? Well, hang in there. I'm sure they're coming. I was just calling to see if you were invited to the Jones and Jones cocktail reception tonight."

"I didn't know there was a Jones and Jones cocktail reception. So I'm guessing I'm not invited."

"Oh. Okay. Sorry. Well, I've got to go get ready. Anyway, chin up!"

Ouch.

Desperate for reassurance, I tried to call Rachel. "Sorry, she's not here," David said.

"Oh. Okay. Well, how are your interviews going?" I asked. "Have any callbacks yet?"

"Callbacks? Martha, I've only got three interviews total. And they're all with firms that I'm sure you Columbia students wouldn't even want to speak to. At Fordham, we don't just get to sign up for interviews like you do. We actually have to submit our résumés and hope firms decide to interview us. And mostly they only want to interview people from Law Review. Three. I've got three goddamn interviews. I don't know what I'm going to do if I don't get a job. And no, no callbacks yet."

"Oh. Geez. I'm sorry, David."

Who's the asshole now? I think that would be me.

"Ring! Ring! Ring!" chirped the telephone again.

Oh! Yes! This has got to be the Lavish Law Firm that I met with earlier today! I aced that interview! And that is one firm I'd kill to work for—it's one of the most prestigious firms in the entire country! They treat their associates like royalty there! I am on the way to realizing my dreams! "Hello?"

"May I speak to Martha, please?" asked a loud but familiar-sounding male voice.

"This is Martha," I said with a smile. *I know that voice—it's got to be the guy from the Lavish Law Firm! I knew he liked me! How could he possibly not have liked me? Woohoo!*

"Hi Martha. This is Bob Ledmiller, from Maritime Lawyers, LLP. We met this morning?"

Oh. Shit. Oh SHIT! Not the Lavish Law Firm. The shoeless freak with the anger management problem. Apparently his name was Bob.
"Hi Bob. So good to hear from you," I croaked.

"Martha, I really enjoyed meeting you today. It's a shame our interview had to end so abruptly, a crying shame. I want you to come visit our offices to meet with some of our other attorneys. As I'm sure you know, you're just not going to find a better law firm than ours. Just call Elaine in the recruiting office to schedule an appointment—she'll be waiting to hear from you."

"Great, I'll call first thing tomorrow. Thanks, Bob." *A callback. A callback that I have absolutely no interest in, but a callback nonetheless. Maybe a life spent practicing maritime law won't be that bad? Oh God, I need another glass of wine.*

Slowly but surely the callback offers did come—even from the Lavish Law Firm. They just took their own sweet time about it. In fact, so many callback offers came that I was able to pick and choose among them. (Which meant no maritime law for me, thank God.) These interviews were an entirely different beast from what the perfunctory on-campus screening interviews had been. Here I would have half-day marathon sessions at each firm that generally would include four long interviews (two with partners, two with senior associates), and a "lunch date" with two more junior attorneys. Stories were passed around the school of candidates who had gotten embarrassingly drunk at interview lunches, said horrific and stupid things, and, to no one's surprise but their own, failed to get job offers handed to them. (No matter what your lunch partners are drinking, you're best off sticking to iced tea or Pellegrino if you know what's good for you.)

I was determined not to be one of those people. I might not have been able to boast about an undergraduate degree from Yale or a college internship at a Fortune 500 company, but I could certainly find a way to plod through a lunch interview without embarrassing myself. Or could I? Actually, I had a lot of boning up to do.

"Joe? I don't eat oysters, do I?" I asked.

"No, dear, I don't think I've ever known you to eat an oyster. Not that we're exactly presented with weekly opportunities."

"I didn't think so. And, for the record, I'm going to make it a new personal policy to avoid all foods that require slurping. But then what am I going to do with the oyster fork in my place setting?"

"What in God's name are you talking about, Martha?"

"Proper dining etiquette! Did you know that a formally set table might well include a fork especially for use with oysters?"

"No. That, I did not know."

"It says so right here in *Emily Post's Etiquette*," I said, gesturing to the three-inch-thick book that sat upon my desk.

"And why, exactly, are you reading Emily Post?"

"Because I've got my first callback interview tomorrow. At the Lavish Law Firm, where I'm dying to work? Where I'll be going out to a fancy lunch with fancy lawyers? And I don't know the first thing about swanky restaurants, because I'm just a hick from Wisconsin whose family considers a night out at Sizzler to be a real treat. But I refuse to be like Julia Roberts in *Pretty Woman,* flinging my escargot across the room by accident. I need to know which fork to use, so I can seem classy and shit. Do you think I eat escargots?"

"I really don't know how to answer that one, honey."

"Me either. But I've got to memorize my silverware. I know that Emily says to 'start from the outside and work your way in,' but what happens if the fork on the outside is an oyster fork and I'm not having oysters? What if that just throws everything out of order and then I end up eating my salad with my oyster fork and my fish with my salad fork and my meat with my fish fork? Emily doesn't talk about that! Am I going to have to force myself to violate my no-oyster-slurping rule just to keep my forks in order?"

"Martha, I think you need to get a grip."

"Get a grip? But I haven't even figured out what to do with my napkin if I need to get up from the table to go to the restroom! Do I put it on the table? Do I leave it on my chair? Do I take it with me so no one uses it while I'm gone?"

"Yeah, um, good luck figuring that out. I'm going to bed."

"Fine, go. I'm staying up. I am determined to make Emily Post proud at this lunch tomorrow."

Whether or not I did in fact make her proud is a question that remains unanswered. The individual interviews at the Lavish Law Firm went well, and I surprised myself with my reasonably articulate answers to the questions posed to me. I think I was at least mildly charming, and I had done a thorough check of my nostrils and my teeth beforehand to make sure there were no errant substances stuck where they didn't belong, waiting to cause me great social embarrassment. The lawyers I spoke with (a very welcoming partner from the firm's litigation department, an overbearing partner from the real estate department, and two tired-looking fourth-year corporate associates) seemed impressed with my grades, pleased with my experience, and excited by my expressed desire to practice law at their firm. It was just a matter of not flubbing the lunch.

With Emily's advice firmly in mind, I walked the four blocks from the firm's offices to the restaurant in the company of the two lawyers with whom I would be dining. We made small talk along the way, and I asked where we were headed to eat. "A great place called Le Colonial," responded the taller of the two men. *Ooh, a fancy French restaurant. It's a good thing I know my soup spoon from my dessert spoon. It pays to be prepared!*

We walked into the restaurant, and it was gorgeous, but not exactly gorgeous in the traditional gold-gilded French way that I had expected. Instead, the room was filled with languorously revolving ceiling fans, exotic tropical plants, and cushioned rattan couches. It gave off an old-world Asian sort of feeling. The atmosphere was so peaceful that I could feel myself relaxing more with each step as we were led to our reserved table. I took my seat, looked down to study my place setting, and was surprised to find there was nary an oyster fork in sight. Nor was there a fork of *any* sort in sight. Instead, I was presented with a bronze warming plate with a burnished patina, upon which sat a beautifully folded napkin and a pair of elegantly carved chopsticks. *Oh. Wait. Le Colonial. Not French. French Colonial. French Colonial Vietnamese. As in Vietnam. Where they eat with chopsticks. Emily said nothing about chopsticks! I know not how to eat with chopsticks!*

With a nervous smile on my face, I opened the menu only to see dishes named Banh Cuon and Goi Bo and Bum Ga Nuong. Well, so much for my oyster slurping dilemma. Unsure as to how to pronounce the names of the foods on the menu, what I should order, or how I was going to eat it, I let my hosts order first. And then I crossed my fingers, hoped for the best, and ordered something called Ca Chien Saigon, as I deemed that to be one of the more pronounceable dishes on the menu. It turned out to be a crisp-seared whole red snapper with spicy-and-sour fish sauce that tasted better than heaven. Within minutes after our food was delivered, my hosts and I had all shed our jackets and rolled up our sleeves, and we were eating dumplings with our fingers and grabbing food off each other's plates while groaning with happiness and urging each other, "Here! You absolutely must try a bite of this!" Emily Post probably wouldn't have approved. But I'd honestly never had a better lunch.

Later that evening, while the taste of red snapper and mushroom spring rolls was still fresh on my lips, my doorbell rang. Hesitantly, I opened the door, but left the chain firmly in place.

"Telegram," said the uniformed man on the other side.

Telegram? People still send telegrams? And why in the world am I getting one? Did someone die? Did I finally win the Publishers Clearing House sweepstakes? I opened the door, signed for the telegram, and went to the couch where I cautiously tore it open.

"CONGRATULATINS. FRIM WOULD LIKE TO EXTEND YOU SUMER OFFER. DETAILS TO FOLLOW." The misspelled telegram had come from the Lavish Law Firm. I sat there in shock, reading the error-riddled message over and over in disbelief. *Screw Emily Post,* I thought, *I just got the job offer of my dreams.*

Nine

Journalicious

*"Nothing changes your opinion of a friend so surely
as success—yours or his."*
—Franklin P. Jones

Conventional wisdom holds that during your first year of law
school, they scare you to death, during your second year they
work you to death, and during your third year they bore you to
death. I already knew from experience that the first part of that
statement was accurate, and it didn't take me long to figure out
that the second part was, too. (It wouldn't be until the next year
that I would learn that conventional wisdom held true on all three
fronts.)

So, during my second year I worked my ass off, and I got to do
it in the middle of a construction zone. Literally. Jerome Greene
Hall was undergoing major and much-needed renovation, and as
the administration's joking way of trying to make light of a bad
situation, we were each handed a bright blue hardhat with the Columbia Law School logo on it as we walked in the front door of
the building to report for classes. We were told that the experience
would require patience, but that we would all reap the rewards the
next year, once the renovation was complete. (Well, except for the
third-year students, who would have to suffer through the inconvenience but would be gone in the fall once the work was done.
Poor bastards.)

As it turned out, the hardhats were only halfway a joke. At

least once a week all year long we would receive e-mails from the facilities director updating us about the construction progress and what we were in for next:

> **From:** Stu Hamilton
> **To:** All CLS Students
> **Subject:** Construction Update
> A new construction wall will be installed next week across from classrooms C and D, rendering them off-limits for the entire school year. Additionally, this will block the law school entrance on 116th Street, and will close off the student café. In order to accommodate this loss of classroom space, we have been forced to alter our class schedule, adding classes over the lunch hour and adding additional class slots at 5:00 to 6:50 p.m. and 7:00 to 8:50 p.m. We apologize for any difficulty that this may cause.

> **From:** Stu Hamilton
> **To:** All CLS Students
> **Subject:** Construction Update
> Terrazzo flooring will be installed in the West hallway on Tuesday and Wednesday, so rooms F, G, and H will be unavailable for use on those days. All classes normally held in those rooms will need to be relocated.

> **From:** Stu Hamilton
> **To:** All CLS Students
> **Subject:** Construction Update
> Construction has adversely affected our e-mail servers, which we understand have been down for the last 18 hours. We apologize for this inconvenience. Normal service has now been restored.

From: Stu Hamilton
To: All CLS Students
Subject: Construction Update
The student locker area will be relocated over spring break. All students must empty their lockers of all contents and remove their locks before March 14. ALL LOCKS WILL BE CUT OFF OF LOCKERS on that date, and the contents will be removed and held in the Student Services Office while the lockers are moved. Thank you for your cooperation.

From: Stu Hamilton
To: All CLS Students
Subject: Construction Update
In order to create a new rare-book room in the law library and to build a larger student study area, ¾ of the books normally shelved on the main floor of the library will be moved to the lower level, and 12,000 volumes of infrequently used books will be sent to off-site storage (but will be available to order through the librarians if needed). We hope and expect that this shouldn't cause any undue problems.

From: Stu Hamilton
To: All CLS Students
Subject: Construction Update
The roof over classrooms A and B is being re-tarred this week, and we are aware that students taking classes in surrounding rooms have been experiencing strong tar fumes. Please excuse this inconvenience, and rest assured that we have confirmed that the vapors are not toxic.

From: Stu Hamilton
To: All CLS Students

> **Subject:** Construction Update
> Construction has once again adversely affected our
> e-mail servers, which we understand have been
> down for the last 22 hours. We apologize for any
> trouble that this has caused, but we want to reiterate
> that—although this entire construction process has
> undoubtedly proved inconvenient for all—we will
> not be offering a reimbursement to offset your
> tuition costs.

So at least I was in an environment conducive to learning and quiet study.

After being force-fed mandatory classes like Contracts, Torts, Property, and Criminal Law the previous year, finally being able to select my own courses during my second year was a more than welcome change. With supposedly nontoxic tar fumes reverberating through my head, I had chosen a roster of classes that I thought would be useful and necessary for the betterment of my legal mind and preparation for my future career. I knew that I wasn't setting myself up for an easy year, but I would be studying constitutional law (the one mandatory class that I had left over to take), evidence (so that I could learn what "hearsay" actually meant), corporations (so that someday I might work on high-powered hostile takeovers and corporate buyouts), federal income taxation (because everyone else I knew was taking it), comparative law (in hopes that someday I might have foreign laws to compare), European Community law and institutions (in hopes that someday I might have some European communities to visit), and taking a trial practice seminar (so that I could practice my technique at yelling "Objection, your Honor!"). In addition, I would be acting as a Moot Court Student Editor and taking a Workshop in Briefcraft, where it would be my job to research and construct a make-believe case for first-year students to work on, as well as to draft a bench memorandum for the Columbia Law School alumni who would serve as judges, educating them about the background of the case and setting out the arguments that each side should present. Finally, I would be serving as a staff member on the *Columbia Journal of Transnational Law.*

Ah, yes, the law journal. Although I hadn't made Law Review, I had applied and received offers to join several of the other "second string" journals to which I had applied. As I was operating under a temporary fantasy that someday I might like to practice international law (not that I really had any idea what that meant, but it seemed like it might allow me to travel to cool places like Paris or Rome or Tokyo), I chose to accept an offer from the *Columbia Journal of Transnational Law,* one of several journals that claimed to be "the next best journal after the Law Review."

Legal journals are odd beasts. Accepting an offer to work as a staff member requires a substantial time commitment, although none require anywhere near the amount of work that the Law Review does. And second-year students receive no credit for their work, just the ability to write "Staff Member, *Columbia Journal of Interglobal Astronomy and the Law*" on their résumé and to see their names written in fine print on the masthead of the journal. Not that anyone ever reads the publication (even if it's the Law Review). Because, seriously, who'd want to? These are hardly magazines filled with glossy pages of celebrity gossip, fashion photos, political commentary, or even recipes for making a healthy tuna casserole in under thirty minutes. These are periodicals filled with the most technical, boring articles that one could possibly imagine. Other than for legal research purposes, there is very little reason to read the articles published in any legal journal. After all, would *you* want to read an article entitled "Education Under Catalonia's Law of Linguistic Normalization: Spanish Constitutionalism and International Human Rights Law" or "Living in Uncertain Times: The Need to Strengthen Hong Kong Transnational Insolvency Law"? (It is an unwritten rule that the title of each article must contain a colon.)

During my second-year tenure, I would have to write a "note" for submission to the journal—essentially, a note is a student-written article (the actual "articles" are written by professors and other legal scholars). If it was good, there was a chance it would be selected for publication during my third year.

As a second-year journal staff member, my main job was to cite-check the footnotes contained in the articles that were to be published. Scholarly legal articles are overflowing with footnotes—it is customary to cite at least one authority to show support for each legal or factual proposition or argument in the article—which adds up to an awful lot of propositions in need of citation, because the articles are *long*. Some authors get quite footnote-happy and have a citation after pretty much every single sentence (or, not infrequently, multiple footnotes in the middle of each sentence); others are more restrained and can sometimes go a whole paragraph without citing any external source.

Checking these citations is a technical, difficult, and mind-numbingly tedious job that involves verifying the substance of what is contained in each footnote (making sure that the source material cited as support for a proposition does indeed stand for what the author claims it stands for) and then making sure that each citation is in proper form according to the rules contained in *The Bluebook: A Uniform System of Citation.*

The *Bluebook* is a three-hundred-some-page book written by the editors of the Law Reviews at Harvard, Yale, Columbia, and Penn that "concisely" sets forth the rules of citation to be used in academic legal writing—it tells you how to write a footnote. The *Bluebook* presents pointedly detailed rules about how to cite every single type of source material that has ever been in existence or may someday be invented in the future. (And the rules vary widely for each.)

To receive my first cite-checking assignment, I met with my managing editor, Vikram, in our journal's shabby two-room office in an annexed brownstone building across the street from the law school. Vikram was a funny, gentle guy with deep brown eyes that peeked out from behind funky eyeglass frames, and he looked at me with a little bit of pity as he handed me copies of pages twenty-two to forty of an article entitled something along the lines of "Throwing Workers to the Wind: Societal Stratification and Unemployment Insurance Programs in the Former Soviet Bloc Countries."

"This assignment will probably take you a while to complete," he said. "But it gets a lot easier, really. It's all a matter of working out a system and figuring out the intricacies of the sections of the *Bluebook* that deal with citing foreign and international sources. If you have any questions, just ask, okay?"

"Okay, no problem," I said. I had gotten familiar with the *Bluebook* during my first-year legal writing course, and was nowhere near as intimidated by the assignment as I should have been. "When do you need this completed?"

"By next Wednesday. Just put it in my mailbox here in the office."

"Okay, will do. Thanks, Vikram."

And so I took my nineteen-page assigned section to a cushy chair in the library and read through it, only to realize that my small portion of the article gave me no real clue as to what the entire article was actually about. Two minutes later, I realized that might just be a good thing. Luckily, understanding of or interest in the article in its entirety was not necessary to complete my cite-checking assignment. To get a better gauge of what lay ahead of me, I flipped through my section and counted 108 footnotes that I needed to verify. *What have I gotten myself into? It's going to take me the rest of the semester to complete this one assignment.*

With increasing degrees of frustration, I spent forty-five minutes in a futile attempt to locate a book entitled *Ancient Soviet Law in Theory and Practice,* which should have been located on shelf C-172 in the library. I wandered through the chaotically reordered shelves until eventually I realized that shelf C-172 was no longer in existence due to the law school construction. Humbled, I resorted to begging the reference librarian for help. After a quick search of the computerized card catalog, she told me that *Ancient Soviet Law in Theory and Practice* had been sent to off-site storage due to reduced shelf space, but that she could place it on order for me. But it wouldn't arrive in time for my assignment deadline of the following Wednesday.

Crap. I've hit a dead end on my very first footnote of my very first journal assignment! What should I do? The author of the article is probably honest and forthright. Just this one time, I can probably trust that pages 437 to 466 of the book Ancient Soviet Law in Theory and Practice *do indeed somehow state or imply that "Russia's severe physical climate undoubtedly affected the early development of the country's legal climate," right? Right.*

With the "substantive" checking of that source out of the way, I consulted the *Bluebook* to check accuracy of the citation form. I experienced inexplicable satisfaction when I was able to pull out a red pen and correct the author's citation, which originally read "B.F. Keeton, Charles Murphy & Edgar Prudhomme, *Ancient Soviet Law in Theory and Practice,* pp. 437-466" to correctly read "B.F. KEETON ET AL., ANCIENT SOVIET LAW IN THEORY AND PRACTICE 437-466, (Richard G. Goldstein, ed., 2d ed. 1965)."

Feeling emboldened, I turned to the second of the 108 footnotes that I needed to check. I spent twenty minutes searching the online library catalog to try and find "Law No. 3.071 of Jan. 1, 1916, amended by Law No. 3.725 of Jan. 15, 1919, I Coleção (1916) (Braz.)," but I could find no reference whatsoever to such a beast. Eventually, defeated, I turn once again back to the reference librarian, gave her an apologetic smile, and was told that the volume was available on microfiche in the subbasement of the library. I realized that I had no idea what "microfiche" was, but that I was about to find out.

I marveled over the strange magnificence of the ancient-seeming microfiche mechanism that was housed in a dim, creepy corner of the empty bowels of the library. With no one around to give me guidance (and I wasn't about to bother the librarian again), I spent what seemed like forever trying to figure out how to work the damn thing, all the while looking over my shoulder at every imaginary noise I thought I heard. *What was that? Did I just hear something? Something creaky? I'm all alone down here. Freddy Krueger could jump out from behind those stacks and slash me to shreds, and no one would have a clue. I bet it would be a week, at least, before anyone even wandered back here to find my tattered remains. I'd better hurry this along if I want to make it out of here in one piece.* Eventually, I located Law No. 3.071 of the whenever as amended by the whatever. By the time I found it, I was too tired to care what it said. I read the text, looked at the proposition for which it was cited as support in a footnote, and decided that it was close enough.

After running back upstairs to join the company of other humans, it was time to consult the *Bluebook* to check accuracy of the citation form. I soon realized what Vikram had been hinting at— the fact that it is truly impossible to figure out how to properly cite foreign legislative materials, no matter how much detail the *Bluebook* might try to go into. Eventually I decided to add a comma in the middle of the citation just for good measure, then I put a red check mark by the side of the footnote and left the rest of it as it was.

Then I realized that I needed to repeat those steps 106 more times.

While doing so, every hour on the hour, I considered resigning from the journal staff. I knew that I couldn't follow through on it, though, because I had heard the rumor that, years ago, someone actually did resign from a journal, and not only did the administration erase the "Staff Member, *Columbia Journal of Interglobal Astronomy and the Law*" credit on that student's transcript, but the journal then actually sent a letter to the law firm the guy was going to work for that coming summer telling them that he was a quitter. There was no way I was going to put myself in such jeopardy.

At about ten that night, with my assignment not even halfway completed, I gave up, realizing that I still had at least five hours of reading that I needed to complete for the next day's classes, and that I was guaranteed to see three a.m. on the clock before I finally headed to bed. It took every minute of my spare time over the next week to complete the assignment, and I had absolutely zero confidence in my work product when I apologetically handed it to Vikram.

All in all, working on a law journal is a pretty miserable job, but most law students do it anyway. I, for one, did it because everyone else was doing it, and I was afraid that someday, somehow, I would look bad if the word *journal* didn't appear on my résumé. Also, I was afraid that people would by default assume that, if I was not on a journal, it meant I had applied and been rejected by each and every one. I suspect I wasn't alone in my motivations. In any case, there aren't many law students who joined journals because the work was compelling, because they wanted to become more intimately familiar with the *Bluebook,* or because they had a deep and burning desire to help further legal scholarship. No, we all did it because we were terrified of being one-upped by someone else.

"Hi, you've reached Rachel and David. We can't come to the phone right now. Please leave us a message, and we'll get back to you as soon as we can. BEEEEEEEP!"

"Hey Rachel, it's Martha. I thought that maybe the four of us could do something this weekend. Maybe go out for some Indian food? Give me a call."

"Hi, you've reached Rachel and David. We can't come to the phone right now. Please leave us a message, and we'll get back to you as soon as we can. BEEEEEEEP!"

"Hey Rachel, it's Martha. I guess last weekend didn't work out, maybe next week? We could all just go to the West End and grab a few beers. Call me."

"Hi, you've reached Rachel and David. We can't come to the phone right now. Please leave us a message, and we'll get back to you as soon as we can. BEEEEEEEP!"

"Hi Rachel, it's Martha. Katie and Elizabeth and I are going out for margaritas on Thursday, want to come? For old times' sake?"

"Hi, you've reached Rachel and David. We can't come to the phone right now. Please leave us a message, and we'll get back to you as soon as we can. BEEEEEEEP!"

"Hi Rachel, it's Martha. Again. Just wondering if you and David might want to come over for dinner on Friday? Let me know."

"Hi, you've reached Rachel and David. We can't come to the phone right now. Please leave us a message, and we'll get back to you as soon as we can. BEEEEEEEP!"

"Hi Rachel—are you alive? If so, maybe you could call me someday?"

"Hi, you've reached Rachel and David. We can't come to the phone right BEEEEEEEP . . . uh, hello?"

"Hello? David? Is that you?"

"Martha? Yeah, sorry, I couldn't get to the phone quick enough."

"How are you doing? God, we haven't seen you guys in ages. What have you been up to?"

"I got a job!" David shouted, triumphantly. "At Lake and Rivers. I know it's a second-tier firm, which probably doesn't sound too impressive to you—it sure didn't to Rachel—but I'm a total goddamn stud now at Fordham. Half my classmates have no jobs at all. I can't believe they even interviewed me, much less gave me an offer."

"Congratulations! We'll have to celebrate! Hey, I've been calling and calling Rachel, and I never hear back. I never see her around school either. Is she alive?"

"I guess. Supposedly, we live together, but I don't see her either. She lives at that goddamn Law Review office. And when she's not at the Law Review office, she's out with her goddamn Law Review friends. Goddamn Art McAsshole and goddamn Lisa VonBitchypants and the worst—the very *worst*—is that goddamn Charlotte Sidwell." David was seething, and he wasn't even trying to hide it.

"Oh, Charlotte Sidwell. She was in my section first semester. I don't really know her, but still, she bugs me. Her little button nose and her little Southern drawl and that saccharine sweetness that oozes out of her pores. Blech."

"Yeah, well, she and Rachel have become inseparable," he grunted.

"What? Not only won't Rachel return my calls, but now she's tight with Charlotte Sidwell? Are you telling me this to purposely *try* to make me feel bad?" I asked.

"No worse than I feel," David said. "Seriously, Rachel's making Law Review is the worst thing that could have happened to our relationship."

"Well, do you think there's any chance of the four of us getting together on Friday night? Could you talk her into it? Just to drink a few beers, hang out, and remember how we used to actually be friends?"

"I'll see what I can do."

On Friday night, David showed up alone (but with a twelve-pack of Miller Lite in hand). Rachel was nowhere in sight. I didn't bother asking why, because I knew the answer. Rachel had other plans. Probably with Charlotte.

When I applied for the position of Moot Court Editor, I figured that it would be a cool opportunity to have some first-year students idolize me and fear my power. Really, it was the first time in my entire life that I'd ever wielded power over anyone, and it felt damn good. Granted, it wasn't like I got to actually assign grades, but, theoretically at least, the students' performing up to par so as to receive credit for the moot court exercise was in my hands.

I struggled to invent some sort of make-believe court case based upon an unresolved legal quandary, and to find somewhat equally balanced judicial opinions that each side could use to bolster their respective arguments. This is much more difficult than it sounds. I needed to identify a theoretical legal issue that had been considered by various courts, but which had yet to be resolved by the U.S. Supreme Court—and if I had any hope of capturing the interest or respect of any of the twelve first-year students assigned to my care and tutelage, I had better not make it mind-numbingly boring.

"Can't you ask a professor for guidance?" Joe suggested, as I whined to him that I had hit yet another dead end.

"I already tried that! I thought: oh, copyrights and trademarks are sexy subjects, right? Intellectual property and all that? So I sucked it up and went to talk to this professor who knows all about the property of the intellect, and I asked him if he had any ideas about interesting unresolved legal issues that I might be able to explore, and he just looked at me sympathetically and said 'Sorry, no.' I think he's hoarding unresolved issues for some future Law Review article he is planning on writing."

"Well, do you remember how, about six weeks ago, you were in this exact same predicament trying to come up with a topic for the note you need to write for your journal?"

"Of course." I had chosen to write a note discussing the issue of whether or not criminal convictions obtained in foreign countries should be considered "prior offenses" when criminals are being sentenced under "three strikes" statutes in the United States and setting forth my thesis regarding the potential constitutional concerns in doing so. "And? Your point is?"

"Well, would it be outrageous for me to say that maybe you should try and work from your note topic? The one you've already spent countless hours hunkered down in the law school library working on? Or is double dipping not allowed?"

I knew I'd married this man for a reason. "Double dipping! *Of course!* I could take the issue I'm writing my journal note about, make up a pretend set of facts to go around it, and use all the research I've already done as the basis for writing the bench memo! That plan is pure brilliance!"

And that's how I ended up guiding twelve students through a Moot Court problem involving a man named Edgar Steele, who had been convicted of burglarizing a pharmacy in the imaginary state of Kent. In my pretend scenario, he had been sentenced to twenty years in prison for his crime instead of ten years, based on an imaginary repeat offender statute that, depending on how you interpreted the wording, might or might not allow a judge to consider the fact that the felonious Mr. Steele had earlier been convicted of a crime in the imaginary foreign country of Ruritania (which had a somewhat sketchy set of made-up constitutional protections for criminal defendants). My students were charged with arguing whether or not the Kent recidivist statute would or would not allow consideration of the criminal conviction obtained in Ruritania.

The students I had been assigned were a mixed bag. There were four who were so smart and so on top of things that they needed almost no help from me whatsoever. Our regular progress meetings basically consisted of them turning in their draft briefs to me, me reading them over, and then giving them back saying "Wow, this looks great. Better than what I would have written! Mind if I borrow some of your ideas to use in my journal note?" Six of the students were of varying degrees of normal: some cared more than others, some tried harder than others, but they all came along fine with some prodding and suggestions on my part.

And then there were the last two students who had been assigned to me. They both had good hearts, and it's not that they didn't care or weren't trying—they did and they were. But they could barely string together a coherent sentence between the two of them. (And yes, English *was* their first language.) A full paragraph? Forget about it. What was I supposed to do with these women? As far as offering substantive suggestions, it was difficult to do that without making mention of the fact that one could barely get past the horrible form in order to try to decipher the substance. And my job was to help them come up with acceptable, well-written and well-researched briefs, not to *actually teach them how to write.* Was I supposed to go to the library and dig up a Grammar 101 book and explain the need for a matching subject and verb in each sentence? The difference between an adjective and an adverb? The importance of personal pronouns? Should I just write "Make Better" in the margins of their draft briefs and hope for the best? And, more importantly, *why hadn't I known during my first year that there were students like this at Columbia Law School?* It would have saved me from an awful lot of paranoia and heartache if I had known that I had a leg up over some other students just because I knew the difference between a direct and an indirect object.

When the phone rang I certainly didn't expect to receive a romantic proposition. I was, after all, a married woman. I made a practice of wearing a traditional gold band on my left-hand ring finger on a daily basis. (Self-conscious in the face of Elizabeth's glaringly large diamond—and several other robust jewels that I had noticed adorning the fingers of various women around the school—I had quietly abandoned regular wear of my miniature-stoned engagement ring, hoping to eschew the implicit statement of social class that the size of one's diamond inevitably proclaimed.)

"Hello?" I said, cradling the phone to my ear.

"Hi ... Martha?"

"Yes, this is Martha."

"Hi, it's Ray Kaplan. How are you doing?"

Ray Kaplan? He was a nondescript guy who had been in my Evidence class the previous semester, sitting in the seat behind me. We had chatted occasionally and we sometimes nodded or said hi to each other in the halls, but I had no idea what would ever bring him to call me. Puzzled, I said, "Oh, hi Ray. I'm good. How are you?"

"I'm good." He paused briefly. "Hey, I was wondering what you were doing this weekend. If you had plans. I thought that maybe we could do something. Maybe get some dinner?"

What? It's almost as though—OH MY GOD—is Ray asking me

out on a date? Weekend? Dinner? Yes, I'm pretty sure that's what he's doing! Crap! Well, this is awkward. "Oh. Wow. Well, um, the thing is, I'm pretty sure my husband and I are pretty booked up this weekend. The two of us—my husband and I—have a lot of plans." *Yes. Good. Stress the word* husband. *Now make a quick and graceful exit. Put a quick end to the pain.* "Maybe . . . um . . . we could get a group of people together from the old Evidence class and all go out for dinner or beers or something some other time?" *Why did I say that? I should have quit while I was ahead. Oh Lord, I've made things worse.*

"Oh . . . yeah." Obviously, the news of my marital status had come as a complete surprise to him. Noticeably flustered, he said, "That's exactly what I meant. Getting a group of us together to hang out, yeah, with the Evidence crew." He was practically panting with discomfort on the other end of the line. "Let me know some other time that's good, and we can try to set something up. And have a good weekend with your husband."

Frankly, I wasn't much more composed than he was. For some reason my discomfort manifested itself in the form of an overly perky affectation as I chirped, "Yes! Oh, absolutely! We will! You have a good weekend, too, Ray! We'll all get together soon!"

Once I finally hung up the phone, I felt rather like I might vomit. I wasn't used to being asked out on dates. At age twenty-four I had already been married to Joe for several years. We had been together since my junior year of college. And hell, Joe had never even really asked me out on a date. We just kind of met and fell in love and that was that. And the last serious boyfriend I had before Joe hadn't ever officially asked me out either. We, too, had just fallen in together. Come to think of it, I hadn't been really asked out on an official date since high school. By the old boyfriend that my ex-best friend Leah had started sleeping with in college.

God, I felt out of touch. It wasn't that being married in law school was altogether uncommon, but most of the married students were a bit older—many in their thirties and some in their forties, mostly looking for second careers—so my relatively young age set me apart from them. At the same time, I felt worlds removed from so many of the students my age who were running loose in the amusement park of law school romance. And indeed, it was like a romantic Disneyland. That's what you get when you throw several hundred young, intelligent people with certain common interests and aspirations into an intense and relatively closed-off environment. Everyone is stressed and needs to find a way to relieve the tension and blow off steam. Drinking excessively and then baring one's soul to a member of the opposite sex who can relate to your troubles (and whose Corporations outline you might be able to borrow) is the natural answer, and if one thing should happen to lead to another . . .

As it turned out, I hadn't really left Wisconsin for the Big City. I had left Wisconsin for what turned out to be a place just like my small town all over again. Although we were in the middle of a city of eight million, most of us mingled only occasionally with non-law students, effectively reducing our population to just over a thousand people. And much like in any small town, everyone knew everyone else's business.

Word about who was hooking up with whom spread quickly around our insular community. (Much like with grades, I suspect someone was keeping a spreadsheet tracking all of the couplings.) The more obvious romantic escapades—a third-year student coming back from a weekend visiting her boyfriend with a new diamond on her finger, two first-year suitemates in the dorms who had instantly fallen in love, a third-year student seen canoodling with someone most decidedly *not* his longtime girlfriend in the middle of the West End—were reported in the law school newspaper's gossip column. The more clandestine tête-à-têtes spread quickly by word of mouth.

And it wasn't just the students. Word in the halls was that my Regulatory State professor had been wooing a popular young tax professor. Two doctoral students who both taught first-year legal writing classes were purportedly engaged. And then there was my Property professor, who had reportedly married a former student years and years before. Hell, the dean was married to a law school clinical professor.

Under the circumstances, I suppose I shouldn't have been surprised that someone assumed I was unattached and asked me out on a date. Possibly I should have been offended that it hadn't happened more frequently.

One sunny spring day after the Moot Court debacle was finally over, in a last-ditch attempt to salvage my friendship with Rachel, I cornered her in the hall and suggested that we do something fun together, like audition for the Law Revue show. She surprised me by saying yes. The Law Revue was a side-splittingly funny show filled with sarcastic skits and musical parody numbers that the students put on each year, poking generally good-natured fun at pretty much every professor, every law school administrator, every outspoken student, and every other aspect of the Columbia Law School experience that you could imagine. And unlike the actual Law Review, they accepted everyone who wanted to participate, no matter how horrible. Case in point: they happily took Rachel and me, even after she auditioned by singing an ear-piercing rendition of "It's a Hard Knock Life," and I auditioned by announcing, "No *way* am I singing on stage. If you want me, you can only give me speaking parts."

The cast was made up of a bunch of good-humored people of questionable talent—out of the forty-one of us appearing in the show, I believe there were exactly seven people who could actually carry a tune. But the show's writer was so smart, so sharp, and so witty that the performance was hilarious despite our collective lack of talent. It made fun of the aged, possibly crazy professor who appeared to be homeless and who always walked around campus carrying a plastic grocery bag filled with his possessions instead of a briefcase. It prominently featured several bits about the Sadistic Professor, jokingly accusing him of trying to overthrow the law school's disheveled dean and reign over the school like a dictator. It ridiculed the professor with the photographic memory who knew the hometowns and life stories of each student in her class, and who would begin a Socratic dialogue by stating, "Mr. Segal, you're from Nevada, right? And you used to be a veterinarian, didn't you? Well, this case originated in Carson City and involved a dog with an injured paw—why don't you tell us the facts of the case?"

The highlight of the show was a song sung to the tune of "YMCA" that was performed by six guys who were dressed as a police officer, an Indian chief, a soldier, a biker, a cowboy, and a construction worker (wearing one of our Columbia Law School-issued hardhats, of course). The song was about the Federal Rules of Civil Procedure (FRCP for short)—the bane of every first-year law student's existence:

> It's fun to read through the FRCP
> It's fun to study the FRCP
> It has everything that you need for Civ Pro
> Nothing else do you need to know
> You can joinder your claims
> You can change your venue
> You can learn to correctly sue
> It's fun to read through the FRCP
> It's fun to study the FRCP . . .

Toward the end of the number, all six of them ripped off their shirts and started doing push-ups on stage while still singing—who knew there were guys with hot bodies and six-pack abs hiding among us? Who had time to go to the gym?

And the best part of all was that I got to play the role of Mrs. Kay, who truly was a Columbia institution, especially around the law school campus. Mrs. Kay was an older woman of indeterminate age with a hip-level monobosom, unkempt hair, disastrous polyester clothing, and giant blue glasses that threatened to swallow her face completely. She was a professional typist who would go to her grave clinging to her Smith Corona—she would have no talk of this "word processing" mumbo jumbo. Mrs. Kay had a strange way of simultaneously appearing 51 percent batshit crazy and 49 percent absolutely sane, and she papered the halls of the school with flyers penned in a flowery hand that advertised her typing services, claiming that Elizabeth Taylor herself had once been a satisfied customer. She claimed to be so busy that she often had to turn away work, but I had never so much as heard of a law student who admitted to using her services.

Perhaps what Mrs. Kay was best known for was her penchant for attending each and every open law school meeting, reception, speech, lecture, or other miscellaneous gathering that might just possibly feature free food. If there was catering, Mrs. Kay was there. If there was a meeting of the International Law Society featuring free pizza, Mrs. Kay was circling the outer edges of the room like a hawk. If there was a barbecue on the law school patio, Mrs. Kay was first in line to get a free cheeseburger. Hell, if there was a card table set up in an abandoned classroom with three stale day-old sandwiches on it, Mrs. Kay was staking that room out. But it turned out that Mrs. Kay was a giver and not just a taker, because after the Law Revue show was over she approached me, raved about my performance, and gave me a bottle of kosher champagne as a token of her thanks. A tough nut to crack, that Mrs. Kay.

As for my hope that doing the show together would repair the rift between Rachel and me, that didn't happen. Because Charlotte Sidwell had joined the Law Revue cast, too. I got to spend weeks with her in rehearsals: watching her wrinkle up her nose in an attempt to be even cuter than little baby Bambi, inwardly cringing as she batted her eyelashes and flirted with every single boy in the cast, and wondering why in the world Rachel needed Charlotte as a friend when she already had the perfect friend in me. And then, the ultimate betrayal, I got to watch Charlotte sing a parody version of the *Grease* song "Summer Nights" onstage along with Rachel. Upon seeing that, I knew The End had officially arrived. I had been replaced.

I knew it had been coming, but still, the rejection stung like hell. Yes, I still had Katie and Elizabeth. But Rachel had been my true best friend. We had been inseparable. Together, Rachel, David, Joe, and I had navigated the dangerous terrain of the first year of law school. We had shared holidays, had each other on speed-dial, turned to each other when things got hard. I couldn't even begin to count the pitchers of beer we drank together as an outlet for our stress. I had been willing to forgive Rachel plenty of personal peccadilloes and shortcomings, but when it came down to it, it seemed like she couldn't forgive me for failing to make Law Review. I know, that's probably an unfair way to put it. But that's exactly how it felt.

And I hated Charlotte Sidwell for being the catalyst of my downfall. Yes, I probably would have found a reason to hate whoever my replacement had been, but the fact that Charlotte had flawlessly bobbed blond hair, a perfect white smile, and straight-A grades made the whole thing just that much worse. Why did Charlotte even like Rachel? They had nothing in common. Charlotte was a Southern belle with fake blue contact lenses; Rachel was a tomboy with sloppy penmanship. Charlotte liked to act demure; Rachel tended toward the brash. Charlotte came from family money; Rachel came from the middle class.

I was the one who deserved Rachel. Me. Not Charlotte. *Me.*

And because irony is a total bitch, shortly after I had been dumped by Rachel because I wasn't smart enough, I received all A's on my second semester exams, and once again earned honors as a Harlan Fiske Stone Scholar. Go figure.

Ten

TURNING OF THE TIDES

"The roots of education are bitter, but the fruit is sweet."
—ARISTOTLE

As I walked through the four-story-high atrium of the midtown Manhattan building that housed the Lavish Law Firm to report for my first day of work as a summer associate, the heels of my conservative black Enzo Angiolini pumps, which were already giving me blisters, echoed off the acres of marble that covered the lobby's walls and floor. My nylons were digging into my stomach, my suit jacket was too tight across the shoulders, and my heart was beating a mile a minute. I was simultaneously marveling at the three-foot-tall flower arrangement of vibrant orange birds of paradise that stood at the lobby reception desk, hoping that the sweat that had drenched me while waiting on the subway platform for my morning train to arrive hadn't left me with irreparable armpit stains, and trying to convince myself that I wouldn't be identified as a total fraud on my very first day of work.

The firm wasn't really going to expect that much from me right off the bat, was it? Because, as I shot up the high-speed elevator on my way to the forty-fourth floor to meet the director of recruiting, I was struck by the simple fact that I had no idea how to be a lawyer, not even a pretend summer lawyer. Sure, my two years of law school and my internship with Judge Lovell had taught me something about the law, but they didn't teach me about lawyering, that's for damn sure. And yes, I'd spent plenty of time watching *L.A. Law* and *Matlock* and *Law & Order* over the years, but I was assuming those shows might not have portrayed the most accurate picture of real-life legal practice, and that my summer probably wasn't going to be spent bedding sexed-up clients, confronting murderers in dramatic courtroom scenes, or arguing with judges in chambers about the admissibility of evidence questionably obtained by Jerry Orbach and Chris Noth. But I had no choice. I was just going to have to hope that they didn't expect me to actually have any practical legal knowledge.

When the elevator doors opened, I stepped out into a reception area featuring sleek, modern granite walls bearing the "LLF" logo in bas relief, which stood in stark contrast to the deliberately weathered dark wood floors covered with fringed, hand-tufted Persian area rugs and burnished leather antique armchairs, which, in turn, made the brightly colored original Andy Warhol prints that adorned the walls look as though they had been hung with a bit of purposeful irony. It was all very Greenwich Country Club meets SoHo meets Harvard meets *Wired* magazine. As I looked out of the full wall of windows that afforded me a view over Grand Central Station, the Chrysler Building, and the Empire State Building, all the way downtown to the then-standing World Trade Center and the New York Harbor, it was clear that I was a world away from Columbia University, even though the physical distance was only about six miles. And I could tell at first glance that *I liked this world better*. Then and there I swore to myself that I was going to work my fingers to the bone in order to make sure I would be given a permanent job offer at the end of the summer.

Before I could even announce myself to the receptionist, I caught sight of Bonnie Bailey, the Lavish Law Firm's recruiting director, scurrying into the reception area. She enveloped me in a giant hug and greeted me as though I was her long-lost best friend. "*Martha!* How *wonderful* to see you! I just know this summer is going to be *fantastic* and you will *love* the work and we have such fabulous things planned and it really is going to be the *very best ever!*"

Bonnie, whom I had met on two prior occasions—once during my callback interview, and once during a cocktail party for law students who had been granted summer offers to work at the Lavish Law Firm—never ceased to amaze me. She was a whirling dervish of energy with a demeanor so permanently cheery that one couldn't help but be a little bit suspicious. But the most bizarre thing about it all was that I really felt that the whole thing was completely genuine—Bonnie truly was the world's most enthusiastic woman.

After she released me from her hug, Bonnie exclaimed, "I've specially picked a *fabulous* office for you! Come on, I'll take you there and you can meet Colin, your officemate, who is just a *darling* and I know you two will just *adore* each other! Let's get this party started!"

We walked together down two flights of marble stairs, and I tried to keep up with her perky steps, despite my rapidly blistering heels. She led me into a large office with two built-in desks, credenzas, and sets of bookshelves, with the same stunning south-facing view as the reception area where I had been standing just minutes before. One of the desks, covered in haphazard piles of papers, legal pads, and Starbucks cups, was occupied by a good-looking, athletically built, sandy blond-haired guy who had a telephone glued to his ear, and who I took to be Colin, my officemate. Bonnie energetically ushered me to my desk, which was equipped with every office supply known to mankind, a complete set of New York City travel guides (despite the fact that I had been living there for almost two complete years) including a Fodor's travel guide, a book of detailed maps of each of the city's many neighborhoods and, most important (as I would soon learn), a Zagat's restaurant guide. On top of the pile was placed a firm telephone directory and a Lavish Law Firm version of the Columbia Law School facebook with each lawyer's photo and alma mater listed underneath.

By way of farewell, Bonnie once again extolled Colin's virtues (he was a second-year lawyer in the firm's corporate department, he was a Columbia Law alumnus, and he had run the New York Marathon five years in a row), gave me another big hug, and told me that the assigning partner would be calling me soon to give me work, but that in the meantime, I should just "acquaint myself."

So there I sat, at my first ever real desk in my first ever real office, without the slightest clue as to what I should be doing. I loaded my stapler. I arranged and rearranged the thirty packets of Post-it notes that were provided. I tried desperately not to eavesdrop on Colin's telephone conversation, even though that was a difficult task. I spent a few minutes marveling at the view, then started paging through the orientation materials that were on my desk. As it turned out, I was one of eighty-three summer associates at the Lavish Law Firm, most of whom were from Harvard, Yale, Columbia, and NYU. There were a decent number of people from the University of Chicago, Duke, Michigan, Stanford, and Virginia, as well as two students from Fordham, both of whom were on the Law Review (otherwise, the LLF probably wouldn't have even bothered to interview them). Once I had exhausted all other activities, I still hadn't heard from the assigning partner, so I turned my attention to listening to Colin's telephone conversation.

As it turned out, it wasn't a conference call or an important client telephone meeting, as I had initially assumed when I walked into our shared office. Colin was just a guy who spent a lot of time on the phone talking to his friends. Most of whom, it turned out, worked at the Lavish Law Firm and were a mere elevator ride away. But talking on the telephone behind a closed office door makes you look busy, while slouching in a chair and laughing in your friends' offices does not, even if you have a legal pad and pen in your hand. This particular conversation seemed to alternate between rehashing recent dates and discussing the most recent episodes of *Beavis and Butt-Head*. Several times, these two topics of conversation became intermingled, and I heard Colin saying "Heh heh heh. Heh heh heh. Boi-oi-oi-oi-oinnngg!" in his best rapid-fire, nasal imitation of Beavis's voice, trying to express his appreciation of the beauty of his most recent conquest.

As my head was about to explode with confusion, the assigning partner, Adam Bryant, finally summoned me to his office. For my first assignment, I would be working on a case for a giant insurance company embroiled in a coverage lawsuit, and I was told to go meet with a seventh-year litigation associate named Jerome Weiss, who would be my direct supervising attorney. Jerome was a giant bundle of nerves, aspiring to make partner at the firm and up for a partnership vote in the fall, and he was killing himself to give one last push to prove his merits to the powers that be. Because it would have been considered bad form to carry around a sign saying "I've billed two thousand hours already this year and it's only June 3," the dark circles underneath his eyes had to suffice as a poor substitute.

Jerome pointed to a foot-high stack of papers and instructed me to take them back to my office and "get familiar with the case." He'd call me when he had something more concrete. I read the complaint, the answer, the counterclaims, the scores of deposition transcripts, the random piles of meaningless, indecipherable papers that had strange numbers at the bottom, like TRS20004832 and FL449298 (which I would later learn were documents turned over in response to discovery requests, and which were specially numbered with Bates codes that began at number 1 and continued to infinity or until the case was settled, whichever came first).

Two days later, having dragged every possible moment that I could out of "familiarizing" myself with the case, I had yet to hear back either from Jerome as to what he wanted me to do or from the assigning partner giving me more work. Although I had accomplished nothing of value, I had managed to bill nineteen and one-half hours of my time for "background reading" that our poor, unsuspecting client was presumably going to have to pay for.

I had also managed to go out to two incredibly fancy lunches: one at Le Bernardin, where I had eaten Maine lobster and avocado salad, Dover sole in a ginger-saffron broth, and a chocolate, cashew, and caramel tart with a red wine reduction, and another at Aureole, where I had feasted on a chilled sugar-snap pea soup, fresh goat cheese ravioli with shaved truffles, and a foot-tall warm chocolate and hazelnut concoction filled with white chocolate custard. It was a summer law firm tradition: regular associates were equipped with LLF credit cards and empowered to take summer associates to lunch as often as they liked, in order to make us feel welcome, get to know people, and fall in love with the firm. There were only two rules: first, we were not to exceed a total of $45 per person per lunch, and second, there needed to be at least one summer associate present for every regular associate at the lunch (this was in order to prevent a group of twelve associates from getting together, planning a four-hour lunch at Il Mulino, and then finding one summer associate to tag along with them as an excuse for the LLF to finance the whole endeavor). The first rule was routinely broken. The second one was iron-clad.

What it meant for us summer associates was that our phones would start ringing at about ten o'clock each morning with lunch invitations. With eighty-three summer associates and over four hundred regular attorneys, it doesn't take a genius to do the math—we were meal tickets, and we were in high demand. Calls would come daily from complete strangers with lunch invitations, hoping to "get to know you and tell you more about the firm." (They were just going down the alphabetical list of summer associates until they hit pay dirt. I do expect that those with last names like Adams received more calls than the Zieglers of the world.) The particularly greedy summer associates would make their own lunch reservations each day at the restaurants they most wanted to visit, and would instruct calling associates that they had "space available" if they wanted to pay for the lunch. I would never have considered being so ballsy. I happily accepted the first invitations that came my way, ate my food, and kept my mouth shut.

At the end of my third day of work, with my belly full and no real work on the horizon, I felt sated but rather useless, and I guessed that I would just pack up and go home.

"Colin, is it kosher for me to go home at six o'clock? Or is there some unwritten law that I don't know about saying that I can't leave before seven-thirty?"

His reply? "Dude, if I were you, I would have been out of here at three-thirty this afternoon. Go home while you can."

At that very moment my phone rang. It was Jerome, asking me to come to his office, because he had some work for me to do on our case. *Excellent! Work! I wish it had come at three instead of at six, but that's fine, no problem! I'm dying to make myself useful.*

I took the elevator down to Jerome's office, eight floors below mine, and he told me that he had some "quick research" that he needed me to do. He was hoping I could have an answer for him by the end of the next day.

"Sure!" I replied, chipper as can be. "Whatever you need!"

"I'm working on writing this brief, and I need you to find me a case that says that if a policyholder doesn't give an insurance company notice of a claim within twenty-four hours of the incident, even if notice is given within the contractual claim period, the insurer can rightfully deny coverage. I know there's at least one case out there—I remember having read it years ago—but I don't remember the name. I think it's a case from New Jersey. Or maybe New Hampshire. Possibly New Mexico. It was from the 1980s. And I think it involved asbestos. So I need you to find that, any other supporting cases, law review articles, or other materials that we might be able to use, and write me a short memo by tomorrow. Sound good?"

"Yeah, good. I'll have it to you tomorrow, Jerome!" I replied.

With assignment in hand, I trotted back up to my office, logged on to Westlaw, and began to do my computerized research. I searched for every case that discussed how soon a policyholder needed to give an insurer notice of a claim. Nothing. I searched for every case that involved asbestos. Nothing. I searched for every case that contained the words *twenty-four hours*. Nothing. I expanded my search back to cases reported since 1920. Nothing. I expanded my search and read every case from New Jersey, New Hampshire, New Mexico, and New York involving notice of insurance claims. Nothing. I expanded my search geographically and read what seemed like every case from every state and federal court dating back to 1910 that involved insurance claims, asbestos, or contained the words *twenty-four hours*. Nothing. I called the Westlaw reference attorneys, whose job it is to help lawyers formulate legal research strategies, and asked for their help. Nothing. I stayed until two-thirty in the morning, dragged my ass back into the office at seven-thirty to keep working and, after performing eighteen hours of legal research, all I had to show for it was a big fat pile of nothing. Well, actually, a big fat pile of cases that said *the exact opposite* of what Jerome wanted them to say. Jerome was wrong. Not only was there no such case, but there were dozens of cases that had each expressly rejected some version of Jerome's argument.

How do you write a memo saying "Sorry, your position has absolutely no support in law or in logic. Although I searched diligently, I am 110% certain that there is no such case as you described to me yesterday. I think you might be on crack?" You don't. Ultimately, I decided that the news of my failure was better delivered in person than on paper. I slipped into Jerome's office, sat there perched at the edge of a visitor's chair waiting uncomfortably for ten minutes while he argued with his wife on the speakerphone, and then tried to break the news to him.

"Jerome, I'm really sorry, but I just couldn't find the case you were looking for. I researched every possible angle and, well, I just don't know that there is such a case."

He didn't believe me.

"Martha, *I know* that this case is out there. Are you sure that you looked thoroughly? I think I said that it was from the 1980s, but I suppose it's possible that it was from 1979. Go back and check again."

"Okay, if you want me to. But really, I swear, I checked as thoroughly as is humanly possible. I checked cases going back to 1920 all across the country—not just limited to that handful of states that you mentioned. I searched legal encyclopedias, law review articles, treatises—you name it. I even called the Westlaw hotline and spoke at length with a reference attorney, who was unable to help me find anything that I hadn't already come up with. All I could find was this one footnote in a dissenting opinion from a case in Puerto Rico written in 1944 that said 'Be there no doubt that prompt notification of claims is a blessing.' And there was an article in the *Journal of Asbestos Law* arguing that insurers should consider shortening the contractual claims periods in their policies. Maybe we could try to use one of those things to support our position?"

"I have a hard time believing this."

"I'm sorry, Jerome. I'm happy to go back and look some more, but I don't want to make poor use of the client's time. Really, I was very meticulous in my research. Here is a list of all of the Westlaw searches that I performed and the exact databases that I searched. Can you think of anything that I missed? Can you recommend anyplace else I should look?"

"I know it's there, Martha. I need you to go back and start from the beginning."

Humbled, I trudged back up to my office. I called and spoke to a different Westlaw reference attorney. Nothing. I redid all the same searches that I had already done, just in case I had missed something the first time. Nothing. I searched in new Westlaw databases that were outside of the firm's flat-rate Westlaw billing plan. Nothing. I wandered the halls of the insurance section of the Lavish Law Firm's library, hoping that something would jump out at me. Nothing. I gave up on computerized research and turned to reading the case digests from the library shelves, just in case one of my search terms was off. Nothing.

Two days (and twenty-seven more billable hours) later, I returned to Jerome, tail between my legs, to tell him that I had once again been unsuccessful. But I reiterated my strong desire to do whatever it took to be a productive, useful member of the team.

"Well, I can't say I'm not disappointed," he said. "I'll just have to get someone else to find it. You can go. I'll call you later to let you know what to do next."

(No one else was ever able to find the case that Jerome was talking about. A week later, after thousands of dollars worth of billable time had been spent on the research, he decided that it didn't really matter anyway.)

I spent weeks pulling my hair out in frustration over "quick" research assignments like this from Jerome, almost all of which were wild-goose chases, and almost all of which were "urgent," requiring me to stay until all hours of the night. One morning, despite the supposedly pressing nature of my assignment, I dared to accept a lunch invitation from an associate who worked in the office next to mine. We purposely kept it fairly quick—instead of traipsing downtown to the Union Square Café, which we had discussed, we went to eat Key West–style seafood at Tropica, which was just two short blocks away. In record time, we ate shrimp ceviche and seared Ahi tuna, accompanied by jasmine rice and beans and followed by Key lime pie with a citrus coulis, and I was back at my desk in an impressively short one hour and eight minutes.

And then I saw the blinking red light on my telephone. In the time that I was gone, Jerome had left me three voice mail messages of increasing degrees of exigency and frustration. Hurriedly, I made my way down to his office and was given a stern lecture.

"Martha, I've been trying to reach you for several hours. Where have you been?"

"Well, I went out and grabbed some lunch. But I was only gone for an hour. Really. I'm sorry that you couldn't get ahold of me. What is it that you need me to do?"

"What I need you to do is to realize the importance of this case you're working on," he said, sternly. "And to understand that when something pressing arises, I need to be able to reach you. I need to know where you are. You can't just go disappearing."

Taken aback by the reprimand, I felt my face begin to burn. "I . . . I'm sorry. In the future, should I send you an e-mail or leave you a message if I'm going to step out of the office?"

"No. What you should do is stick around so I can find you. Got it?"

"Yes, Jerome. I've got it."

I never found out why Jerome was originally trying to reach me. Possibly—just possibly—it wasn't really all that important in the first place.

Nevertheless, beginning on that day, I turned down handfuls of fancy lunch invitations every day. I skipped almost all the extravagant after-work events that the LLF had planned for us summer associates: tickets to Shakespeare in the Park and a private reception afterward with the actors, a cocktail party held at the Ellis Island museum complete with a guided tour by the curator, dinner in a private room at Sardi's followed by a Broadway show. And I never felt like I could complain much because, no matter how late I was in the office, Colin was always still there when I left. I left at ten p.m.; he was still there working. I left at eleven-thirty p.m.; he was still there working. I left at one forty-five a.m.; he was still there working. I left at two-thirty a.m.; he was still there working. *Is this really how things go around this place? I mean, everyone has heard the rumors about the big firms working you to death, but is this really what my life is going to be like? It's one thing to be doing this every day as a summer associate trying to prove myself, but is this the way it will be forever?*

One day, I asked him. "Colin, are you *always* here until the middle of the night?"

"Yeah," he replied, dejectedly. "It sucks ass, and it makes it hard to keep a girlfriend. But it is what it is, you know? One thing I've learned, though: the security guard turns off the lights in the empty offices when he makes his rounds. So if you wait until after three a.m. to leave—after he's made his last rounds—you can leave your office light on when you go and it will still be on when the early folks get here in the morning. So people will know you pulled an all-nighter. Then they cut you some slack. Sometimes I'll stay an extra half hour just to wait out the security guard."

"I'll make sure to file that tidbit away, Colin."

The next morning I arrived at work before Colin did, and couldn't help but notice his monthly billing statement sitting in the middle of his newly cleaned desk. I was insanely curious. *Should I peek? Can I peek? Would it be awful to peek?* I mean, Colin was at work until all hours every single day. How many hours per month must he have billed? Two hundred fifty? Three hundred? More? *No, it wouldn't be awful to peek. Consider it a learning experience. A way to find out more about life at the Lavish Law Firm. That's what this summer is all about, right?* So, I peeked.

You know how many hours Colin had billed during the month of June? One hundred twenty. An average of thirty hours per week. How was that possible? He was always there in the office! I sat and contemplated this great mystery, and then it came to me. Yes, he was always there, but he was always there *talking on the phone.* Not working. The only reason he had to stay at the office until two each morning was because he spent all day yammering away in his Beavis voice with his friends, calling them ass munches and butt dumplings and then laughing so hard he could barely breathe. Then he'd have to stay half the night to do the work he should have been doing during normal business hours. If he had actually worked during the day, he could have left at six every evening. And all this time I thought he had his nose to the grindstone. A smart girl I was not.

Curious, I asked Colin about his Lavish Law Firm plans when he came in later that morning. Did he hope to make partner? Did he plan to stay for the long term? If not, then what?

"Hell no, dude. I'm serving my time for three years to the day, then I'm out of here. I'll go in-house at Goldman Sachs or Credit Suisse First Boston or something. Investment banking is where it's at. This shit is for suckers."

"Suckers like me?" I asked.

"No. That's not what I meant. Because, really, this gig isn't so bad. If you're not a Jerome worried about making partner, it's easy enough to let yourself fall between the cracks. Take it easy. Do the work they give you, but don't do more than you have to. I mean, no one ever gets fired. Sure, if you're a sixth-year associate and they have no intention of ever making you partner, they'll find a gentle way to usher you toward the door, but for the first few years, it's a piece of cake. And everyone gets paid the same—your salary just depends on what graduating class you were in. Whether you bill eighteen hundred hours per year or twenty-eight hundred hours, the same paycheck goes in your pocket. So why be one of the twenty-eight-hundred-hour suckers?"

"I have no idea how to answer that question, Colin. Food for thought, though. Food for thought."

Just when I thought my mind was about to explode with the inane research, Jerome told me that a document production had come in, and he wanted me to help with the document review. Not even knowing what a document production was, I asked a woman in the office two doors down from me, a kindly fourth-year litigator, who told me it was a giant bunch of papers that the opposing counsel sent to you after you had sent "document requests" asking your opponent to send you all the information they had in their possession relating to certain stated subjects. Then, I understood: those were the endless papers marked with the bizarre numbers like BVV499216 and SGT900455.

Jerome ushered me into a large conference room that was stacked with at least a hundred large boxes of papers. I was there with a first-year associate named Clay, who I was to assist in reviewing the documents. On call was a paralegal named Omar, who would later catalog the documents after we reviewed them. Jerome told me to keep an eye out for any documents that "looked funny" or for anything that was "privileged," and to put those documents aside for Omar to index. He offered no further instructions. Ten minutes after Jerome left, Clay left to "go take care of something," and he didn't return for hours. That was fore-shadowing of the amount of time Clay would be spending in the conference room over the next weeks.

Luckily, I knew what "privileged" meant. They had taught that much to me in law school: any piece of paper with a lawyer's name on it—whether it was a memo written to the company's lawyer, a letter from the lawyer, an e-mail with the lawyer bcc'ed on it, a handwritten note that vaguely alludes to the existence of a lawyer—that shit was *privileged*. Or "work product." I wasn't sure exactly what the difference was, but that was okay. With no one to turn to with questions (I wasn't going to let the paralegal know that I had no clue as to what I was doing), I pulled out every document that was ever touched by an attorney and said they were both privileged *and* work product. I was zealously representing my client!

But as to the documents that Jerome referenced that might "look funny"? I had no idea what to make of that. I knew that by "funny" he didn't mean "bust a gut because you're laughing so hard" funny. But I didn't know exactly what he did mean, because he hadn't bothered to explain before he ran out of the room. And I didn't dare ask anyone—it might let them in on the fact that, despite my Ivy League education, I really didn't have the slightest clue as to what I was doing.

So I spent the next weeks looking through seemingly endless boxes of papers, hoping to find a piece of paper that said in giant letters "WE KNOW THE INSURANCE COMPANY REALLY ISN'T LIABLE FOR OUR PURPOSEFUL MISDEEDS" or "WE DUMPED THAT WASTE INTO THE ESTUARY EVEN THOUGH WE WERE FLAT-OUT CERTAIN IT WAS TOXIC." I never found such documents.

But then I got to thinking. What if those documents *were* in the giant pile of boxes but I had just missed them? What if the insurancey-type jibberish on those pages of forms, invoices, notes, reports, memos, and letters had just confused me, and I had missed critically important documents that would have been obvious to anyone with half a brain in their head? The more I thought about it, the more I was certain that was the case. If the documents in all of those boxes weren't relevant and important, why would opposing counsel have produced them? Surely there were all sorts of "funny looking" documents in there, vitally important to the case, which I had omitted in error. What if we lost the case because of the things I had missed? What if, later on, someone else came across things that I had overlooked? Jerome would *freak*. What should I do? Should I start over from the beginning?

"Colin, I think I've messed up big time. Should I tell Clay? Omar? Should I suck it up and tell Jerome?"

"What are you talking about?"

"This document review. I'm pretty sure I've missed some really important stuff." I began to really panic. My breathing became labored, my chest constricted.

"Why?"

"Well, I don't know what I'm doing. Jerome never really told me what to look for. I'm afraid that there are all sorts of important documents in there that I've overlooked. *Wheeze.* Should I tell him? If I do, he'll kill me."

"Martha, calm down."

"But if I don't tell him myself, and he finds out somehow on his own, it'll just be worse. Shit! I can't believe I messed this up! I just know this is going to ruin my chances at getting a permanent job offer here! *Wheeze.*"

"Martha. Dude. *Breathe. Everyone* gets an offer. You'd have to burn down the building or have a lesbian love affair with the hiring partner's wife or skip work for an entire month in order to not get an offer. Relax a little bit. Christ almighty."

"Really? You think so?"

"Why do you think they allow us to take you summer associates out to $400 lunches every day? Why do you think they're taking you on ushered museum tours and to country club parties every week? With a turnover rate that has to be bordering on twenty-five or thirty percent per year, they're fighting a war of attrition. They're desperate to have you love it here. They want you more than you want them. They *need* all of you to accept your offers to replace the midlevel associates who are leaving in droves. Right now, you've got the upper hand. So take advantage of it, already."

"The upper hand? I don't know about that."

"You know what you need to do? You need to get yourself off that stupid case. If you don't, Jerome Weiss is going to beat your ass into the ground all summer long just to further his own partnership neuroses, and you'll never have one bit of fun."

"Get off the case? I would *kill* to get off this case. But how?"

"Talk to Bonnie in recruiting. She's bending over backward to make sure everyone has a wonderful summer, she'd for sure step in on your behalf. Or else find a way to get yourself another assignment, then slowly disengage yourself from this one, claiming you're too busy. The partners won't care, only Jerome will. And who gives a shit about Jerome?"

"Really? You think that could work?" My eyes were lit up with excitement.

"Martha, you just have to make it work. *Strategize,* dude."

So although it was against my nature, I schemed myself out of the case. I called Adam Bryant, the firm's assigning partner, and let him know that I was looking for more work. A few days later, I received a return call from him.

"Martha, this is Adam Bryant. Do you have a valid passport?"

"Well, yes. Sure, yes, I do." *Not that I've ever used it, but a girl can dream, right?*

"Excellent. Then I have an assignment for you."

"Oh, fabulous!"

"I need you to go to Slovenia. You can stop by my office to pick up your tickets—your flight leaves from JFK in three and a half hours. I'll have my secretary call a car to take you home so you can pack a bag, and then on to the airport."

"Oh. Okay. I'll be there in just a minute."

"Good."

"Just one more question, sir?" I asked, nervously.

"Yes, Martha?"

"Where exactly is Slovenia?"

"I don't know. Just come to my office."

"Yes. I'll be right there."

When I arrived, he handed me a set of plane tickets, a hotel reservation at the Holiday Inn Ljubljana, several million dollars' worth of bearer bonds, and instructions that someone from the Slovenian government would meet me at the airport upon my arrival. I was told that, in the wake of the dissolution of the former Yugoslavia, several of its constituent nations were refinancing their national debt, and the Lavish Law Firm was somehow working to help this happen. I was to transport the bonds, get some papers signed, and then get on a flight back to New York the next day. He told me that once I returned, he had a different corporate deal that he wanted me to begin work on.

I had no idea where the former Yugoslavia was, and I didn't have time to check. My awaiting car sped me uptown to my apartment, where Joe met me to give me a good-bye kiss and to warn me not to drink the water. I threw a few articles of clothing, my toothbrush, and my camera into a bag, then I was driven out to Kennedy Airport in Queens, where I barely made my plane. As I was standing in line to board, I realized that I had a business-class ticket—a whole new ball game for me. *Business class? Isn't that like first class? Doesn't that mean free-flowing champagne and heated washcloths and chocolate sundaes with cherries on top? So far, I'm liking this trip!*

After enjoying a gourmet meal served on fine porcelain dishes, drinking a steaming mug of Swiss hot chocolate, and selecting a movie to watch on my own personal video screen, I fell asleep in my comfortably reclined leather seat somewhere over the Atlantic Ocean. I woke up as my ears began to pop when we began our descent into Geneva, where I would switch planes to continue on to Ljubljana, Slovenia. When I awoke, still in a sleepy haze, I looked out the small plane window and thought I was looking down on Antarctica or something—as far as the eye could see, there were nothing but icy tundras and snow-covered mountains. *Did I get on the wrong plane? Damn it, I knew I didn't know what I was doing with this whole "international travel" thing. But* Antarctica? *Accidentally getting on a plane to the South Pole is a pretty big screw-up, even for me.* But then I came to a bit more and realized I was looking out at a thick blanket of clouds, with the Swiss Alps poking through and protruding what seemed like miles into the sky. *Oh, not Antarctica. Alps! Swiss Alps! Holy cow. I'm a long way from home.*

I got off the giant, comfortable Swiss Air jet in Geneva, and switched to the tiniest, ricketiest plane I had ever seen, where I proceeded to chew every single one of my fingernails down to their quicks during the flight to Slovenia. About fifteen minutes before we landed, I thought to ask a flight attendant exactly where it was I was going. (Until that time, I seemed to think I was going to Czechoslovakia.) She replied in broken English something about "Slovenia . . . near . . . Croatia . . . Bosnia . . . Kosovo . . . Montenegro . . ." *Bosnia? Croatia? Kosovo? KOSOVO? Where they have guns and bombs and armed resistance and civil war? Is the assigning partner trying to punish me for my attempt to escape from Jerome? A year slaving away on the* Journal of Transnational Law *and taking classes in European Community Law and Comparative Law, and* this *is what I get in the way of "international" work?*

When I arrived at the airport in Ljubljana, it was utter chaos— arriving at the same time as my flight was a plane full of Slovenians who had just finished climbing Mount Everest, and there was a veritable parade throughout the airport welcoming them home and celebrating their accomplishment. (It made surviving two years of law school seem a bit pale by comparison.) I sat back and waited for my escort. And waited. And waited some more. After an hour had passed, I began to wonder. After two hours had passed, I began to worry. After three and a half hours had passed,

I began to panic. I didn't have the phone number, or even the *name* of the person I was supposed to meet. And I didn't know who to ask for help—everyone was speaking some strange, unknown language. It wasn't French. It wasn't German. What was it? (It was Slovenian.)

What should I do? I'm stranded in a possibly war-torn country! I've been here for hours and no one has come to my rescue! Calm down. Call the office. Phone. I need a phone. Oh look, there's a sign with a picture of a telephone and an arrow pointing down that hall! Okay, a phone. How the hell do I work this phone? I have no Slovenian money. Must find Slovenian money. A currency exchange! Yes, here's the phone and here's some Slovenian money. But the phone doesn't seem to take money. Only cards. And it won't take my credit card. Do I need some special card? Would it kill them to have some signs in ENGLISH around here?

Eventually I figured out how to buy the special card and how to use the phone—no small feat, mind you—only to realize that it was about six a.m. in New York, and there was no way I was going to catch anybody in the office, not even Colin. So I sat back and waited some more. Eventually, I got Bonnie Bailey on the phone, explained that I was stranded in a strange and possibly dangerous nation where everyone spoke an unknown language, and that nobody was there to pick me up and I didn't even have a telephone number or a contact name and *God please help me NOW.* Within an hour, my escort was there. I expect there had been some behind-the-scenes yelling, because the gentleman was very apologetic (and in English, no less!).

My job consisted solely of riding to a very important-looking government office, handing the bonds over to some nicely dressed men, and signing a few papers—I was the world's best-paid and most highly educated courier. When I was done, it was only about three in the afternoon, and my flight back to New York didn't leave until noon the next day. Thrilled at the chance to do my very first official European exploring, I hoofed it over to my hotel, unloaded my bag, grabbed my camera, and set off.

And it turned out that Slovenia was not a dangerous, war-torn country—it was the most beautiful place I had ever seen.

I walked along narrow pathways beside a meandering river, marveled at the stately red-roofed homes and graceful willow trees flanking each side, wandered down cobblestone streets past tiny green-awninged sidewalk cafés, crossed a dozen foot-bridges—each with a more stunning view down the narrow river than the last—stared at candy-colored Baroque buildings, lost count of the number of quaint town squares I walked by (all with exotic names like Mestni trg and Stari trg), and marveled over the fact that each time I turned a corner, I had a new and different view of the small, tree-covered mountain at the center of the town, upon which was perched a giant, ancient stone castle. *Yes, I am a long way from Wisconsin. Hell, I'm a long way from New York. Shit, at this point, I feel like I'm a long way from earth—I had no idea there was anyplace this beautiful on my home planet.*

I bought a necklace from a vendor who sat on one of the foot-bridges—I had no idea how much it cost, nor did I know how to ask, so I just held my money out in the palm of my hand, and he took some of it from me in exchange for the jewelry. I ate dinner and drank coffee at a sidewalk café overlooking the Ljubljanica river. Afterward, I drank cheap beer and smoked Slovenian ciga-rettes at some sort of outdoor music festival in one of the town squares, watching a band play while men and children danced, and women sat at small tables gossiping. By that point, I was so tired that I wasn't sure if any of it was real, or if I was partly hallu-cinating.

Reeling with exhaustion, I crawled back to my hotel and climbed into my surprisingly comfortable bed. And then I was unable to sleep. I took a bath, I read a book, I sat on my hotel room balcony and I tried to wrap my mind around what was hap-pening. Around the fact that I was actually in Europe. Around the fact that in the last twenty-four hours I had gone from slaving away in a depressing conference room doing document review for Jerome Weiss to sitting on the balcony of a hotel room in Slovenia, watching the sun slowly rise over a mountaintop castle. Even now, I'm not sure I would believe it was real if I hadn't taken pictures and if I didn't have a Slovenian stamp in my passport.

When I finally made it back to the office, I had thirteen voice mail messages from Jerome asking where I was. *Shit. Shit!*

"Colin, what do I do? Jerome is going to eat me alive!"

"Martha, you've got to change your whole mind-set. Stop apologizing. Start acting entitled. Tell Jerome you're off the case. Or at the very least, tell him that you've gotten another assignment that is going to be keeping you really busy—too busy to be very involved anymore. Then tell him he's an asshole."

Stop apologizing? Start acting entitled? Since when have I been entitled? I never even considered the possibility that I might be entitled. But hey, entitled doesn't sound that bad. I mean, after all, I am an Ivy League law student. Right? Right! At one of the most elite institutions in the country! And now I am a world traveler, to boot! Perhaps I am entitled? Yeah! ENTITLED!

"Jerome Weiss," he answered his phone perfunctorily.

"Jerome, it's Martha. I'm sorr— I apolog— I just got back from an emergency trip to Europe at the request of the assigning partner, and now he has put me on a corporate deal that urgently needs my help. I'm afraid I'm not really going to have time to keep working on the case. I hope it won't be too much of a problem, because I do know there are seven other associates staffed on the case, along with the two partners in charge. But it's been a pleasure working with you, Jerome. A real treat. Bye now."

With shaking hands, I put down the phone and let out a giant sigh of relief. *My first act of entitled defiance!* And I knew he wouldn't dare complain. Adam Bryant was on the Partnership Committee, about to vote on Jerome's fate in a few short months. Who was he to question the assigning partner's decisions? Jerome could just go beat up on someone else.

Once extricated from the case of misery, I spent the rest of the

summer working on the corporate deal, which I didn't understand in the least. It was a "high-yield debt offering" (a fancy way
to say "a sale of junk bonds"). I had taken Corporations in law
school the previous year, but it was full of things like "fiduciary
duty" and "classes of stock" and "shareholder derivative suits" and
"proxy contests" and "supermajority voting." I had gotten an A,
but nowhere had I learned anything about drafting prospectuses
for high-yield debt offerings. Nor had I been taught that low-level
corporate legal work amounted to nothing more than document
review and proofreading, which I had gotten plenty enough of
working on the staff of my journal.

I was working for a young partner named Ruth Gibbons, who
appreciated my hard work, but who, unlike Jerome, also understood the importance of the pampering that was supposed to be
going on during one's summer associate tenure. Lavish lunches?
Yes. Evening social events? Yes. Late nights? On occasion. Working
until I'd outstayed the security guard's last rounds? Never.

On my third day of working for Ruth, as I sat proofreading the
nineteenth draft of our client's prospectus, I got a lunch invitation. And I thought, "What the hell." I gave a tentative yes, and
called Ruth to get official clearance.

"Hi, Ruth, it's Martha. I'm in the middle of working on the revisions to the prospectus, but I just got invited to a lunch that I'd
really like to go to. That is, if you don't mind."

"What?" she asked.

"Well, I wanted to make sure that you didn't have a problem
with me leaving."

"Martha, go. Absolutely! As long as the work is getting done, I
don't care when you do it. I'm not your mother. I don't need to
keep tabs on your every move."

"Oh, right." I felt silly for having asked.

"The client isn't expecting the document to be turned around
until Thursday, anyway. So go! Eat! Enjoy yourself!"

"Thanks, Ruth. I think I will."

Over the next weeks, with Ruth's gracious blessing, in between document review (which was called "due diligence" by the corporate lawyers) and proofreading infinite drafts of the prospectus, I managed to lunch at most of the best restaurants in the city. I acquired a taste for sushi at Nobu, experienced the ecstasy of a perfect chocolate soufflé at Bouley, ate a steak the likes of which I'd never ever tasted before at Peter Luger, had lunch at a table next to Donald Trump at the Four Seasons, and spent three hours stuffing myself with fresh, handmade pasta at Il Mulino. I was introduced to sashimi, oysters, truffles, foie gras, sweetbreads, and Beluga caviar. *Why didn't I know about these things earlier? I have wasted twenty-four years of my life going without sushi or caviar. How did I manage? Colin was right. I am entitled! These are the things I was meant to eat! Finally, I am realizing my destiny!*

It was heaven to actually have time to attend most of the summer events. Although I had missed out in the beginning, I made up for it in the end. There was an all-day party at one of the partners' country clubs in Westchester, where we played tennis, had private golf lessons, lounged by the pool, and had cocktails and dinner outside underneath the stars. *A country club—someday maybe I, too, will be a member of a country club!* There was a guided tour through the secret catacombs and catwalks of the magnificent Grand Central Station. *I am now filled with knowledge of the history of one of the city's most venerated Beaux-Arts edifices!* There was horseback riding on the trails in Central Park. *When I'm rich someday, I wonder if I should board my horses here in the city or in my country home in Connecticut?* There was an outing to a Yankees game, where we had box seats right behind the dugout. *This was fun and all, but couldn't they have arranged for us to meet some players? I'd really like to get Derek Jeter's autograph.* There was a catered wine tasting, where several summer associates got embarrassingly drunk on premier cru wines. *Ahh, Château Lafite Rothschild—I was born to drink Château Lafite Rothschild! I deserve nothing less than opulence!*

And on yet another front, Colin was right. When I was reveling in the excess, I got paid the same $1,650 per week that I had earned when I was slaving away for Jerome and missing out on all the fun. All it took was a little entitled defiance on my part. As I walked out of the Lavish Law Firm's marble-covered lobby for the last time that summer, with an offer to return for permanent employment upon graduation in hand, I couldn't help but marvel at the change I had experienced over the course of the last few months. *Entitlement—what a wonderful thing. God bless Colin and the little smackdown he gave me. Because I like life better this way. What was it with that self-doubting, hardworking, subservient attitude I'd been carrying around all my life? God, I was such a sucker! Self-doubt is for losers, not for Ivy League law students! I'm one of the best of the best! The cream of the crop! Entitlement! Yeah! That's where it's at!*

Eleven

SLACKER SAVANT

"My problem lies in reconciling my gross habits with my net income."
—ERROL FLYNN

When I returned to law school for the beginning of my third and final year, my checkbook was full of money and my heart was full of attitude. Back inside the familiar corridors of Jerome Greene Hall, I looked around at the naïve entering first-year students, their eyes wide with fear, exploring the law school for the first time. I watched as the second-year students hurried down the halls dressed in their freshly dry-cleaned suits, briefcases in hand instead of the usual backpacks, running out of classes early to go to callback interviews. I listened as the first-years whispered in the hallways, speculating about which professors would be difficult, which would be frightening, and which would be kind, too afraid to simply ask an upper-class student about the faculty reputations. I smelled the scent of superiority that positively oozed from some of the second-years who had just made Law Review, and witnessed the disappointment in the eyes of those who had expected to make it but hadn't.

Instead of feeling empathy, compassion, or even pity for these people (myself not being very far removed in time from their exact positions), I just felt disdain. Instead of marveling at the beautiful new student lounge, café, library space, and updated classrooms that the completed renovation had provided, I couldn't muster up the energy to care. Every bit of it made me want to put my hands on my hips, roll my eyes, and scream "I am so totally *over* this!"

Not all that long before, I had myself been one of those wide-eyed entering first-year students, so obsessed with my studies that I could barely see the outside world. Although it had only been two years before, it seemed like it was in a different lifetime. All that stressing about assigned reading and case briefs and class outlines and study groups and grades and making Law Review—it was just so *first year.* Having acclimated myself to the excesses that had been lavished upon me over the summer, school really seemed more than just a little bit beneath me.

After all, was the dean offering me his box seats to the Yankees playoff games? Were the people at the Career Services Office inviting me to meals at four-star restaurants? Was the registrar asking me to accompany him to the ballet, where we would go backstage afterward and meet the principal dancers? Was the director of admissions inviting me to a behind-the-scenes cooking demonstration at the Union Square Café? Was anybody at law school paying me a damn penny? No, no, no, no, and *no.* Simply put, there was no wooing going on back at Columbia. And I had really come to like the wooing. I *deserved* the wooing.

"Can you guys believe that we have to do this for another year?" I whined to Katie and Elizabeth, as we sat drinking margaritas and catching up on the events of the past couple of months, during which Elizabeth had been a summer associate at a large Boston firm, and Katie had been an intern at the Public Defender's Office in Los Angeles.

"No kidding," moaned Elizabeth. "I'm done with this shit. I'm ready to get working."

"So how was your summer?" I asked.

"It was great," Elizabeth answered. "Who can complain about the fabulous restaurants and the parties?"

"I know," I answered. "I think I gained seven pounds."

"I was lucky to get my mentor attorney to accompany me to

the cafeteria once a week for a tuna fish sandwich between seeing clients in the county jail," Katie said.

As though she hadn't even heard Katie, Elizabeth added, "Plus I got to do some really significant work on two different M and A transactions for very high profile clients. I always thought I was going to want to focus on structured finance, but I've definitely decided that I want to do M and A work when I go back."

I couldn't believe she found that stuff interesting. "I worked on a high-yield debt offering, and even though I loved the partner I was working for, it gave me nightmares," I said. Corporate work just wasn't for me. I had accepted the Lavish Law Firm's offer, and had decided to join the litigation department, crossing my fingers and hoping that my experience with Jerome Weiss was an aberration.

"You guys are just lucky that you both have offers," Katie chimed in. "I'm not going to find out for months whether or not the Public Defender's Office wants me back. I know they liked me, but there's some sort of budget weirdness going on and they can't make offers a year in advance like law firms can. I hope it works out. I hate not knowing."

"It'll work out, Katie," I said.

"Yeah, I'm sure it will," Elizabeth added. "But still, I'm amazed that that's what you want to do for a living. Don't get me wrong, it's great and all, I just never really had you pegged as a girl who would interact with felons."

"Well, me either," Katie answered, twirling a strand of her hair, which was several shades blonder than it had been back in May. "I mean, when I went to work for Legal Aid the summer after first year, I was totally bummed about it. I only did it because I couldn't find a firm job. But I turned out to really like it. And this summer with the Public Defender's Office was fabulous!" she exclaimed, with a look of genuine excitement in her face. "I know— if I even get a permanent job there—I'm going to get paid nothing and I'm going to defend criminals, most of whom are probably guilty. But they need someone to help them, and I can help. Plus I'd get great trial experience. Within a couple months of passing the bar, I would be in an actual courtroom arguing in front of an actual judge!"

"Wow," I said, honestly blown away at the thought. Although I was heading back to be a litigator at the Lavish Law Firm, I knew I'd be lucky to see the inside of a courtroom before I turned forty. When the stakes were as high as they were for companies willing to pay LLF billing rates, no one was willing to risk going to trial. Almost every case settled, even if it wasn't until the eleventh hour. Hell, I had the impression that half of the litigation partners had never even gotten the chance to utter a word aloud in a courtroom—all they did was draft briefs, file motions, and take depositions. "You know, when I first came to law school, I thought I wanted to do nonprofit work," I reminisced. "Maybe work for the ACLU or something. Or the Department of Justice. But I've borrowed so much money that I can't imagine paying it back on a $35,000-a-year salary." I felt a bit jealous of Katie's decision to do something so risky and unexpected.

"Well, Columbia has a loan forgiveness program for people doing public interest work," Katie said. "If you're not making much money, they help you pay your student loans back."

Still, my jealousy only went so far. "Sorry, but I'm just not willing to sacrifice all that cash. I'm going back to the Lavish Law Firm, raking in my gigantic salary, and staying until it begins to drive me insane. And meanwhile I will live in a nice apartment, buy expensive shoes without feeling guilty, and go on tropical vacations with Joe. I don't think I could stand slumming it any longer. I've been poor long enough. After suffering through all of this, I deserve some riches."

"It's up to you," Katie said, as she reached for her bag. "I'm sure you'll be happy there."

Was there a hint of judgment in her statement?

"You guys, I've got to run," she said. "Josh is coming to visit and his plane lands in two hours. I'm going to surprise him at the airport."

As Katie walked away, Elizabeth leaned over to me and whispered, "I don't know how happy she's going to be a year from now when she and Josh are living in some crappy apartment in Reseda and eking out a living on a combined $60,000 per year."

I couldn't help but wonder if Elizabeth was right—partly just to assuage my own misgivings about having strayed from my intended path—but I felt too bad to actually agree with her out loud. Instead I took a long drink, licked a few chunky granules of salt off my upper lip, and said, "You know, that ring you wear. I've always admired it. It's really beautiful. Is it a family heirloom?"

"Do you want to know the truth?" Elizabeth asked. "I wouldn't be telling you this if I wasn't on my third margarita. It's fake. Cubic zirconia. But don't tell anybody."

"Oh, wow. I had no idea."

"I bought it when I worked at Smith Barney, so I could put it on my left hand and ward off boys at bars. I just didn't have the time or energy to get into it with men. Actually, I still don't. I've got a career to worry about. And I like the ring, so I keep wearing it."

My years-long rumblings of jealously evaporated and I began to feel kind of sorry for Elizabeth.

When I had perused the course catalog to select my schedule for my final year, I was torn. First, there were the courses I *wanted* to take. By and large these were classes that sounded interesting but would either be too hard or of absolutely no practical use to me in the working world. Criminal Investigations? A fascinating topic, but probably not too applicable to a woman headed to a firm whose litigation practice concentrated on insurance defense, antitrust, and securities cases. Copyright Law? A field I really wanted to study, but the professor was renowned for giving both a four-hour in-class exam *and* a two-day take-home. So, no. Not during my third year, thank you very much. Human Rights Law? Unless I was planning on staging an uprising to protest the working standards at the Lavish Law Firm, it probably wasn't going to get me too far.

Then, there were the classes I thought I *should* take. These were mostly "commit hara-kiri to save yourself from the boredom" type of courses, but I suspected that at least some knowledge of these subjects would probably be expected of me at some point. Corporate Reorganization and Bankruptcy? Misery. Administrative Law? Intolerable. Financial Statement Analysis and Interpretation? I could feel myself falling asleep as I read the course description.

Finally, there were the classes that sounded fairly ridiculous but looked as if they might be really *easy.* Feminist Theory Workshop? No. I was a firm believer in shaving my legs on a regular basis. Seminar in Law and Theatre? Despite its spot-on relevance and usefulness within the context of a corporate law firm, I decided to pass. Welfare and Poverty Law? Although I would soon be graduating with $100,000 in student loan debt, I didn't think that would qualify me for welfare.

In the end, I picked a hodgepodge of courses, making one concession to necessity by reluctantly choosing Antitrust, making a rash decision by—for altogether inexplicable reasons—enrolling in a seminar called Selected Aspects of Bioethics, throwing myself a bone by signing up for a no-brainer-sounding class called Negotiation Workshop, choosing Criminal Adjudication just because it sounded interesting, no matter now irrelevant to my future career, and otherwise focusing on courses that either required final papers instead of exams, or at least offered take-home exams instead of in-class finals.

But of all the classes I selected during my third year, by far my smartest choice was Spanish for the Legal Profession. According to the description, this was "an intensive first-year language course with an emphasis on legal terminology, designed for students with absolutely no or extremely limited knowledge of the language." I had taken Spanish for four years during high school and for two semesters in college, and I was confident that my knowledge of the language was rather broad. Which meant that this class should be easy. So I knew that this was definitely the class for me. And better yet, I could take it for two straight semesters, eight credits of Remedial Legal Spanish in all.

Rumor had it that if you had a decent grasp on the Spanish language, you could easily skip two out of four classes per week and still pull down a four-credit A. If you didn't have a background in the language, you'd probably drop out within the first week, because it was positively insane to think that in four short months you could somehow learn conjugations of regular verbs, irregular verbs, and stem-changing verbs in the present tense, preterit tense, imperfect tense, conditional tense, future tense, and present and past subjunctive; basic vocabulary, nouns (including memorization of which nouns were feminine and which were masculine), adjectives, adverbs, prepositions, direct and indirect objects, idiomatic expressions, and Spanish legal jargon. Luckily, I fell into the first camp. To me, the class sounded like a third-year law student's dream come true.

It turned out I wasn't the only one who had heard these rumors. When I walked in, the small classroom was bursting at the seams with third-year students, almost all of whom already spoke Spanish at some level of proficiency and were looking to coast by on their prior knowledge, yet who were claiming total ignorance of the language. (Hell, one of the men in our class bore a distinctly Hispanic first name and surname and, from his perfect pronunciation and diction, I know I wasn't the only one who wondered if Spanish might have actually been his first language.) Our profesora didn't seem to suspect a thing.

About five minutes into the first class session, Rachel snuck into the room and took a seat near the door. When the class ended, I hesitantly approached her.

"Hey Rachel. How've you been?" I asked, picking at the wire on my spiral notebook.

"Good. Good. I mean, busy, but good. You know—Law Review and all."

"Yeah, Law Review."

"I'm a managing editor this year. So, that's a lot to do. And this summer was really busy—I was working for a firm out in San Francisco," she said.

"Yeah, David told me you went out there."

"Oh. Sure. Anyway, I just found out that I got a clerkship with a Second Circuit judge, so I'll be here in New York for at least a year after graduation. I'm not sure if I'll go back to San Francisco after that or what."

"Great. Congratulations. Hey, I haven't talked to David in a while. How did he enjoy his summer?"

"Oh, I think it was good," Rachel answered, uncertainly.

"Well, um, say hi to him for me, okay?"

"Sure. I will. And you say hi to Joe."

The conversation left me feeling itchy and incredibly awkward. As Rachel went walking off toward the Law Review office, I wondered if she felt the same way.

"They've offered me a new position at the business school," Joe said, with a smile.

"A promotion?"

"Not just a promotion, a totally different job. A way better job. A position came open in the Student Affairs Department, and the vice dean personally asked me if I'd be interested. I would be running the Student Activities Office, dealing with the B-school equivalents of you law school crazies."

"Wow, congratulations! Did you say yes?"

"Not yet. I wanted to tell you first. But this is pretty much a formality. I'm taking the job no matter what you say. I'm just pretending to consult you so as not to piss you off."

A wise man. "Are you sure you'd enjoy it?" I asked. "I mean, over the past couple of years your exposure has been limited to alumni and donors and stuff. I don't know that you've yet experienced the full extent of the craziness that emanates from students."

"I've spent plenty of time with you and your friends over the past two years, haven't I? I think I'm well equipped." A real comedian. "I think I'd be good at it."

Joe was right. He would be good at it. He had an outgoing yet laid-back personality students could relate to. He had the patience of Job. He could get along with anybody. Joe had always been That Guy whom everyone likes.

"I'm sure you would be. I'm just afraid that you underestimate the evil that lurks within some students. I've seen the condescending way they treat some of the administrators at the law school—it's horrifying. I can't even count the number of times I've heard students whipping out the 'Do you have any idea how much money I pay in tuition?' line when they're unhappy with the tiniest aspect of something going on at the school. I can't imagine having to deal with that day in and day out."

"Martha, I've been dealing with donors for the past two years. Some of them make a fifty-dollar annual pledge and think that should give them the power to dictate how the entire school is run. Don't think I don't know what it's like to deal with obnoxious people."

"I suppose you have a point there."

"Plus a lot of the work I would be doing would be advising the student government, clubs, and athletic teams—I figure the joiners aren't the ones causing trouble. They're the ones having fun at school."

"I wouldn't know. I've never really joined much of anything."

"Yeah, case in point. And as a bonus, I'd be running the Thursday-night happy hours at the business school. Five thousand dollars' worth of sponsorship money each week from Goldman Sachs and Morgan Stanley and Arthur Andersen and the like—and I'd be in charge of it all. Nobody can act too insufferable toward the guy who's putting out eighteen kegs of beer every week, right?"

"*Five thousand dollars* every week to throw a party?" I was floored. The law school hadn't tapped into the sponsorship market, and we had nothing like the business school happy hours. A few times each year we had an event called "Keg in the Hall" that consisted of, quite literally, one lonely keg of beer sitting in the middle of the hallway, usually with about thirty bored students gathered around. I was jealous. Didn't the law school have any idea how much money we paid in tuition? Why couldn't they throw fabulous parties for us each week? "Could you sneak me in?" I asked Joe.

"Absolutely. I'd be in charge."

"Take the job, honey. Congratulations."

Despite the fact that I hadn't really enjoyed my work on the law journal, at the end of my second year I had applied for a third-year editorial position. I really wanted to be able to write something impressive like "Editor in Chief" or "Head Articles Editor" on my résumé, instead of just "Staff Member, *Columbia Journal of Transnational Law*." In the spring of the prior year, we had all been given application materials asking us to rank the editorial positions we were interested in (which ranged from editor in chief, the most prestigious position, to special projects editor and book review editor—neither of which carried much weight). I was looking for something important-sounding but without too terribly much responsibility. And certainly nothing that would require me to read and evaluate the articles sent in for submission—my eyes glazed over just reading the titles of most of the pieces we published. Ultimately, I set my sights on the position of executive editor. It was the second-in-charge position, just under the editor in chief, so it sat impressively high on the masthead. But in comparison to the EIC job, it entailed far less substantive responsibility. I could handle it, I thought. At least I would earn credit for my journal work third year, and that would be one less exam I would have to take each semester.

I sat on pins and needles in my apartment the night the senior staff were to cast their votes and make their decisions.

"You'll get a good slot, Martha," Joe said, reassuringly, as I paced our living room floor.

"I hope so. I can just picture them up there in the journal office, carefully analyzing everyone's application materials. I hope mine hold up. Although I kind of hated it, I did good work for the journal all year. But I know I'm not the only one with my hat in the ring for the executive editor position."

"Well, you'll just have to wait and see, I guess. Are you sure you'll find out tonight?"

"Yeah. Kyle, the editor in chief, said they would call everyone with their decisions," I answered. "I hope I don't end up with something like topical issue editor or special projects editor. Those sound so lame. I want something on my résumé that has pizzazz."

"Wait and see, Martha. Wait and see."

"Although, equally, I hope I don't get elected editor in chief. I'd shit a brick. I mean, I put it down as a position I was interested in just because I felt I had to in order to make myself look serious and committed. But truth be told, I'm not all that serious or committed. I'm banking on them passing me over for someone smarter."

"Heh, it would serve you right if you got it," Joe laughed.

"Shut up! I'm aiming high, but not that high. If I got that job, I'd be miserable. And I'd make you miserable by extension. So you might want to consider placing an anonymous call right now to Kyle telling him that I'm not really all that smart."

Pretending to call my bluff, Joe began reaching for the phone. In mid-reach, it rang. I jumped for it, but he snatched it up, smiling at me playfully.

"Hello?" he answered. "Martha? Hrmmm. I'm not sure if she's home. I think she might have just gone out."

"You give me that phone right this minute, mister," I hissed, quietly.

Joe paused while I did my best to glare a hole straight through his forehead, all the way through to his occipital lobe.

"*Now.* I mean it," I repeated.

Finally, he gave in, smiled at me, and said into the receiver, "Oh, I was wrong, she's here right now. Can I tell her who's calling?"

He smiled, handed me the phone, and said, "It's Lorenzo calling from the journal."

Lorenzo! He's the current executive editor. Please let me have scored his spot! Martha Kimes, Executive Editor. Martha Kimes, Second in Command. Martha Kimes, Very Important Person.

"Oh, hey Lorenzo," I said, in what I hoped was a breezy, nonchalant manner. "What brings you to call?"

"Well, you know that the journal elections were this evening," he began.

"Oh really? I knew they were coming up, but I've been so busy I didn't even remember the exact date," I lied.

"Well, I'm happy to tell you that we chose you to be the next executive editor of the *Journal of Transnational Law.*"

"That's fabulous," I answered. "I'm really excited about taking on the position."

"Now, I know you had your sights set on the editor in chief job. Although it was a hard choice, we decided to give that to Naomi Hayes. I hope you're not too disappointed. Like I said, it was a very difficult decision."

"Not at all," I said, with what was probably an audible sigh of relief. "I mean, of course I was hoping . . . but I know this executive editor position will be a fabulous opportunity. Thanks, Lorenzo."

When it was time for me to assume my executive editor responsibilities at the beginning of my third year, I quickly found out that, despite the respect my position theoretically commanded, my job mainly consisted of making sure the articles looked pretty and were laid out correctly before I sent each edition of the journal off to the printer. I carefully formatted and reformatted the masthead, created tables of contents with pretty dotted tab leaders, made sure there were even margins and consistent fonts, counted spaces after periods, and aligned footnotes correctly.

While not particularly mentally taxing, it involved a lot more work than you'd expect, because I had to do it in WordPerfect 5.1—an ancient word processing program invented a long time before there were Windows and WYSIWYG and pretty graphic displays of exactly what your printed page would look like right there on your computer. No, this was like back in the days of Pong, with nothing but a bunch of pixelated letters on a blue screen with a white flashing cursor. Although the law school's main computers had been upgraded along with the building renovation, our journal wasn't included in the overhaul. So I got to spend hours upon hours in our overheated second-floor office highlighting article titles and hitting "[Shift]+[F6]" to center them and "[Ctrl]+[F8]" to change the font and "[Ctrl]+[F7] 1, 1" to edit the footnotes and, of course, the all important "[Alt]+[F3]" to "reveal codes" and try to figure out what the hell was wrong with the entire document. And then, when I was reasonably sure things looked right, the "[Shift]+[F7]" to print, look it over, notice a few small errors, throw the entire 269-page document into the trash, and start all over. Entire forests were killed during my tenure as executive editor of the *Columbia Journal of Transnational Law.*

"Naomi, do you ever wonder why we signed up for this?" I asked the editor in chief after a particularly frustrating day.

"Are you kidding?" she answered. "We get to shape the direction of the journal—one of the best international law publications in the country. We get to interact closely with faculty and with the authors. We get to learn so much!"

"Oh." *She's one of those?*

"Plus I had a job at a really subpar firm last summer. I'm interviewing again right now, and hoping that having this title on my résumé will get me at a top-tier firm. I'm gunning for the Lavish Law Firm."

Aha! The truth came out.

Despite my occasional frustration over my work at the journal, I enjoyed my opportunity to laugh at the poor second-year students who were stuck cite-checking the note that I had written the previous year, entitled "The Effect of Foreign Criminal Convictions under American Repeat Offender Statutes: A Case Against the Use of Foreign Crimes in Determining Habitual Criminal Status," which had been accepted for publication by the journal. (Note the long, unwieldy title, complete with colon—I'm certain that's why the piece was published.) It was 27 single-spaced pages long with a total of 153 footnotes, many of which contained upwards of 20 individual citations each. I had spent almost a full year writing the piece, and I rued the fact that I had been pretty meticulous in my *Bluebook* form when I had submitted the note for consideration, later realizing that I was depriving the second-year students of the joyous "learning experience" of correcting the form of my footnotes. Oh well, they still got to spend hours on end digging around in the subbasement microfiche looking for the articles I had cited, like "Constitutional Problems in the Execution of Foreign Penal Sentences: The Mexican-American Prisoner Transfer Treaty" from a 1977 edition of the *Harvard Law Review,* and "The Effect of Foreign Criminal Judgments in the United States" from a 1964 edition of the *University of Missouri-Kansas City Law Review,* as well as a book on comparative criminal procedure by an author named Fré Le Poole-Griffiths that was written half in French and which probably was still in off-site storage, even though the library renovation was long since finished.

I was sitting and sweating in the overheated journal office one gray January day when several large cardboard boxes arrived from the printer, addressed to me in my capacity as executive editor. Excitedly, I tore them open and reveled in the beauty that was Volume 35, Issue 2 of the *Columbia Journal of Transnational Law,* on pages 503 through 530 of which appeared my published note. It looked so *official* when formatted and bound in journal form. I had seen the note a million times on a computer screen, or printed out on plain white paper and stapled together. But this was different. I let out a squeal of delight: I was a published author! Someday I was sure to have my own footnote in someone else's unread journal article that, in proper *Bluebook* form, would officially read "Martha Kimes, Note, *The Effect of Foreign Criminal Convictions under American Repeat Offender Statutes: A Case Against the Use of Foreign Crimes in Determining Habitual Criminal Status*, 35 COLUM. J. TRANSNAT'L L. 503 (1997)." Surely the fame and fortune I had long deserved would soon fall in my lap! Would Supreme Court justices call to congratulate me? Would the Sadistic Professor stop me in the hall, just to shake my hand? Recognizing my writing prowess, would Simon & Schuster offer me a book deal? Or, sensing that I had abilities far beyond my legal writing prowess, would William Morris offer to be my talent agent?

Oddly enough, none of those things happened. I was able to walk the streets without adoring fans stopping me for my autograph. No paparazzi were jumping out from behind bushes in an attempt to ambush me. The only people who called to congratulate me were my parents. For my trouble, I got one writing credit on my law school transcript, five full copies of the journal edition that my piece was published in, and twenty-five individually bound copies of the note itself. I paged through those copies dozens of times, marveling at the perfect-looking pages, then sent one to each of my parents. I gave another one to Joe and forced him to take it to work, making him promise that he would show it off to everyone who walked by his office. The remaining twenty-two copies still sit on my bookshelf at home.

"Joe, I want to move," I announced one late January evening.

"Why?" he asked, rather befuddled. "Where?"

"Somewhere. Anywhere. *Off campus.* I can't take it up here anymore. There's no Starbucks nearby, the closest ATM machine is eight blocks away, the restaurants up here suck, there's only one decent bar—we're living in the Manhattan version of Siberia."

Joe tried to respond, but I kept plowing on. "I'm so sick of walking around campus in a sea of undergraduates all dressed in flannel shirts and pants so baggy they're about to fall off. I'm tired of looking at the boxer shorts of nineteen-year-old boys. And I'm tired of the Ph.D. students who have the permanently forlorn looks on their faces after realizing their degrees in medieval literature are never going to get them paying jobs. And the business school students with their shiny laptop cases and rimless eyeglasses—I'm sick of them, too. And let's not mention the law students."

"But Martha, *you're a student,*" Joe pointed out.

"I don't care. I am done with this place."

"Martha, I don't want to move. We've got a great apartment. We've got high ceilings and three whole closets and about seven hundred square feet of space in a doorman building, all for only $935 a month."

I tried another tack. "Well, we're going to have to move anyway once school is over. What's the big deal about leaving a couple of months early?"

"It's only January, and our lease isn't up until the end of June. We're rent stabilized! We're a three-minute walk from both your school and my job! Why would we leave this place a day before we had to?" he asked, quite reasonably.

"Because I don't even feel like I live in New York. It's embarrassing to live up here. I'm practically a Lavish Law Firm lawyer, and you just got a promotion at your job. It's time for us to get a real address. I deserve better. *We* deserve better. Come on, we're entitled to it!"

"Martha, an apartment off-campus would cost a lot more money. I don't want to start living beyond our means. You know how they say, 'If you live like a lawyer when you're still a student, you'll have to live like a student when you're a lawyer?' They say that for a reason."

Joe had a point. But I wasn't giving up. "Just think how great it would be to live on the Upper West Side."

"We already live on the Upper West Side!"

"Well, I suppose you could call this the Upper-Upper-Upper West Side. We need to lose two of those Uppers. I'm calling a realtor and, at the very least, we're going to look at some apartments in the Eighties. You'll change your mind, I know it."

"Don't hold your breath, Martha."

Within the month we had an address on West 83rd Street right off Central Park West, and a duplex apartment with shiny hardwood floors, a working fireplace, exposed brick walls, a real kitchen complete with dishwasher, a wrought-iron spiral staircase that led from the main floor to the bedroom below, and full baths on both levels. We were also paying $1850 a month in rent—double what we were paying up at our subpar Columbia apartment—and we had paid the broker 15 percent of a year's rent for having shown us that one place (that's over $3,000, if you're counting). But it didn't matter. We lived off-campus! It was like we were actual grown-ups!

Never mind the fact that Joe still worked on campus at the business school and I still had classes on campus, and each morning we would trudge all the way back up to 116th Street together. We would wait somberly on the subway platform, marinating in the smell of urine and chicken wings. We would sit stuck in the subway tunnel staring at the innumerable ads for Dr. Zizmor's dermatology services, with his sad-looking smile next to boldface proclamations that "Now YOU can have beautiful, clear skin!" and for "1-800-FOOT-PAIN—We treat feet!" We would wonder aloud exactly how many people had torn earlobes. Neither of us could recall ever seeing anyone with this particular affliction, but we gathered that the number must have been large in order to justify the prevalence of ads for earlobe repair surgery. We would try to decipher the Spanish language public-service serial comic strip "Julio y Marisol," which extolled the virtues of having safe sex, and then scratch our heads at the various poems plastered on the subway walls as a part of the New York City Transit Authority's "Poetry in Motion" campaign. Between the two of us, we got to pay six dollars a day in subway fare to commute, thanks to Martha's Grand Moving Plan.

As the weather began to warm and the trees that lined College Walk slowly began to bloom, spring fever hit me big time. I would walk through campus, watching soccer games on the lawn in front of Butler Library, gazing at the sun-worshipping undergraduates crowding the steps of Low, and feeling terribly sorry for myself and the fact that I was headed back into the bat cave that was the law school to memorize Spanish legal terminology and do yet more [Shift]+[F6] journal formatting.

And then, as I was sitting in the journal office talking to Naomi, I got an idea. Back in December, just after exams were over, she had asked me a favor. She had gotten an offer at the Lavish Law Firm and wanted to celebrate. She found an incredibly cheap last-minute vacation package to Paris, and she and her boyfriend wanted to go for a five-day trip. Would I keep an eye on things at the journal and make sure everything stayed under control? I had said yes, and I was overcome with jealousy when she returned and showed me her pictures of the Louvre and Versailles and the Eiffel Tower and riverboats on the Seine.

Then it dawned on me. If Naomi could take a Parisian vacation, why couldn't I? Sure, she had gone off-season and on the cheap, while I was itching to go to Paris in the springtime, which isn't exactly budget travel season. And sure, she had gone over break and hadn't even missed one class, while I would have to play hooky in order to accomplish my mission. And yes, she and her boyfriend had been saving money for just such a trip, while I would be forced to rely on all of those preapproved credit card offers that had recently begun to flood my mailbox in order to fund my journey. But possibly I should be looking upon those offers as a sign from God telling me I deserved to take such a trip! When again in my life would I be so free and unencumbered, able to skip out on responsibility at a moment's notice?

It really wasn't that difficult to beat Joe into submission and force him to acquiesce. He'd been at the business school for two years and had yet to take any real time off, and he seemed to have a touch of spring fever, too. Before I knew it, we had booked our vacation to Gay Paree. With several weeks to anticipate the trip, I decided to concentrate on learning a little French instead of studying Antitrust. I was determined not to stand out as a tourist, and this necessarily entailed being able to say important things like "Je voudrais une bière très grande" or "Nous avons besoin beaucoup plus de vin, s'il vous plaît" with a thoroughly convincing French accent worthy of Catherine Deneuve or someone equally French and equally chic. I could picture it perfectly: instead of sitting in class or in my down-at-the-heels journal office, I would sit with Joe at a sidewalk café, sipping wine and discussing existentialist philosophy. We would be the absolute pinnacle of sophistication and worldliness. Passersby would mistake us for a reincarnation of Jean-Paul Sartre and Simone de Beauvoir. If only Columbia had offered French for the Legal Profession instead of Spanish, I would have been in primo shape.

When it was time to go, I packed two giant suitcases full of chic clothes (yes, I had used the new credit cards for those, too, but I had kept that a secret from Joe), cute handbags, and impractical shoes. No matter how much walking we might be doing, I steadfastly refused to be the stereotypical American tourist trekking about in a T-shirt and white sneakers. So instead I was a nicely dressed woman with seeping blisters all over my feet hobbling around with my husband—a guy who spent the entire week comfortably walking around in a T-shirt and white sneakers.

But it didn't matter. In Paris, I felt somehow in my element. Although I might not have really spoken the language, understood the culture, or had the slightest clue as to what was going on there, I felt as though it was a place I was meant to be. Surely I would soon be sent on business trips to Paris by the Lavish Law

MARTHA KIMES

Firm, so it was a good thing I was familiarizing myself with the City of Light beforehand, *non? Oui!* As I strolled the Place des Vosges and ambled through the Tuileries gardens, I began to think of it as a prebusiness business trip. Research. Studying. Due diligence! See, I wasn't really shirking my law school responsibilities. I was actually going above and beyond to prepare myself for my burgeoning career.

On one of the first nights we were there, Joe and I went out to dinner at a lovely old hole-in-the-wall bistro, a real neighborhood place that was not at all touristy. As I glanced around the room, looking at the tables covered in white butcher paper, the crusty and ancient waiters, and the chalkboards hanging from the walls featuring the daily menu haphazardly scribbled *en Français,* I silently congratulated myself for picking out a place so very *authentique.* I felt worlds away from Columbia University. And that was a very good thing.

Something about the atmosphere put me in the mood to eat some meat. A nice bloody steak, maybe? A bacon-wrapped beef tenderloin? Possibly some veal? Oh yes, veal! Now, I'm not usually a veal eater, but it was vacation, after all, and nothing counts while you're on vacation. Damn the baby calves who are penned up in those tiny little cages and not ever allowed to take a free step because it would make their muscles less tender when eaten, right?

My eye honed in on the "rognons de veau" listed on the chalkboard menu. "Veau!" I knew that word! Veal! Yes! I wasn't about to consult the French-English dictionary that I had stashed away in my cute little purse—I wanted to seem as though French came naturally to me, as though I was a true Parisienne. Without looking at the dictionary or asking my waiter, I was secure in the knowledge that I would soon be supping on thinly sliced and tender veal lightly breaded and sautéed and served in some sort of wonderful buttery white wine sauce. It would be all self-indulgent and fun and so very different from what I would do in everyday life! Was there veal on the menu at the Hamilton Deli next door to the law school? No, indeed.

A half hour (and a goodly portion of a bottle of wine) later, our food was delivered. Joe, being a man with far greater common sense than me, had ordered steak frites, and got exactly what he expected. Then our waiter deposited a giant tin bucket, complete with a big metal handle, of something that looked like a genetic mutant combination of cauliflower, brains, and mushrooms on a plate in front of me. With nothing else. Except for a big spoon. And then he left, perfunctorily.

I looked at Joe. Joe looked at me. We were quiet for a few moments. Then I said to him, "Maybe it's an appetizer? Mushrooms or something like an *amuse-bouche* to whet my appetite for when they bring out the lovely cutlets of veal in just a few minutes?"

Hesitantly, I took a bite. Quite, um, liverlike. Or maybe not liverlike, but intestinelike. Like a turkey gizzard. Slowly, interminably, about fifteen more minutes went by. I had managed to munch down two or three of my "mushrooms," but was anxiously awaiting my actual meal. Finally, as our waiter passed by, Joe flagged him over. In a voice more akin to a shout (because you *know* foreigners understand you better the louder you talk, right?) and with a horrific and exaggerated fake French accent designed to do nothing but embarrass me, Joe asked, "What . . . no meat for zee laydee?"

The crusty Parisian waiter looked at Joe, scowled, said something unintelligible (unintelligible because we don't speak French), gestured toward my bucket, and left. Frustrated, I decided to do the unthinkable and resort to the dictionary. I pulled it out of my purse and surreptitiously looked up the word *rognons* underneath the cover of the tablecloth, hoping that none of my neighbors would notice what I was doing. And that's how I figured out that I had indeed ordered a big bucket of veal kidneys on purpose. Only by accident. What to do? I was too embarrassed to ask for something else and openly admit my mistake. Similarly, I was loath to let them sit there uneaten, because that would be a tacit admission of error. There was nothing left to do but suck it up, suffer in silence, and cram a sizable bucket of veal kidneys down my throat, because that was definitely preferable to facing the scorn of the waiter.

We spent the rest of the week wandering around Paris, taking in museums, drinking wine in cafés, and eating more cheese than I previously thought humanly possible. I spent the week trying to speak French to poor, unsuspecting taxi drivers, answering *"oui, oui"* (which I pronounced "way, way" in my attempt to sound authentic) to all of their questions because I didn't understand them and didn't know how else to respond. After it became clear on each taxi trip that we were about to become hopelessly lost due to my inept instructions, Joe would finally jump in and, in his fake-accented English, inform the driver of exactly where it was we were trying to go ("Zee laydee mean zat we go to zee Latin Quarter! But do not drive by zee Sorbonne, for zee laydee wants not to be reminded of zee studies zat she is skeeping!").

After a full week of this protocol, we had been all but laughed out of the country, and we were lucky to find a taxi driver willing to take us to the airport. ("To zee airport of zee Charles de Gaulle, please—not zee airport of zee Orly!") On the way home, I made a mental note of the fact that, when it comes down to it, wearing uncomfortable shoes and carrying tiny purses may make you look cute, but it doesn't make you French. Nor does it erase the fact that you're going to have to head straight back to law school upon your return to the great U.S. of A.

The email that awaited me upon my return was short and to the point:

> **From:** The Dean
> **To:** All Third-Year CLS Students
> **Subject:** Mandatory Pro Bono Requirement
> This e-mail is to remind you that all candidates for a
> Columbia J.D. degree must complete 40 hours of

mandatory pro bono legal work as a prerequisite to graduation. Certifications of completion must be turned in to the Dean's Office on or before May 5. A description of qualifying public interest service programs may be obtained from the Director of Public Interest Programs.

I hope this experience will be a rewarding one for everyone and that it will help to remind you all of our collective duty as lawyers to give back to society.

Students' feelings on this "mandatory volunteering" matter were mixed. The students in the Federalist Society were up in arms:

From: Timothy Frankel
To: The Dean; All Third-Year CLS Students
cc: All First-Year CLS Students; All Second-Year CLS Students
Subject: Re: Mandatory Pro Bono Requirement
As I sit looking out my window at the sweeping view of the Statue of Liberty and all of the freedoms that she stands for, I simply cannot stand silent. This "mandatory pro bono" requirement that has been thrust upon us at Columbia Law School is nothing more than an abhorrent attempt at indentured servitude toward the orthodox liberal ideology that this institution blindly supports.

As Alexander Hamilton stated in Federalist Paper Number 78, "It can be of no weight to say that the courts, on the pretense of a repugnancy, may substitute their own pleasure to the constitutional intentions of the legislature. . . . The courts must declare the sense of the law; and if they should be disposed to exercise WILL instead of JUDGMENT, the consequence would equally be

the substitution of their pleasure to that of the legislative body." In this case, the administration of
our school, the school that exists to serve and edu-
cate its students, is substituting and imposing its
own WILL for the collective will of its constituents,
and attempting a logical fallacy by forcing us to
"volunteer" our service.

I cannot and will not stand silent in the face of
such oppression, and I hope my fellow students will
let their voices be heard as well.
—Timothy Frankel

The do-gooders were gleeful:

From: Francesca Giovanni
To: Timothy Frankel; The Dean; All Third-Year CLS
Students
cc: All First-Year CLS Students; All Second-Year CLS
Students
Subject: Re: Re: Mandatory Pro Bono Requirement
I would suggest that the people (yes, I mean YOU,
Timothy) who have such a sense of moral outrage
over the requirement that they give back a small bit
of their time to benefit the less fortunate are probably the ones who could benefit the most from doing
so. Possibly by spending some time aiding victims of
domestic violence, political refugees who have been
subject to human rights abuses, or low-income resi-
dents of our neighboring communities who need
representation in fair housing cases, they might be
able to stop and realize that we at Columbia Law
School are a privileged few, and that we are under a
duty to share the benefits of our place in society
with those in need of our help.

If we need to make a small personal sacrifice for

the greater good (and I seriously question the judgment of anyone who looks at performing a few hours of pro bono work to be a real sacrifice), then I, for one, am happy to do so.

I am considering sending a petition around to other top 20 law schools urging them to adopt mandatory pro bono requirements along the lines of Columbia's. If anyone would be interested in joining me in this endeavor, please respond by e-mail.
—Francesca

p.s. Timothy, I know where you live, and you DON'T have a view of the Statue of Liberty from your apartment window on 112th Street.

The rest of us were all over the map:

From: Natalie Sommer
To: Francesca Giovanni; Timothy Frankel; The Dean; All Third-Year CLS Students
cc: All First-Year CLS Students; All Second-Year CLS Students
Subject: Re: Re: Re: Mandatory Pro Bono Requirement
Francesca, sign me on to the petition. I'd be happy to do whatever it takes to make the conservative zealots that run all too rampant throughout our white male–dominated legal culture realize that it is not only our right, but also our DUTY to mobilize to provide justice for all, not just justice for those who can afford it! Together we can sow the seeds of equity!

From: Jennifer Kohl
To: Francesca Giovanni; Timothy Frankel; The Dean; All Third-Year CLS Students

cc: All First-Year CLS Students; All Second-Year CLS Students

Subject: Re: Re: Re: Mandatory Pro Bono Requirement

Lord knows I hate to agree with Timothy on anything in life, but seriously—doesn't anyone else see the irony in forcing someone to volunteer their time? I've already completed over 80 hours of pro bono work, but I've done it because I wanted to, not because I had to.

—Jen

From: John Balthazar

To: Jennifer Kohl; Natalie Sommer; Francesca Giovanni; Timothy Frankel; The Dean; All Third-Year CLS Students

cc: All First-Year CLS Students; All Second-Year CLS Students

Subject: Re: Re: Re: Re: Mandatory Pro Bono Requirement

Does anybody know if we can just pay a fee or something instead of having to do this pro bono thing?

—John

From: Natalie Sommer

To: John Balthazar; Jennifer Kohl; Francesca Giovanni; Timothy Frankel; The Dean; All Third-Year CLS Students

cc: All First-Year CLS Students; All Second-Year CLS Students

Subject: Re: Re: Re: Re: Re: Mandatory Pro Bono Requirement

MY GOD, JOHN. COULD YOU POSSIBLY BE MORE OF AN ELITIST PRICK?

From: Christopher Banks
To: John Balthazar; Natalie Sommer; Francesca Giovanni; Timothy Frankel; The Dean; All Third-Year CLS Students
cc: All First-Year CLS Students; All Second-Year CLS Students
Subject: Re: Re: Re: Re: Re: Re: Mandatory Pro Bono Requirement
You're all acting like a bunch of assholes. We knew about this requirement when we enrolled at Columbia. Just shut up and do it, already. Personally, I thought being forced to sit through an entire semester of Rosenberg's Property class to be a far more onerous and offensive requirement than this stupid pro bono thing.

From: The Dean
To: Christopher Banks, Natalie Sommer, Francesca Giovanni, Timothy Frankel; All Third-Year CLS Students
cc: All First-Year CLS Students; All Second-Year CLS Students
Subject: Re: Re: Re: Re: Re: Re: Re: Mandatory Pro Bono Requirement
While we here at CLS like to foster an environment that promotes healthy debate, this discussion has deteriorated to a level not befitting this forum, and I will now consider the matter officially closed.

As I stated in my earlier e-mail, certification of completion of 40 hours of qualifying pro bono service must be submitted by each student to my office by 5:00 p.m. on May 5. No exceptions will be made, and extensions will not be granted.

There are a wide variety of qualifying public interest service programs that should suit students of

> any political, religious, or philosophical persuasion, and information on all of these programs may be obtained from Suzanne Riley, Director of Public Interest Programs. Please note that Ms. Riley is not authorized to grant any waivers to the mandatory pro bono requirement or to authorize any nonconforming projects.

Upon my arrival at Columbia, I had lofty intentions of doing tons of pro bono work, but it hadn't panned out that way. As it turned out, I think I liked pro bono work more in hypothetical portions than in actual ones. But I had no choice.

Begrudgingly, I walked into the Center for Public Interest Law and began to peruse their lists of available pro bono placements. At first glance, it seemed as though the opportunities were limitless. I paged through long lists of positions, and started to convince myself that maybe this whole mandatory pro bono thing wouldn't turn out to be so bad. The law school offered options to advocate for international human rights laws; to represent complainants reporting police misconduct; to handle uncontested divorces for needy spouses; to help the homeless with immigration, employment, and family law issues; and to assist claimants appealing the denial of unemployment compensation, just to name a few.

Encouraged, I dug in to make my choice. *Let's see . . . should I help coach junior high school students from Harlem in a mock trial program? That sounds like it might be fun! Oh, wait. The deadline for that project was back in November. Oh well. Should I conduct intake interviews with political asylum seekers? No. Too late for that one, too. All right. Should I assist low-income clients in preparing their tax returns? No—tax season is over next week. Hrmmm. Should I staff a legal clinic at New York Presbyterian Hospital? No, training for that started back in January. Shit. There's got to be some kind of good left to do.*

As it turns out, procrastination gets you nowhere. Which is

how I became a Family Court Advocate: it was one of the small handful of options that were still open to me. I signed up for the program and was given an orientation packet, which explained that my job was to sit in on and observe various Family Court proceedings and to fill out reports after each hearing. The idea was that this would ensure that the Family Court judges weren't giving the shaft to people who were representing themselves without the benefit of attorneys. It wasn't our job to act as actual representatives for any specific party; instead, the idea was that the Family Court judges would be aware of our presence and would be mindful to act in a fair and even-handed way. Which should have been a given, because I'm certain that the word *fair* is in the "judge" job description, but I'm assuming that there were problems somewhere along the line—otherwise, there would have been no need for a Family Court Advocate Program.

So, in late April, I skipped an entire week of classes to perform my civic duty. I trudged downtown through the rain to a building on Lafayette Street, stood in a long, snaking line to pass through a metal detector, and then carefully sought out Room 13C. It was a dismal linoleum-floored room, filled with flimsy plastic chairs that sat facing an ancient spindly wooden desk, behind which sat a middle-aged female judge with a pinched expression on her face. As instructed by my orientation booklet, I introduced myself to her and told her my purpose, and she told me to make myself at home in a plastic chair of my choosing.

Ick. This looks more like the inside of an underperforming urban elementary school than a courtroom. Judge Lovell's courtroom didn't look anything like this. His courtroom had plush, patterned carpet and rich mahogany benches. Here, I'm stuck in a wobbly plastic chair for an entire week. It's only been ten minutes, and my ass is already falling asleep.

I spent exactly forty hours, to the very minute, sitting in that uncomfortable chair and watching proceedings for restraining orders, domestic violence hearings, custody hearings, and various other family law disputes. During many of these hearings, neither party was represented by an attorney. During many, neither party bothered to show up. More often than not, the women looked at me with "Who the hell are you and why are you sitting in this tiny room with me, my ex-husband, and the judge listening to the private details of my personal business?" stares. More often than not, the men looked at me with "Are you writing shit down about me? Are you? You'd better watch it, girlie, or I'll knife you in the hallway" stares. Through it all, I desperately wished I had gotten my act together earlier so I could have done something less miserably depressing. In the end, I wasn't left second-guessing my choice to forgo a career in public service.

As the semester drew to a close, it was time for the third-year editors on my law journal to choose the staff who would be the senior editors the following year. The twenty-seven of us met at the Hell's Kitchen apartment of the head articles editor, ate pizza, drank beer, and talked trash about the second-year students who had applied for our positions.

"I like Alexa Martin. We should make her EIC."

"She didn't even apply for the job! She wants to be head notes editor."

"But the other EIC candidates suck."

"They do not. Marcus Speyer is good."

"But he's got those weird glasses. Also, I hear he's a Republican."

"Well, what about Jacob Burnett?"

"I don't really care, as long as it's not Lori Blanchard. She's such a disaster."

"Well, we've got to give Lori some position. What are we going to do with her? She applied for every single slot."

"I don't know. She's the only one who applied for the financial editor position. But there's no way she's getting near our books. We're going to have to talk someone else into doing it."

"Get me another beer, would you?"

We spent several hours debating, arguing, gossiping, drinking, and coming up with a roster of students who would become our successors. The previous year, I had envisioned the decisions being made so officially, with careful consideration of résumés and qualifications, nominations made following Robert's Rules of Order, secret ballots, and official tallies. Instead it was more like a high school popularity contest. I guess I shouldn't have been surprised.

From: Roberta Harr
To: All Third-Year CLS Students
Subject: Graduation Tickets
I have a large extended family coming in to town to attend graduation. If anyone has extra tickets they're not planning to use, please let me know.
Thanks in advance.
—Roberta

From: Kyle Hoffman
To: All Third-Year CLS Students
Subject: Graduation Tickets Needed
I need six more graduation tickets. If anyone has extras, please let me know. Thanks!

From: Amar Desai
To: Kyle Hoffman
cc: All Third-Year CLS Students
Subject: Re: Graduation Tickets Needed
Me too. I need five more tickets.

From: John Balthazar
To: Kyle Hoffman; Amar Desai
cc: All Third-Year CLS Students
Subject: Re: Re: Graduation Tickets Needed
I have two extra tickets that I'm willing to sell for $40 each. Let me know if you're interested.

From: Zach Webster
To: All Third-Year CLS Students
Subject: Graduation Tickets For Sale
Four graduation tickets for sale. $35 each or best offer.

From: Tricia McConnell
To: All Third-Year CLS Students
Subject: Graduation Tix
I have 3 tix to sell. $34 each.

From: Amar Desai
To: Tricia McConnell
cc: All Third-Year CLS Students
Subject: Re: Graduation Tix
I'll take them.

From: Robert Glatzer
To: All Third-Year CLS Students
Subject: Graduation Tickets
I've got two. $30 each.

From: Jon Atillo
To: All Third-Year CLS Students
Subject: Graduation Tickets
I have four tickets to sell for $28 each.
—Jon

From: The Dean
To: All Third-Year CLS Students
Subject: Graduation Tickets
Importance: High
Due to space limitations at Alice Tully Hall, each graduating student has been allotted six tickets to the commencement ceremony. We realize that some

students have larger families that plan to be in attendance and need extra tickets. We also realize that
other students will have fewer guests and will not
need to use all of the tickets allotted to them.

Nevertheless, let me make it clear that **graduation tickets may NOT be sold, bartered, or otherwise exchanged**. Anyone who is not planning to use
all of their tickets should inform the Student Services
Office, and all extra tickets will be assigned at random to students in need.
Thank you.

From: Charles Whitmore III
To: The Dean; All Third-Year CLS Students
Subject: Graduation Tickets
I still need two more tickets. And I don't appreciate
being called a "student in need." If anybody's still
selling, I'm buying.
—Chaz

Both of my parents had decided to come to New York for my
graduation—a fact that made me both excited and terrified. Neither of them had been to New York before, neither were exactly
what you would call "cosmopolitan," both had the potential to
embarrass me greatly in front of my classmates, and, to top it all
off, the two of them weren't on speaking terms. I didn't begin to
relax about the situation until I realized that I was going to be on
stage most of the day—it was Joe who would have to play inter-
mediary between the warring parties. For that, I didn't envy him.
But this is what husbands are for.

Despite my eagerness to graduate, I found myself less than
excited by most of the pregraduation activities. Somehow I just
couldn't picture myself going on a group trip to an amusement
park in New Jersey or on a "final farewell" canoe adventure or to
a class picnic where we would inevitably end up playing dizzy

bats and having tricycle races and briefcase-tossing contests. Couldn't we have class wine tastings or farewell dinners at Lutèce or group cocktail parties at the Rainbow Room? Apparently not. What were we? In junior high school? No! Despite the obvious similarities, we were about to be Ivy League Lawyers, so weren't such shenanigans beneath us? I, for one, knew they were beneath *me*. No dizzy bats were going to be touching *this* girl's forehead, that was for sure.

The one graduation event I did go to was the Graduation Ball—a formal affair held at a rented-out mansion somewhere in Murray Hill. Joe and I dressed to the nines and sprang for a taxi ride downtown. As the music played and the liquor flowed, the atmosphere in the entire venue slowly changed through the night until, when it approached the midnight hour, everyone in the whole place was like one extended family. Antisocial people had come out of their shells, Law Review demigods had stooped to talk to us mere mortals, the cool folks were mixing with the geeks, everyone reminiscing about our time together and discussing postgraduation plans. The hundreds of us there were all buddy-buddy and sentimental with people we hardly knew.

"Martha! It's been so awesome knowing you. All the best to you after graduation!" exclaimed a guy who I vaguely remembered from first year.

"I'll miss you, too, Robert!" I replied.

"Actually, it's Jack."

"Jack! Yes, Jack! Are you staying here in the city to work? We should have lunch!" I said, in what seemed like a brilliant idea at the time.

"That sounds great. Let's do that!"

"Okay, Robert, let's!"

Just as the liquor had forged friendships on our orientation cruise, it seemed to be reestablishing them on the eve of graduation. Everyone was reunited—except for me and Rachel, who hadn't shown up. Deep down, I had hoped that possibly our friendship could be rekindled, if even for an hour or so, in the sentimental, booze-filled atmosphere. I guess it wasn't meant to be.

Meanwhile, Katie, Elizabeth, and I, along with a bunch of other friends who we had tacked on over the years, downed scotch and soda at the open bar as we opened ourselves up to a bit of sap, reminiscing about our first-year fear, our second-year insanity, and our recent third-year boredom. We gave each other teary, sentimental hugs, and then we trickled off on our separate ways. I think we were all worried we'd end up losing touch. We had been close during school, but distance often doesn't bode well for friendships. Elizabeth was headed off to a giant firm in Boston, and Katie was headed back to work for the Public Defender's Office in Los Angeles, where her boyfriend, Josh (who had recently proposed), awaited her.

Long after midnight, Joe and I decided that it was finally time to pack it in and haul our asses back uptown. As we wound our way toward the exit, we were physically stopped by a drunken, slurring Sean Jacoby, hands down the biggest partier in our class, as witnessed by the fact that early on in our tenure, he had been voted "Most Likely to Go to Betty Ford." Sean, who I had not known well in the first place and who I don't think I had talked to in at least two years, had run up behind me and goosed me. As I tried to crane my head around to see who had assaulted me, he announced, "Martha! *Martha!* I gonna misssss you. You're an awesome friend. Remember Civil Procedure classss? I loved Civil Procedure classs. Sometimes I hardly went to Civil Procedure classs though. I got a C in Civil Procedure class. But anyway, let's do a shot."

"Oh, Sean, I don't think so," I replied, knowing that I had already passed my limit. *A C? He got a C? I didn't think they gave Cs!*

"We're graddddduating! This may be the lassst time we ever see each otherrr! Bartender, two shotss of Jägermeister, please!" he demanded.

"Sean, I can't drink that stuff. I can't!"

"You mussst! Oh, wait, there's your boyfriend. Tom, come do a shot with us!" Sean shouted. "Bartender, make that three shots!"

"Joe. He's my husband and his name is Joe," I corrected him.

"Joe! Yesssss, Joe! I'll miss you so much, too! Are you guys staying in the city to work? We should all get together for lunch sometimessss!" he announced.

As soon as the bartender set the shots of Jägermeister in front of us, Joe and Sean promptly put theirs back while, without concern for the fancy clothing of anyone who might have happened to be standing right behind me, I tossed the sticky brown liquid from my shot glass straight over my shoulder. And then we departed. It was time to get this graduation thing over with.

On the morning of graduation, I donned my slate blue satin gown with black velvet lapels and my puffy, octagon-shaped cap, brimming with excitement that the end was finally in sight. In the morning, there was a university-wide commencement ceremony for all the undergraduate, graduate, and professional students receiving degrees that semester—close to eight thousand students total. It was a sunny but rather chilly May day, and the entire main campus quad was a sea of thousands upon thousands of tiny white chairs that facilities people had spent the past week setting up. We all sat in groups by school, and there were fifteen Columbia schools in total represented (everything from Columbia College to the School of Dental and Oral Surgery to the School of International and Public Affairs).

The president of the university stood on the steps of Low Library and gave an address, then the deans of each respective school gave separate speeches introducing their school's students: "Mr. President, it is my pleasure to present to you the finest group of soon-to-be dentists in the history of Columbia University!" "Never again will you find a more accomplished group of future architects!" When the Business School graduates were recognized as a group, they all threw Monopoly money into the air; when the dean of the Medical School spoke, the med students tossed around inflated surgical gloves; when the Journalism graduates were introduced, they tossed newspapers high into the sky. When we Law School graduates were recognized, we did nothing special because, really, were we going to throw ten-pound casebooks into the air? Do you know what kind of liability that would open us up to?

That evening's graduation ceremony, which was held at Alice Tully Hall in Lincoln Center, was ours and ours alone. I felt almost regal as I walked past the giant fountain, gazing into the brightly lit windows of the majestic Metropolitan Opera House that stood across the courtyard. We law students were carefully broken down into groups, given different stations at which to line up, inspected as to the straightness of our caps and gowns, and instructed by a drill sergeant as to when to begin our procession to our assigned seats on stage—each group arriving from a different direction, but all of us somehow ending up seated alphabetically. Balanchine himself couldn't have choreographed it better.

Speeches were given by every person imaginable: the dean, who congratulated us and stressed our collective duty to give back to society; our elected class speaker, who reminded us of our duty as lawyers to speak up in the face of injustice and wrongdoing; Marion Wright Edelman (president of the Children's Defense Fund), who gave a politically charged speech that seemed a little bit inappropriate for a graduation ceremony; various students and professors who had won awards, who gave words of appreciation; and the president of our student senate, who presented the dean with our class gift—an embarrassingly small amount of money that we had managed to scrape together as a class, with probably only about 25 percent of the students participating. And then our names were called, one by one. We each got to file individually across the stage, shake the dean's hand, get our photograph taken with him, and proceed backstage to receive our actual diploma.

When my name was called, I was surprised to hear what

seemed to be a cacophony of hoots and hollers from my fellow students, instead of just a polite clap from the audience and a little whistle from Joe and my parents. Who were these people cheering for me? Did I have more friends than I knew about? Or were people still feeling friendly and sentimental like they had been at the Graduation Ball? Was everyone still drunk?

I smiled as I walked across the stage, shook the dean's hand, and posed for my photo, and then I ran backstage to get in line for my diploma. Until that sucker was in my hands, it wouldn't seem real. And once I got it, it still didn't seem entirely real, partly because the diploma itself made no sense at all:

CVRATORES·VNIVERSITATIS·COLVMBIAE

NOVEBORACENSIS

OMNIBVS ET SINGVLIS AD QVOS PRAESENTES LITTERAE
PERVENERINT SALVTEM SCIATIS NOS

MARTHA HELEN KIMES

CVM EXERCITATIONES OMNES AD GRADVM

IVRIS DOCTORIS

ATTINENTES RITE AC LEGITIME PEREGERIT AD ISTVM GRADVM
PROVEXISSE EIQVE OMNIA IVRA PRIVILEGIA ET HONORES QVAE
ADSOLENT IN TALI RE ADTRIBVI DEDISSE ET CONCESSISSE
IN CVIVS REI PLENIVS TESTIMONIVM CHIROGRAPHIS PRAESIDIS
HVIVS VNIVERSITATIS ET DECANI COLLEGII IVRIS NEC NON
SIGILLO NOSTRO COMMVNI DIPLOMA HOCCE MVNIENDVM CVRAVIMVS
DATVM NOVI EBORACI DIE VICESIMO PRIMO MENSIS MAII
ANNOQVE MILLESIMO NONGENTESIMO NONAGESIMO SEPTIMO

Despite all the Latin terms that had been shoved down my throat during the previous three years, the only words I recognized were *Martha Helen Kimes, Diploma,* and *Die.*

As I was contemplating the words *Cvratores Vniversitatis*

Colvmbiae and wondering whether that was the name of the school at which I had suffered these last three years or whether it was the name of some sort of gum disease, I was struck with a realization: IT DOESN'T MATTER ANYMORE. *It doesn't matter! A diploma is a diploma! I SURVIVED! It's all downhill from here! As God is my witness, I'll never have to study again! Suck on that, you first-year students!*

After the ceremony came to a close, Joe found me in the crowd in the lobby and ran up to me with a giant embrace. "You did it!" he shouted, right before he gave me a giant kiss.

"No, honey . . . *we* did it," I answered. "Together. You kept me sane through it all."

"*That* was you being sane?"

Twelve

BELLY UP TO THE BAR

"There is nothing so stupid as the educated man if you get him off the thing he was educated in."

—WILL ROGERS

"Woohoo!" I yelled to Joe the morning after graduation as I jumped out of bed. The champagne bubbles were still resonating through my head, and I was manic with excitement. "Finished! I graduated! I can't believe I'm really free! No more studying! No more books! No more outlines! No more classes! I'm done!" I was speaking so quickly that I was tripping over my own words. "I've got to start making plans for the summer. I've got a $15,000 advance on my salary from the Lavish Law Firm burning a hole in my pocket, and I don't start work until the end of August—that's three months from now. What should I do with all my time? Start watching soap operas all day? Take up Rollerblading? Learn origami? Oh, I know, let's plan a vacation! It's been two whole months since we were in Paris. We deserve another vacation!"

"Well, I don't know, honey—"

"We could go somewhere nice and romantic. Italy, maybe, the Amalfi coast! We could stay at Le Sirenuse and swim in that gorgeous-looking pool atop the pale rocky cliffs overlooking the Mediterranean and eat fresh fish and homemade pasta and take drives along the winding Italian roads. We could take a day trip to Capri!"

"Martha—"

"What, you don't like that? Okay, we could go to the Caribbean. Find an upscale resort on the white, powdery sands of Anguilla and drink mai tais while we watch the sun set over the turquoise ocean. We could learn to scuba dive!"

"But—"

"No good? Well, what about Provence? We could stay in the Lubéron in a hilltop village surrounded by fields of rosemary and lavender, visiting wineries, drinking Pernod, and eating produce handpicked by local farmers each and every day!"

"I don't think—"

"No? What about Belize? We could spend half the trip at some deserted beach, snorkeling over the second-largest coral reef in the world, and then the other half we could spend at a spa in the rain forest, getting massages and mud wraps after a long day of hiking and watching howler monkeys!"

"*Martha!*"

"What? Stop interrupting me!"

"What about the bar?"

"The bar? Joe, I know it's Saturday, but it's only eleven o'clock in the morning—a little bit early to start drinking."

"Not that kind of bar. The *New York Bar Exam.* Hello? Have you forgotten that you have to take the bar exam in July?"

"Oh. Shit. Yeah. That."

"Yeah. That."

"Well, that kind of throws a wrench into that whole 'As God is my witness, I'll never have to study again' crap that I've been spewing, doesn't it?"

"Kind of."

As it turns out, graduating from law school alone wasn't really going to get me very far. Because until I'd (1) passed the bar exam, (2) undergone a character and fitness examination, and (3) been officially sworn in to the bar by a judge, I couldn't actually call myself a lawyer. (Since I had never been arrested, indicted, or disbarred in another state, steps two and three would be mostly formalities, but step one most definitely was not.) The bar exam is a two-day-long test, and I had to pass if I wanted to justify all the money I borrowed in order to attend law school and the three years of blood, sweat, and tears I put into my studies. So there was no pressure involved or anything.

Some states are known for having fairly easy bar exams. New York is not one of those states. New York and California are widely regarded as having the most difficult bar exams in the country. Each July, approximately nine thousand people sit for the bar exam in New York. Usually, somewhere around 70 percent of them pass. (An additional three thousand or so people take the exam each February, many of them people who failed it the previous July. The pass rate for the February exam is usually only about 50 percent.)

One full day of the exam is dedicated to what is called the Multistate Bar Exam portion, which is a set of two hundred multiple-choice questions asking about generally accepted rules of law (as opposed to the law of any one particular state), testing applicants on contracts, torts, constitutional law, criminal law and procedure, evidence, and real property. The questions require test-takers to analyze complex fact situations, take positions as advocates, interpret statutory language, and offer advice as to structuring transactions. The Multistate Bar Exam is given to students sitting for the bar in every state across the country on the same day.

The other day of the exam is devoted to New York substantive and procedural law, and it focuses largely on a set of essay questions. It covers New York–specific law as to all six of the subject matters covered on the Multistate Bar Exam, and additionally addresses the New York laws of agency, commercial paper, conflict of laws, corporations, domestic relations, equitable remedies, federal jurisdiction and procedure, mortgages, New York practice and procedure, no-fault insurance, partnership, personal property, professional responsibility, secured transactions, wills, trusts, and workers' compensation. One would note that this is *a lot* of subjects. And, conveniently, much of New York law differs from the "common law" that is tested on the Multistate portion of the exam. So that leaves you having to remember picky little differences: on the Multistate day of the exam you should say that lifetime employment contracts *are* within the statute of frauds, but on the New York day you should say that such contracts *are not;* for the Multistate portion of the exam there are *four* different types of torts relating to the invasion of privacy, but on the New York portion of the exam there is only *one.*

I, personally, had several problems with this whole setup.

First of all, in law school I had not studied three-quarters of the subjects that the bar exam would test. Commercial paper? *What?* No-fault insurance? *Huh?* New York practice and procedure? *Excuse me?* Wills and trusts? *I don't think so.* Agency? *What's that?*

Second, even as far as the subjects that I *had* studied in school, I didn't begin to know what was necessary to pass the bar. They don't teach you what you need to know in law school, at least not in my law school. Columbia, like most elite institutions, prides itself on teaching students how to "think like lawyers," not necessarily how to *be lawyers* or how to *do what lawyers do* or how to *sue someone* or how to *give someone legal advice.* For example, in my Torts class, we had learned about the economic impact of various tort reforms, wrestled with questions about who should properly bear the costs of life's misfortunes, and argued about whether a comparative negligence system or a contributory negligence system was more societally correct and just. But we hadn't learned one lick about battery or trespass to chattels or conversion or defamation—the types of things the bar exam would be testing us on.

Faced with this complete lack of relevant knowledge, there was only one reasonable option: to take a professional bar review course (and to let the Lavish Law Firm pay my $2,000 tuition, of course). Most applicants sitting for the bar exam take a prep class—in light of all the material tested, you'd have to be crazy not to—and the most popular course is run by a company called BAR/BRI. They offer a six-week-long crash course in all things bar-related: a comprehensive program of outlines, lectures, workshops, and simulated tests to maximize students' ability to pass the bar exam.

The class was offered at numerous locations around the city, including a daily lecture at Columbia Law School, where most of my friends were planning to study. I spent about five minutes contemplating taking the class at my alma mater, but then thought better of it as soon as I remembered the intense mindfuck competition that had been my first year of law school. I had a sneaking suspicion that studying for the bar would bring out the evil in people even more than the first-year experience had, and I saw no need to put myself through that ordeal all over again. Instead, I decided to take the class in a Times Square location, hoping that would allow me to study in an environment that would perhaps be a bit more rational than that of Columbia Law School.

Ready to take on the world, I walked into the Times Square skyscraper where the BAR/BRI offices were housed, poised for my first class. I took my place in a giant, snaking line, and eventually presented my ID, signed in, and was handed close to forty pounds of books and course outlines, all stuffed into a canvas BAR/BRI tote bag. I lugged them all into the classroom where, instead of seeing a lecturer in front of the class, I saw a large television set. Soon, a real live woman walked into the room, introduced herself, and gave us an overview of how the course would run. Our classes would meet for four hours daily, Monday through Friday, for the next six weeks, where we would watch videotapes of lectures delivered by professors. (After she left the stage, there were no more live people for us.)

In order to stay on track, we were expected to spend between five and nine hours each day studying the materials, in addition to our class time. We should review the appropriate BAR/BRI subject matter outline before each class, and after class we should review and digest our class notes and complete the assignments listed in our program guide. We would be assigned various sample New York essay questions to complete each week, which would be graded and returned to us, and toward the end of the six-week class, we would take a simulated Multistate Bar Exam at the Jacob Javits Convention Center, where we would be taking the actual bar exam in late July. After the prep class was over, there would be a two-week period where we would need to devote ourselves 100 percent to studying and memorizing.

After delivering this news, the woman announced that we would be diving right into our first of three lectures on evidence, pressed the "play" button on the VCR, and walked away, leaving us alone with a man on the TV who was discussing the definition of "relevance" and trying painfully hard to be funny.

But at least I had taken Evidence in school. I had even liked it. I had even *remembered* much of it. So I felt free to let my mind wander a bit. I surveyed the room around me, wondering if I would catch sight of a familiar face, but instead I was surrounded by a sea of strangers.

And then I smelled my advantage. *Wait. Those aren't just strangers. They're strangers wearing CUNY LAW T-shirts. CUNY is a Tier 4 school . . . And those strangers over there are carrying Pace Law School backpacks. Pace is Tier 4, too. Look, there's a girl with a New York Law School sweatshirt. That's third tier! And over there are a bunch of people drinking from insulated Hofstra coffee mugs. Hofstra is ranked #95 compared to Columbia's #4! Doesn't that mean that I am, by definition, smarter than all of these people? Better than all of these people? MORE LIKELY TO PASS THE BAR than all of these people? Maybe this whole thing won't be so bad after all!*

That night, after I returned home, I was beaming. "Joe, you're not going to believe this. I'm in a class surrounded by a bunch of people from these subpar law schools. There wasn't one person from Columbia there! This is going to be a piece of cake. Cake, I tell you! I'm getting ready to sit back, relax, and enjoy my summer."

"Don't get ahead of yourself there, dearie. I've heard that the New York bar exam is plenty tough."

"Whatever. It's not like I've got very stiff competition. Get me a beer, would you?"

Briefly (and oh so wrongly) confident in my intellectual superiority, I sat through hours and hours and hours of videotaped lectures on domestic relations, secured transactions, wills, trusts, and New York practice. I was taken aback by the sheer volume of material. For each subject, there were lectures, lecture notes, BAR/BRI big outlines, BAR/BRI small outlines, BAR/BRI bulleted lists, BAR/BRI charts, Conviser Mini Review mini-outlines with bulleted lists and charts, and practice essay and multiple-choice questions, complete with model answers and explanations. And there was no time to let it sink in: before I could even finish reviewing the materials on one subject, we were already on to the next.

I would sit in the daily lectures, trying to take note of picky, incomprehensible rules that I was expected to memorize: an interlocutory paper is deemed served when it is mailed (not when it is received); both "leave and mail" service of process (where the server delivers process to a person of suitable age and discretion at the defendant's residence, and then mails a copy by first-class mail) and "nail and mail" service of process (where the server affixes process to the door of the defendant's residence and then mails a copy by first-class mail) are complete ten days after proof of service is filed. (And yes, I laughed out loud when our videotaped lecturer uttered the words *nail and mail*, because I had the emotional sophistication of a twelve-year-old boy. Quite possibly, I still do.) But, I thought, if *I* was having trouble grasping all of this, surely all of the academic plebeians around me were, too. They were undoubtedly having much, much more trouble than I was, right?

And then I listened to the whispers coming from the people around me. Slowly, I began to realize exactly how wrong I had been.

From my right, a girl in a CUNY LAW shirt said to her friend, "I swear, this is so useless. I mean, didn't we learn all this already during New York Procedure class second year?"

What? At CUNY, they took a class called New York Procedure? Before this class, I'd never even heard *of New York Procedure.*

From my left, I heard a guy with a New York Law School notebook whisper, "I thought the statute of limitations for medical malpractice was two years, not three and a half. I remember it being on Professor Korn's exam."

How does that guy know this stuff? Did someone teach him this stuff already?

From behind, someone with a giant Pace Law backpack that was overflowing into the middle of the aisle and pushing up against my desk grumbled, "That guy forgot to mention that the plaintiff can make an ex parte motion to the court for an order allowing an improvised method of expedient service if the other methods aren't practicable."

Am I the ONLY ONE HERE who is clueless about New York practice? I'm an IVY LEAGUE GRADUATE! I'm headed off to work at the Lavish Law Firm! I'm supposed to be superior! Where is the justice?!?

As it turned out, while I had been busy at my fancy school cite-checking lofty journal footnotes and taking negotiation seminars and studying European Community law and blowing off Spanish for the Legal Profession and having my mind filled with legal theory, those people from the "lesser schools" had been learning actual, practical, useful, bar exam–relevant law. They had been taking classes in wills and trusts and New York procedure. While I had been learning how to think like a lawyer, they had been learning how to *be* lawyers. And that put them in far better shape than me.

And to add to the humiliation, they traveled in packs. While I attended class alone each day, away from my former classmates who were studying on campus, everyone around me attended bar review class with friends. On more than one occasion, I was asked if I'd mind switching seats, so as to allow a pack of St. John's students to sit together and whisper through the lecture. Alone and embarrassed, I acquiesced.

My group of friends had dissipated after graduation. Katie was studying to take the bar in California, and Elizabeth was off in Boston. Rachel and David had broken up—one week before they were set to move off-campus to an expensive new Upper East Side apartment together. By that point, it seemed as if it had been ages since I had really been friends with Rachel, but I was still in regular contact with David. (Throughout the third year of law school, David had showed up at our apartment almost every Friday night with a twelve-pack of Miller Lite in his hand—that right there is true friendship.) That summer, however, he was even worse company than I was: depressed over being dumped, frantic over studying for the bar, and freaking out that Fordham's pass rate was lower than Columbia's. Whenever we did talk, he would spend the majority of the conversation lecturing me about how I had a 7 percent better chance of passing than he did (overall, Columbia had around a 93 percent pass rate to Fordham's 86 percent), and things usually went downhill from there. But David, too, had taken a class in New York procedure at Fordham, putting him at least a few steps ahead of me.

So, aside from the four daily hours of class time, I spent the rest of the summer holed up at my desk, studying all alone, apologizing to God and mankind for the elitist thoughts I had allowed to inhabit my soul, and secretly wishing I had gone to Hofstra Law School.

In bar review class, we were repeatedly told that we should not be aiming for perfection. Far from it: the exam was pass or fail, and achieving a score that was 20 points above the passing mark meant that was 20 points worth of studying you had wasted. Minimal proficiency was the goal—enough to pass, but nothing more. They told us that BAR/BRI students set the curve for the bar exam: since over 50 percent of test-takers took that very course, if the test addressed an issue that we hadn't covered, a majority of the test-takers would all be in the same boat and, ultimately, it wouldn't matter. We should just concentrate on what they told us to study, and forget about trying to master the rest.

Do you have any idea how hard it is to transfer your entire mode of thinking from "if it's not better than a B, it's akin to failure" to "minimal proficiency is fine, because a D is still a passing grade"? For me, it simply wasn't possible. I've always been skilled at taking multiple-choice tests, so I wasn't so terribly apprehensive about the Multistate portion of the exam, relatively speaking. There were so many questions that if I had to guess at some of them, it wasn't the end of the world. But the thought of the New York essays had me lying awake at night with fear. What if they asked me to write an essay about something I wasn't even minimally proficient in? There weren't many essays, so each one counted for a big chunk of my score. What if I took BAR/BRI's advice and just skimmed over the rule saying that unwitnessed, handwritten wills are invalid except when written by mariners at sea and by members of the armed forces during declared or undeclared war, and then I got hit with an essay question testing that very fact? What then? I would be stuck staring at a blank answer book, guaranteed complete failure. I would have to admit my defeat to the Lavish Law Firm, retake the bar exam in February, and forever go down in history as an Official Loser.

No. It wasn't going to happen to me. I refused to participate in a minimum proficiency curve. Instead, I spent every waking moment with my nose buried in my books and outlines. I lived and breathed bar prep. I rewrote my notes each day after class in multicolored pens, I memorized arcane details of the law of domestic relations that I'm certain even the New York Bar Examiners knew nothing about, I had vivid dreams about UCC Article 9 secured transactions, and I occasionally awoke in the middle of the night to write out the answers to random practice essay questions. I stopped eating. I re-restarted smoking. I quadrupled my caffeine intake. I ignored Joe's repeated exhortations to chill the fuck out, already. In short, I was even more crazed than I had been before my first-year law school exams. And for good reason. This was The Big One.

The people at BAR/BRI had repeatedly stressed that, on the day before the exam, we should all quit studying by five in the evening, that we would have learned all that was humanly possible by that point, and it would benefit us to relax, go out for dinner, get to bed early, and get a good night's sleep so we would wake up rested on the day of the exam. They likened the bar exam to running a marathon, and pointed out that reasonable people aren't going out for one last training run at eleven o'clock the night before the big race.

I tried to listen to them. I really did.

I shut the last of my books at 4:59 p.m. on the day before the exam. But I couldn't help myself from sitting on the couch, chewing my fingernails, rocking back and forth, and silently reciting mnemonic devices in my head until Joe finally arrived home from work. (What are the testamentary substitutes to which the elective share rule applies? *TS LEG UP. T*otten trust accounts, *S*urvivorship estates, *L*ifetime transfers with strings attached, *E*mployee pension plans, *G*ifts made within one year of death, *U*.S. government bonds, and *P*owers of appointment.)

I made Joe take me to dinner at my favorite neighborhood Mexican restaurant, in an effort to follow the BAR/BRI "have a relaxing dinner" edict, but I don't know if I would describe the scene as particularly relaxing.

After we were seated at our table, I opened my menu and promptly ignored it, instead imagining myriad creative doomsday scenarios involving myself, a newly sharpened number two pencil, and a bar exam answer booklet.

"Martha?" Joe asked.

No response. I was lost in thought.

"Martha?"

Again, I didn't even hear him.

"*Martha?!?*"

"Huh? What?" I finally answered, snapping out of my night-mare fantasy.

"Are you okay?"

"Joe, I'm anything but okay." I was both sweaty and cold at the same time. I could feel the pressure building up behind my temples.

"You've got this thing in the bag. You'll do fine."

"What if I don't? I'm going to die if I'm one of *those people* who fails. I mean, I can name for you right now the four people from Columbia who didn't pass last year's exam. Within two hours after the results were announced, their names had been gossiped around the whole school and forever immortalized. I can't be one of those people, Joe. I can't!"

And then I started sobbing into our complimentary basket of tortilla chips, my face bright red, my shoulders heaving, and the people around us staring.

"Honey, stop," Joe said quietly. "You're just exhausted. You've studied so hard all summer. You know this stuff inside and out. I have confidence in you."

"I'm not trying to be irrational here," I said, trying to catch my breath. "I'm really not. But it's just too overwhelming. It's *so much material.* I'm afraid I'm going to forget it all overnight. I've already forgotten what the statute of limitations for shareholder derivative actions is."

"Don't worry. It will all come back to you when you need it."

"You know what I need?" I said, trying to crack a joke. "I need a drink. But the BAR/BRI people said no alcohol the night before the exam. And when could you possibly need alcohol more than the night before the bar exam?" I laughed weakly.

"Martha? If you're not up for this dinner, maybe we should just go home and go to bed."

"Yeah, maybe we should. I guess I don't really need the remnants of some cheap enchiladas rumbling around in my stomach tomorrow. And I'm not really very hungry anyway."

So I let Joe take me home. Before I went to bed, I decided to pack the things that I would be taking to the exam, to save myself some time in the morning. I got out the admission ticket that I had received in the mail several weeks earlier, and perused the detailed list of rules pertaining to the exam that had been enclosed along with it. Specifically, as per the New York Bar Examiners, the rules state:

> Applicants are not permitted to bring any items into the examination other than a clear plastic food storage type bag (maximum size one gallon) which may contain: admission ticket, government issued photo ID, wallet, quiet snack/lunch, hygiene products, earplugs, pens, #2 pencils, erasers, highlighters, beverage in plastic container or juice box (20 oz. maximum size), medications, and tissues.

Hygiene products? I guess that means I can bring some tampons. I don't really need them, should I bring them anyway? Nah. And I can bring a twelve-ounce box of Juicy Juice. But not a can of Diet Pepsi, because aluminum is verboten. Are they afraid we're going to go crazy during the bar exam, rip the cans apart with our teeth, fashion homemade shanks, and then lunge for the proctors? And more important, how can I survive this two-day exam without Diet Pepsi? I suppose I could bring in a little plastic bottle of Diet Pepsi, but I hate the way it tastes out of a bottle. And I'm going to need some sort of snack, otherwise I get that dizzy low blood sugar thing. What counts as a "quiet snack"? Probably not carrot sticks—too crunchy. That probably rules out apples, too. And Doritos. Crap, those things right there, along with SlimFast, pretty much constitute my entire diet. And the SlimFast is out because of the whole aluminum-can thing. What

MARTHA KIMES

am I supposed to bring? Pudding? String cheese? A bento box of sushi? I know: grapes! Yes. Juicy Juice and grapes: THE ACCOU-TREMENTS OF CHAMPIONS.

After I packed my things and set out my clothes for the morning (the BAR/BRI people had strongly advised us to wear layers, because the temperature at the Javits Center was notoriously unpredictable), I tried for the restful night's sleep, but it didn't happen. I defy you to find anyone who had a restful night's sleep before the bar exam. Unless, of course, they broke the BAR/BRI rule and drank themselves into a brain cell–killing slumber.

The Jacob K. Javits Convention Center is a giant exhibition hall that is rather ill-suited to host thousands of crazed recent law school graduates sitting for the New York Bar Exam. It contains over 800,000 square feet of exhibition space, taking up more than five acres of prime Manhattan real estate. The entire complex is generally rather dirty, it is made of a Tinker Toy–like construction that has resulted in leaky ceilings, and it is alternatingly freezing cold and boiling hot, often within the same fifteen-minute span of time. Oh, and it's almost impossible to get to without being hit by a bus while you try to run across Eleventh Avenue.

When I arrived, an hour before the exam was to begin, I felt as if I was walking into a combat zone. Security guards stood before each entrance door and in front of all the restrooms, there to ensure that no one was stashing cheat sheets in the potty stalls. An ambulance was on standby for medical emergencies. An armored car, complete with armed guards, had delivered the official test packets earlier that morning. Hundreds of proctors were patrolling the exam halls. And all of the test-takers had a look of terror in their eyes, as though we were being sent off to war.

Through the echoing hallways, terrifying rumors were passed around. One guy was swearing that, the previous year, a man had a heart attack in the middle of the exam, and the gentleman sitting next to the victim tried to resuscitate him. Rumor had it that the heart attack victim survived, but the good Samaritan wasn't given any extra time, and he failed the exam. Another woman was telling a story of an applicant who simply went crazy during the middle of the Multistate exam and began running up and down the aisles of the test center screaming "I'm a covenant and I'm running with the land!" Someone else said they heard that a woman had jumped off the top of the New York Hilton hotel after the exam one July, and the storyteller's companion responded, "Yes, but I heard that her jump lacked organization and missed several crucial points, so she was forced to jump again the next February." I wasn't amused.

At eight-fifteen we were allowed to enter our testing rooms. I'm sure that at least some of the space in the Javits Center is superbly outfitted for the myriad trade shows and expos that it hosts each year, but my particular seating assignment was in a giant room that was basically a warehouse space with cement floors, metal walls, and no sound insulation whatsoever. The stifling-hot space was filled with long tables and folding chairs, and it took me a ridiculously long time to find seat number 37822. When I finally did find my place, I unpacked the pens, pencils, erasers, Juicy Juice, and grapes from my clear-plastic food storage–type bag. I sat down next to a woman who seemed to speak no English whatsoever, and consciously resisted the temptation to revel in a feeling of superiority given the fact that my native English-speaking skills might give me a small leg up over at least one person, because I had learned my lesson as far as the superiority went. And then I began to freak out.

The exam instructions had explicitly prohibited us from bringing in notes, books, or bar review materials of any sort into the exam area, so when my mind went blank—just as it had during my first law school final exam—I was shit out of luck. With Xanax in hand (thankfully, the rules did allow for medications), I tried desperately to recover some sort of composure and inner Zen.

Then I saw it—my lucky pencil (well, the entire three inches of it that were left after years of use), still wedged into the corner of my bag. I fished it out, gazed at its beauty, and cupped it in my hand. I closed my eyes, rubbed my thumb over the "Woodbine" name embossed into the base, and tried to conjure up its magic powers.

A minute later, I heard a noise. A terrifying noise. The noise of a giant, industrial metal garage door slowly being lowered, barricading our exit from the cavernous exam hall. We were in. We were stuck. There was no way out. (Nor was there any way in for latecomers.) At nine a.m. on the dot, a booming, Oz-like voice announced from a far-away speaker "You may now begin the New York State portion of the exam." I kissed my pencil, said a little prayer, and kind of wished that I had a frightening miniature troll doll with soulless black eyes and neon orange hair to add to my karma, just like that crazy woman in my Civil Procedure class had three years before.

I wrote my seat number on the front of my examination booklets, flipped quickly through the test, suppressed a minor heart attack upon realizing that yes, the exam looked every bit as hard as I had feared it might, and dug in—there was no time to waste. I kept careful track of time (a lesson learned in that infamous Civil Procedure exam), and stayed on pace while I scrawled out essays answering questions about breached contracts, criminal law and procedure, corporations, and fiduciary duties.

And then, strange things began to happen.

As I was in the middle of writing an essay about mortgages and recording acts, something caught my eye from far above. I tried to ignore it. But then it started making noise. Finally, I relented, let my eyes wander upward, squinted to focus a bit, and realized that I was staring at a large, flapping pigeon.

A pigeon? Aren't we indoors? Granted, this is nothing but a glorified warehouse, but still . . . Am I not taking the most important exam of my life? Only to have a rat with wings trying determinedly to distract me?

And then I saw another one. And another.

Okay, ignore the pigeons, already, Martha. Focus. WRITE.

And then one of them landed on the floor, not more than four feet in front of my seat, and began slowly meandering up and down the aisle, making its clucky pigeon noise.

Oh my God. I can't believe this! How am I supposed to ignore a giant breeding ground of pestilence and disease that is casually strolling about at my feet?

And then another one joined the first. And another.

God is testing me! I wonder if they're after my quiet snack? But pigeons don't like grapes, do they? Oh, who am I kidding? Pigeons would eat corroded batteries if given the chance. Those bastards had better stay away from my food.

I probably wasted the better part of ten minutes staring at the birds with my mouth agape, and I wasn't the only one. I made momentary eye contact with the woman sitting next to me, whose face was filled with absolute terror. I scanned the room and saw dozens of people staring in wonder, precious minutes of bar exam writing time slipping through our fingers. Finally, mercifully, the trio of pigeons took flight to the far side of our giant warehouse room, and began to distract others.

It took a while to regain my concentration and composure, but soon enough I was back at it, finishing my essay about mortgages and recording acts. Still on pace, I moved on and had just begun to outline my answer to a torts question about a negligent contractor when something else demanded my attention. A forklift, carrying large pallets of some unidentifiable contents, being driven down the side of the room by a gigantic man who was almost spilling out of the sides of his small vehicle. Incredibly slowly, he "beep, beep, beeped" his way through the length of the enormously large room and through some super-secret warehouse door.

I can't believe this. With all of the test-taking advice and strategy that BAR/BRI gave us, why didn't anyone tell us that the exam would be in the middle of an industrial warehouse with all sorts of distractions? This is surreal. And although I wasn't sure about the motives of the pigeons, from the size of that forklift guy, I can pretty much guarantee he is after my food.

Five minutes later, he emerged to make the return journey with a newly emptied forklift.

As it turned out, once the pigeons made their fourth visit to my side of the room, and once the forklift guy made his eighth "beep, beep, beeping" round-trip, they both became easy enough to ignore. Somehow I motored through the rest of the essays, answered the small handful of New York State nitpicky multiple-choice questions, and then, at precisely four-thirty p.m., the Oz-like voice announced, "This examination session is concluded. Stop writing, close your examination books, and stand silently at your desks." I waited until the door was raised, and then navigated through a sea of stampeding test-takers all desperate to escape.

As I made my way outside, I passed several people weeping over their abysmal performance, many people looking lost, dazed, and confused, and one guy throwing up into a trash can. As for me, I went home jubilant. Not so much because I thought I had done well, just because it was halfway over. And it was the hard half that was over—the half that required me to remember the New York distinctions to the rules that I had learned for the Multistate half of the test, the half that tested twenty-three subjects instead of just six, the half that required me to write essays instead of just answering multiple-choice questions. That night, I actually got a semidecent night's sleep.

The next morning, I filed past the guards and the proctors and the other crazed test-takers back into the Javits Center to take the Multistate portion of the bar exam, and I was happy if for no other reason than it meant that I got to use my lucky pencil all day. (The New York essay part had been a pen-and-ink endeavor.) Once the industrial garage door had locked us in and the Voice of Oz had announced we could begin, I put my lucky pencil to my bubble sheet and began coloring in circles. B, A, A, D, C, C, D—*it's only been three minutes, and already this tiny pencil has my hand all cramped up. But I can't stop using it! D, B, C, C, A, D, B, B, C— why are all of these questions about constitutional law? C, C, A, B, D, A, C, D. Should I eat my grapes now? A, D, B, C, A, A, A, A, A, A, A, A—okay, I've screwed up something here, because there's no way that there are eight "A" answers in a row. B, B, D, A, B, C, D, B, A. I would kill someone without hesitation for an actual Diet Pepsi right now. C, A, B, A, D, D, A, A, C. Why can't I remember the UCC rule about the battle of the forms?* And so on. For six and a half grueling hours. And then, as quickly as it had started, Oz told us that the whole thing was over.

I fought my way out of the examination room and past the myriad party promoters handing out flyers advertising postbar celebrations at clubs across the city. I ran into various friends from Columbia and we exchanged exhausted looks and recounted our plans to go home and sleep for days on end. I looked around the halls and saw the Hofstra and NYU and Pace and Brooklyn Law School and St. John's versions of the Gunner lying in wait for former classmates whose souls they would attempt to destroy with sinister comments about how that one question had a really sneaky point in it about mandatory injunctions, and how it would have been really easy for some unsuspecting soul to miss it, surely leading to imminent failure of the bar. Thankfully, my own Gunner was nowhere in sight. By that point, I was beyond caring. I didn't know if I had done well; I didn't know if I had done poorly. I thought I had put in a decent showing, but it was difficult to say—the test had been *brutal.* Had I been minimally proficient? The odds were that I had been. But who knew? All I knew was that the results wouldn't come out until November, so I had a whole lot of waiting to do.

On my long walk from the Javits Center to the subway, I wasn't surprised so much by the presence of the tears that were rapidly forming behind my blinking eyes, but by their nature. I wasn't crying out of sadness or even out of frustration—I was crying out of relief. I could feel every moment of lost sleep that I had experienced over the last three years, every chewed-off fingernail, every moan of worry over the possibility of failure slowly trickling down my face in the form of hot, salty tears. It was Over. The hard part was officially behind me. And I was going straight home to use every last one of those BAR/BRI outlines as kindling in my fireplace.

Epilogue

The End of the Innocence

"The first thing we do, let's kill all the lawyers."
—William Shakespeare

It would be four months before I found out I had passed the bar exam, but in the meantime, I had a job to do. It was time to head back to the Lavish Law Firm, and this time it was for real. There would be no more easy assignments, no more daily three-hour lunches, no more events and parties designed specifically to make sure my every experience there was 100 percent enjoyable. They had me where they wanted me: I had accepted their job offer. They would continue to pay me well and to offer plenty of nice perks, sure, but the blatant ass-kissing of my summer associate tenure was over, and I knew it as soon as I walked back through the revolving door.

I felt a warm sense of familiarity as I passed through the lobby to report for my first day of work. The click of my heels still echoed off the marble in the atrium, but (thanks to that generous salary advance) now my shoes were sumptuous buttery leather Stuart Weitzman pumps that weren't making my feet bleed. I finally had a suit that was nicely tailored and well-fitting (no more shiny elbows and oversized shoulder pads), but my nylons were still digging into my stomach—some things never change. I walked past the stunning floral arrangement that sat atop the lobby reception desk, said hello to the security guard who I recognized from my earlier tenure, and pressed the elevator button to take me up to the forty-fourth floor for my orientation.

When I arrived, the large conference room was filled with little clusters of people standing around chatting, some of whom I recognized from the previous summer, and some of whom were new faces altogether. I grabbed a glass of orange juice and said hello to a few friends, with whom I swapped bar exam war stories and talked about how glad I was that the whole horrible ordeal was finally over.

At nine o'clock on the dot, the hiring partner walked into the room. He was an extraordinarily tall, strikingly good-looking man with piercing blue eyes, and his presence undoubtedly overshadowed that of everyone else he ever encountered. He walked to the front of the room to officially welcome us all to the Lavish Law Firm. He began by extolling the virtues of the firm and telling us how privileged we were to be joining an institution with such accomplished attorneys, with such a diverse practice, and with such an esteemed history. He told us that those who chose to stay at the firm would be richly rewarded, but that no matter where our careers took us, having started out at the Lavish Law Firm would put us on a path to greatness: former LLF lawyers had gone on to be high-ranking politicians, presidential advisers, federal judges, law professors, and helmsmen of some of the largest and richest corporations in the world. We were joining a very elite group of professionals, and we should be proud.

This speech sounds strangely familiar. Have I heard it somewhere before? Hmmmm . . .

Quickly, he moved on to praising the distinctive backgrounds, intellectual abilities, and unique accomplishments of my entering class of attorneys, proclaiming us "the most talented and promising group of young professionals in the firm's illustrious history." He pointed out the editors of both the *Harvard Law Review* and the *Yale Law Journal* who sat in our midst, the artist who had her paintings shown at a SoHo gallery over the summer, the man who had successfully started and grown his own software company while in law school, and the former BBC correspondent who had been at the scene when the Berlin Wall came down. He told us he was certain that, given the high caliber of the applicants for LLF jobs, he wouldn't be hired if he had to apply all over again that day—his résumé coming out of law school didn't even begin to compare to ours.

I felt an overwhelming sense of déjà vu as I thought back to the dean's speech on my first day of law school orientation. *Did those two compare notes or something? Freaky.*

Out of nowhere, I was wrapped in a hug. "Martha! It's so incredibly *fabulous* to have you back! I just know that everything will turn out *wonderfully* and that you are going to absolutely *love* being back here!" trilled Bonnie Bailey, the firm's recruiting director, who was as enthusiastic as ever. "Here, let me introduce you to someone," she said. "She's new, and she could probably use a friendly word."

Bonnie then ushered me over to a tall blond woman standing alone nearby, who was wearing a boldly striped shirt under her black suit jacket. Bonnie introduced her as Sandra Connelley, from Stanford Law School, who had spent the previous summer working at a firm in San Francisco before deciding she wanted to move to New York.

And then, as quickly as she had arrived, Bonnie excused herself to continue on her journey of embraces.

Sandra seemed a little shy and skittish, and quietly said, "I can't believe I'm so nervous. After having been in school for so many years now, it's strange to think of myself as a professional instead of a student, you know?"

"I know what you mean," I answered, appreciatively surveying the room around me. "Well, here's to the beginning of what will hopefully be long and happy careers at the Lavish Law Firm," I said, raising my glass of orange juice in a toast.

Suddenly, Sandra didn't sound nervous anymore. "Oh, you've got to be kidding. Not for me. I'm only here for two years to build up my résumé before I go off to do public interest work. I can't believe some people actually intend to try and make partner here. It's sheer, unmitigated greed, is what it is. There's no excuse for it. No excuse at all."

Wow. Somehow this woman seems strangely familiar. Have I met her somewhere before?

After I managed my escape, I wandered through the room to go grab a bagel, and I couldn't help but overhear a short, pointy-looking guy wearing suspenders and a crimson pocket square in his jacket speaking to a frightened-looking woman who, while wearing her conservative navy pumps, had at least four inches on him.

"I'm Andrew Brooks. I'm from Harvard," he proudly announced. "Undergrad *and* law school. What about you?"

"Oh, hi, I'm Michelle. Michelle Sanders. Nice to meet you."

"Where did you go to school?" he asked while shooting his cuffs.

"I'm from Brooklyn Law," she answered.

There was a long pause.

"Really?" Another long pause. "I didn't know the Lavish Law Firm hired people from Brooklyn Law School," he said, in a voice clearly intended to intimidate.

What an asshole. But a familiar-sounding asshole. Do I know him?

I kept walking before I could hear Michelle's embarrassed reply.

As I wound my way toward the front of the room in my quest for nourishment, I saw a guy wearing a red bow tie and carrying a shiny new briefcase lecturing the hiring partner about how deeply glad he was to be at the Lavish Law Firm and pointing out how far superior his credentials were to everyone else's, building himself up and cutting everyone else down simultaneously.

And then it hit me: *building himself up and cutting everyone else down simultaneously.* Todd Sebastian—the Gunner. Brian Peters—the Show Off. Chaz Whitmore—the Boarding School

Bastard. Christine Hsu—the Self-righteous Do-Gooder. After everything I had been through, I hadn't really left any of my old classmates behind. I had just graduated on to newer versions of them. And it wasn't until that very moment that I realized: maybe the hard part isn't behind me. Maybe the hard part has just begun.

Acknowledgments

First of all, I owe a debt of gratitude to Columbia Law School for giving me an invaluable education and, despite everything, a very memorable and enjoyable learning experience. Columbia really is a special place, and I consider myself privileged to have been able to attend. I'm still not sure exactly why I was admitted, but I'm thankful that I was. I truly want to thank the faculty members, administrators, and students who took the time to meet and talk with me during the writing of this book.

While I was working on this project, my family was more supportive and patient than I had any right to expect, and I couldn't have done it otherwise. My husband, Joe, spent many a weekend dealing with two whining, cranky young children who missed their mother while I sat holed away in my office, trying to ignore their cries. I owe this book to all three of you.

All of my friends have offered encouragement from the very beginning, but I owe special thanks to Jen Lancaster, who provided me with much insight into the process of writing, and who talked me down off the ledge more than once.

Both my agent, Laurie Abkemeier, and my editor, Suzanne O'Neill, helped make this book into something far better than it otherwise would have been, and I am truly grateful for their guidance (even if it was painful at times).

Finally, I'd like to thank my parents for always supporting me, even when I had crazy ideas like getting married without telling them first or moving off to New York to go to law school. My father passed away in January 1998, and the last time I saw him was the day after my law school graduation, as I was hugging him good-bye at the door of my overpriced Upper West Side apartment before he headed home to Wisconsin. I'm glad he got to see me in one of my proudest moments. And I'll remember the exact feel of that hug forever.

Made in the USA
Middletown, DE
23 July 2020